CONVERSATION

$29.95 → $23.96

Volume 34

T. Givón (ed.)

Conversation: Cognitive, communicative and social perspectives

CONVERSATION
COGNITIVE, COMMUNICATIVE AND SOCIAL PERSPECTIVES

Edited by

T. GIVÓN
University of Oregon

JOHN BENJAMINS PUBLISHING COMPANY
AMSTERDAM/PHILADELPHIA

TM The paper used in this publication meets the minimum requirements of American National Standard for Information Sciences — Permanence of Paper for Printed Library Materials, ANSI Z39.48-1984.

Library of Congress Cataloging-in-Publication Data

Conversation : cognitive, communicative, and social perspectives / edited by T. Givón.
    p.   cm. -- (Typological studies in language, ISSN 0167-7373; v. 34)
    Papers: all except one were originally presented at the Symposium on Conversation held July 1995 at the University of New Mexico.
    1. Conversation--Congresses. 2. Oral communication--Congresses. 3. Discourse analysis--Congresses. I. Givón, Talmy, 1936- . II. Symposium on Conversation (1995 : University of New Mexico) III. Series.
P95.45.C665   1997
302.3'46--dc21   97-4488
ISBN 90 272 2929 5 (hb.) / 90 272 2930 9 (pb.) (European; alk. paper)   CIP
ISBN 1-55619-643-1 (hb.) / 1-55619-644-X (pb.) (U.S.; alk. paper)

John Benjamins Publishing Co. • P.O.Box 75577 • 1070 AN Amsterdam • The Netherlands
John Benjamins North America • P.O.Box 27519 • Philadelphia PA 19118-0519 • USA

Contents

Editor's Preface

The papers in this volume were originally presented at the Symposium on Conversation, held at the University of New Mexico in July 1995. The symposium itself brought together scholars who work on face-to-face communication from a variety of perspectives — social, cultural, cognitive and communicative. In organizing the symposium, we wanted to challenge some of the prevailing dichotomies in discourse studies. First is the cleavage between the study of information flow and the study of social interaction. Second is the theoretical division between speech-situation models and cognitive models. Third is the methodological split between the study of spontaneous conversation in natural context and the study of speech production and comprehension under controlled experimental conditions. Last is the genre distinction between narrative and conversational discourse. All four dichotomies have been useful either methodologically or historically. But important as they may have been in the past, the time has come to work toward an integrated approach to the study of human communication, one that will be less dependent on narrow reductions.

Both the primacy and the supreme challenge of natural face-to-face communication are beyond serious doubt. Human language has evolved, is acquired, and is practiced most commonly in the context of face-to-face communication. Most past theory-building in either linguistics or psychology has tended to ignore face-to-face communication, a fact that is indeed regrettable and in need of rectification. We can only hope that this volume represents a move in the right direction.

The paper by **Anderson, Robertson, Kilborn, Beeke** and **Dean** presents an experimental study of communication between aphasic and unimpaired speakers. It demonstrates that the collaborative accommodation that is natural in grounding unimpaired communications is even more pervasive and indispensable when communication takes place in the presence of severe impairment.

Wallace Chafe's study concerns itself with the collaborative nature of the development of topical coherence, likening the resultant performance to polyphonic music. The paper argues that collaborative face-to-face discourse is not

merely the creation of a jointly constructed artifact, the text, but more profound-
ly a dynamic process of bridging over the cognitive gap between two minds.

In a similar vein, **Jennifer Coates** presents a study of the collaborative
construction of both conversational turns and the "floor" or framework, within
which face-to-face communication gains its coherence. The paper likens playful
conversation among friends to a musical jam-session, noting the important social
function of such activity.

Connie Dickinson and **T. Givón** present a pilot experimental study of the
effects of conversational interaction on episodic recall of a video film. They
argue for a cognitive approach to understanding the process — rather than the
product — of face-to-face communication, framed in terms of mental models
found in working memory and early episodic memory.

The paper by **Susan Ervin-Tripp** and **Aylin Küntay** deals with the
function and structure of narratives embedded within, and shaped by, conversational contexts. The study thus calls into question the rigid distinction between
narrative and conversation.

Per Linell and **Natscha Korolija's** paper is the only one in the volume not
presented at the original Symposium. It deals with the coherence of conversational discourse, arguing that cross-participant episodes rather than single-
participant "turns" are the appropriate units of conversational coherence.

Linda Moxey and **Tony Sanford** present an experimental study of the
communicative function of quantifier choice. While working with non-conversa-
tional language materials, the authors argue that their observations are fully
extendable to face-to-face communication.

The paper by **Stein, Bernas** and **Calicchia** is an experimental study of
natural face-to-face communication during conflict mediation. The authors report
strong difference between the communicative behavior of winners and losers and
women and men, as well as strong differences in memory for conversations. The
more combative context of winning or loosing seems to sharpen memory for
who said what, while the more collaborative context of compromising seems to
dull memory for such detail.

Tom Trabasso and **Asli Özyürek** present an experimental study of the
evaluative aspects of text comprehension. The authors probe the communicative
function and context under which evaluative judgements are made, suggesting
that the evaluative component of narrative interpretation is not different from
evaluations occuring in conversation.

Eugene, Oregon
March 1996

Dialogue despite Difficulties

A Study of Communication between Aphasic and Unimpaired Speakers

Anne H. Anderson, Alasdair Robertson, Kerry Kilborn
University of Glasgow

Suzanne Beeke and Elizabeth Dean
Queen Margaret College, Edinburgh

1. Background

1.1. *Introduction*

Psychological research on dialogue has highlighted its collaborative nature (Clark and Wilkes-Gibbs 1985) with speakers working together through their contributions to the conversation to establish 'mutual knowledge' (Clark and Marshall 1981). Speakers have been shown to adjust the linguistic form and content of their utterances to ensure that the references they make are intelligible to their listeners (Clark 1985; Clark and Schaeffer 1987; Garrod and Anderson 1987; Isaacs and Clark 1987; Anderson and Boyle 1994). Similarly scholars from the conversational analysis tradition have shown how speakers cooperate to prevent or repair trouble in conversation by the fine-tuning of the timing and structuring of their contributions (Sacks, Schegloff and Jefferson 1974; Sacks and Schegloff 1979; Schegloff 1980; Goodwin 1981, 1995). These two schools of research have shown how skilfully speakers use a wide variety of linguistic resources to achieve successful communication. In the present paper we will explore what happens to the communicative process when the speaker's linguistic resources have been damaged as the result of brain injury.

Speakers who have developed aphasia for example as a result of stroke or head injury, show a wide variety of linguistic impairments of differing extents and severities. Standard clinical tests of linguistic abilities have been developed to chart the language skills and impairments of individuals, for example the Western Aphasia Battery (WAB) (Keretz 1982) and the Boston Diagnostic Aphasia Examination (BDAE) (Goodglass and Kaplan 1983). The resulting scores across a wide range of language production and comprehension subtests provide the clinician or researcher with information about the nature and extent of the patient's linguistic impairment. Yet several researchers have noted that aphasic individuals who exhibit a range of difficulties as scored on such tests, often display relatively effective communication skills. Feyereisen (1991) has claimed that "aphasics communicate better than they speak", and several studies suggest that standard clinical tests of linguistic abilities may underestimate these skills (Holland 1980, 1982; Davis and Wilcox 1985; Howard and Hatfield 1987).

We will investigate whether aphasic speakers adopt communicative strategies which compensate for their linguistic impairments, the nature of such adaptations and whether these are common across different aphasic individuals. In addition we will examine whether the conversational partners of aphasic speakers adjust their contributions to the dialogue. Isaacs and Clark (1987) and Wilkes-Gibbs and Clark (1992) have shown how speakers make sensitive modifications to their utterances in the light of the expertise or knowledge of their listeners. The large body of literature on child directed speech or 'motherese' has shown how adult speakers make a whole range of adjustments to the immature language processing skills of their young listeners, both in terms of the syntactic forms used and the way in which the conversation is 'scaffolded', see for example Snow and Ferguson (1977), Gleitman *et al.* (1984) and Snow (1994). Similarly 'foreigner talk' can be seen as the modifications made by native speakers to the perceived linguistic limitations of non-native listeners (Ferguson 1975; Hatch *et al.* 1978; Brulhart 1986).

These findings would lead us to expect that the language production difficulties which aphasic speakers manifest, may well elicit modifications in the communicative behavior of the unimpaired conversational partner. In our study we will not only examine the utterances of partners for communicative modifications, but we will also attempt to determine if such adaptations are beneficial to the success of the dialogue. Anecdotal accounts of the difficulties faced by many aphasic individuals feature the frustrations of making their communicative needs known in the face of 'helpful' but dominating conversational partners.

1.2. Studies of the communicative abilities of aphasic speakers

Evidence that supports the proposition that aphasic individuals may retain effective communication abilities comes from several studies. Busch *et al.* (1988) investigated the efficiency and accuracy with which aphasic and non-aphasic individuals communicated the information necessary for referent identification. They concluded that aphasics are not significantly different from non-aphasics. Prinz (1980) found that aphasic speakers are capable of communicating a broad range of intentions and employing pragmatic strategies such as gesture to assist their communication. Holland (1982), in a study of communication in the home, found that the frequency of aphasic individual's successful communicative acts was far greater than that of communicative failure. A wide range of compensatory strategies were used by different individuals including non-verbal gesture, circumlocutions, self-cueing with high association words, spelling out loud; using pen and paper to write; imposing self delay by pausing and signalling listeners to wait, consulting word lists, actively searching for objects, requesting help from listeners.

In a lab based study which attempted to explore communication in naturalistic dialogues, Ulatowska *et al.* (1992) investigated the conversational skills of aphasic subjects engaged in role-playing activities. Conversational structure was found to be comparable in aphasic and unimpaired speakers in terms of the distribution of turns, the range of speech acts used, and the structuring of adjacency pairs.

Milroy and Perkins (1992) used conversational analysis (CA) to investigate how communicative trouble is dealt with by aphasic speakers. They found that aphasics employ different mechanisms to repair breakdowns in conversation than those used by non-aphasics. Both types of speakers however adhere to the 'principle of least collaborative effort' (Clark and Schaefer 1987, 1989). Dialogue partners attempt to minimize the total effort invested in a given contribution. The difference in aphasic/non-aphasic dialogues is the precise nature of collaboration involved.

1.3. Studies of non-verbal communication in aphasia

One possible way of compensating for impaired linguistic abilities, such as word finding difficulties is through the use of gesture. Several studies have explored to what extent aphasic individuals can use such gestures to assist their communication, for a review see Feyereisen and Seron (1982). Unfortunately the results from such studies have been equivocal, with some studies reporting more use of gesture whilst others find no difference. Glosser *et al.* (1986) in a study of

informal conversation found no differences in gesture rates between aphasic and
non-aphasic controls. Yet Cicone *et al.* (1979), claim that Wernicke's aphasics
use more gesture than unimpaired speakers who in turn use more gesture than
individuals with Broca-type aphasia. Feyereisen (1983), Smith (1987) and Le
May *et al.* (1988), all found that aphasic speakers use more gesture than non-
aphasics but report different patterns of results for the different aphasic syndromes.

Earlier research has illustrated several important aspects of aphasic communication, but many studies have been restricted in the size of the sample of
speakers and the scope of the communication task which was studied. In many
studies the tasks used elicited very little dialogue and it was hard to assess how
well the speakers had achieved their communicative intentions. This means that
it is difficult to draw general conclusions about the generality or explanation of
the claim about aphasic individuals' communicative abilities. In our study we
attempt to overcome these methodological shortcomings by testing a reasonably
large number of individuals and by using a communicative task which elicits
extended dialogues. These dialogues are comparable across different speakers
and can be subjected to detailed dialogue analysis. In addition the task provides
for each dialogue an associated measure of communicative success in the form
of an objective non-linguistic performance score. From this study we hope to
provide answers to the following questions:

Do some or all aphasic individuals communicate successfully despite their
linguistic impairments? How is this communicative success achieved? What does
such an achievement mean for our views of communication?

We explore the nature of aphasic communication on a collaborative
problem-solving task which elicits extended speaker-determined dialogues (Map
Task, Brown, Anderson, Shillcock and Yule 1984). We study a sample of
aphasic speakers (N = 16) and age and education matched control subjects. By
analysing the way the dialogues are structured in terms of the communicative
functions which speakers are attempting to convey, we can determine how
dialogues between aphasics and normal speakers differ from those between two
unimpaired speakers. From such analyses we can also explore to what extent,
and in what ways, aphasics compensate for their linguistic impairments, and
what role non-verbal communication plays in this process. We examine if
aphasic speakers can achieve more successful communication than we would
predict from an assessment of their linguistic abilities and what communicative
processes may underpin such achievements. We hope that such analyses will be
informative not just for the study of aphasic communication but also for our
general models of dialogue.

The data presented in this chapter are drawn from an ongoing research project on the relationship between communication and language processing in aphasia. Over the course of this two year research program our aphasic subjects have been tested and retested on a wide range of real-time language production and comprehension tasks, as have age-matched and young control subjects. Our long term research goal is to explore the relationships between various language processing abilities of aphasic speakers and their communicative abilities, see Kilborn, Anderson, Dean, Robertson and Beeke (1995) for an initial exploration of such relationships. In the present paper we focus on the detailed analysis of the communicative performances themselves. The data we have gathered on communicative behavior are immensely rich and the potential range of analyses is correspondingly wide. We present only a sample of the possible explorations of these data. We hope these preliminary findings capture some of the most salient features of the communicative strategies adopted by aphasic speakers and their conversational partners.

2. Method

2.1. *Subjects*

The subjects in the study were a group of 16 individuals aged between 31 and 71 years of age who had become aphasic following cardio-vascular accident (CVA) in the left hemisphere of the brain. The subjects were assumed to be clinically stable as their CVAs had occurred between 3 and 16 years prior to testing. All were formally assessed by trained speech therapists using the Boston Diagnostic Aphasic Examination (BDAE) (Goodglass and Kaplan 1983). In addition to providing scores for performances on specific language tasks, the BDAE allows the therapist to rate the severity of the individual's aphasia. This score relies on impressionistic classification into one of six descriptive categories. The scale is from 0 to 5, where 0 indicates very severe aphasia with 'no usable speech or auditory comprehension' 2 indicates 'conversation about familiar subjects is possible with help from the listener but there are frequent failures to convey the idea' to a rating of 5 which indicates very mild difficulties or 'minimal discernible speech handicaps'.

The aphasic patients were all part of an on-going programme of speech and language therapy at Queen Margaret College in Edinburgh. This programme aims to develop three main areas: (a) metacommunicative awareness; (b) overall communicative competence; and (c) individual non-verbal modalities. This therapeutic regime was developed before the research program began and as yet no modifications have been introduced in the light of the findings we report in this chapter.

Subject details details are given in Table 1. Control subjects who were matched with each aphasic subject for age, gender and educational background were also tested.

Table 1. *Characteristics of aphasic subjects*

Subject	Boston Classification	Boston Severity Score	Diagnosis	Age	(Former) Occupation	Gender
AJ	Broca's	3	Left CVA	64	Salesman	M
AM	Broca's	1	Cartoid	66	Insurance	M
BA	Broca's	4	Left CVA	54	Actuary	M
CR	Broca's	2	Left CVA	47	Electrician	M
DW	Broca's	2	Left CVA	63	Shop Supervisor	F
GM	Anomic	4	?	38	Gardener	M
HL	Anomic	4	Left CVA	76	Printer	M
IB-G	Anomic	4	Left CVA	38	Civil Servant	M
IE	Conduction	4	Left CVA	62	Lt. Colonel	M
IH	Transcortical	2	Left CVA	64	Farmer	M
JM	Broca's	3	Left CVA	49	Army Major	M
JN	Broca's	4	Left CVA	64	Docker	M
MD	Anomic (WAB)	4	Left Parietal	30	Doctor	M
MS	Conduction	4	Left CVA	58	?	F
RS	Anomic	4	Left CVA	52	Business Owner	M
SMcA	Anomic	4	Left CVA	48	Teacher	F

Partners for the aphasic subjects in the communication study were recruited from the student population at Queen Margaret College, Edinburgh. The students were all in their first year of a speech and language therapy degree but were not known to the aphasic subjects nor had they experience of communicating with aphasic individuals. Each partner took part in a pretest training session where they were shown video tapes of a pilot study of aphasic subjects participating in the map task. The partners were instructed to be generally supportive, to communicate as naturally as possible being helpful but avoiding dominating the dialogue. Partners for the age-matched subjects were recruited from the student population at the University of Glasgow.

2.2. *The Communicative Task*

To assess communicative abilities each subject was asked to attempt two versions of a an interactive communication task, the Map Task (Brown, Anderson, Shillcock and Yule 1984). This task was been used widely to explore the communication skills of unimpaired children and adults (Anderson *et al.* 1991a, 1991b, 1993, 1994). It has also been successfully piloted with aphasic subjects by Merrison (1992). In the Map Task pairs of subjects are presented with copies of a schematic map. One member of the pair is assigned the role of instruction giver (IG) and his task is to describe the route shown only on his copy of the map so that his partner the instruction follower (IF) can reproduce this accurately on her copy of the map. Although the basic map and most of the landmarks are common to both copies, the participants are warned that as the maps have been produced by different explorers, some landmarks differ between the two copies of the maps. By comparing the original route on the instruction giver's map and that drawn on the instruction follower's map we can derive an objective non-linguistic measure of communicative success.

In this study we produced maps which contained landmark pictures which were adapted from pictures used in a number of aphasia assessment instruments. On the maps all landmarks are labelled but in a pretest we ensured that the pictures alone would successfully elicit the intended names from aphasic subjects. As part of a battery of other tests all the pictures to be used as landmarks were presented to our aphasic subjects, 82% were correctly named without prompting, 95.4% were correctly named after a semantic or phonological prompt.

Each version of the maps showed eleven landmarks with eight of these being common to both instruction giver's and follower's maps. Three landmarks were shown only on IG's map and three only on IF's map. Shared features were interspersed with unshared features along the route. Each map included a mixture of high, medium and lower frequency words used as landmarks. High frequency words occurred more than 40 times per million, medium frequency words between 20–40 times per million and low frequency words less than 20 times per million. An example of the map task is shown in Fig 1.

All subjects were given the following task instructions:

To the instruction giver:

> You and your partner have both got a map of the same place. Your map has got a route on it. It's the only safe route through all the dangers. Your partner hasn't got a route on her/his map. Your job is to describe the route to your partner so that (s)he can draw it on her/his map. You must describe it exactly because it's the only safe route. The maps have been drawn by different explorers, so they might not be quite the same; there might be some differences.

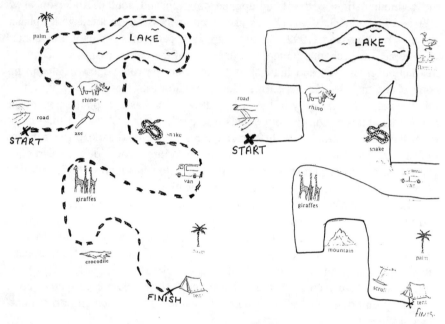

Figure 1.   *On left: Instruction giver's map, original 12" × 16". On right: Instruction follower's map, completed from BA's instructions*

To the instruction follower:
> You and your partner have both got a map of the same place. Your partner's map has got a route on it. It's the only safe route through all the dangers. (S)he's going to tell you what the route is. Your job is to draw the route on your map. Listen carefully to what your partner says, and ask questions if there's anything you're not sure about. You must draw it exactly because it's the only safe route.
>
> The maps have been drawn by different explorers, so they might not be quite the same; there might be some differences. Do you understand what you're supposed to do?

All subjects, aphasic and age-matched controls, were assigned to the instruction follower's role for task one, with their partner giving the instructions. They then swapped to the instruction giver's role for task two where they attempted a different version of the map task. For the aphasic subjects testing was conducted in a quiet clinic room in Queen Margaret College which the subjects attended regularly for speech therapy sessions. Subjects were seated at a sloping table which prevented either participant seeing their partner's map. Subjects sat about four feet apart. Testing was arranged to compensate for any peripheral visual difficulties or limb apraxia of the aphasic subjects so the map was placed in a position where it was fully visible to the speaker and the seating was arranged so that gesturing was possible.

Age-matched subjects were tested in the Human Communication Research Centre laboratories in the University of Glasgow. Subjects again sat about four feet apart at a sloping table to prevent seeing their partner's map.

All performances were recorded on audio and video tape. Full verbal transcriptions of all the dialogues were then produced and checked by trained transcribers. An example of a map dialogue is shown in Extract 1. All the videotapes were studies and all the hand gestures and head nods were recorded and added to the dialogue transcripts.

Extract 1. *BA is the Instruction Giver (IG) his unimpaired partner is the Instruction Follower (IF)*

< Indicates the start of a turn containing overlapping speech
/ Indicates the point at which a speaker interrupts
> Indicates the end of the turn containing overlapping speech
... Indicates a pause

IG : So start

IF : Mhm

IG : Third. One two three third

IF : A third from the top?

IG : Yes and eh

IF : Mhm. At the ... we're going right

IG : This

IF : Uh huh. Right.

IG : Difficult because me and you are different

IF : We're a mirror yes

IG : So here

IF : Uh huh

IG : And here

IF : Uh huh

IG : Start

IF : Right

IG : And eh

IF : Go to the right?

IG : Yes

IF : Right

IG : <And eh/

IF : For how long?

IG : Road. Road. Just here>

IF : Is the road the starting point?

IG : Yes. Yes

IF : Is the road ...? Uh huh. So we're starting just below the road?

IG : Yes

IF : And going right

IG : So uh maybe three inches

IF : Mhm

IG : That way

IF : Right

3.   Results

3.1. *Communicative performance*

To assess overall communicative performance all map performances were
scored. This is done by placing a squared transparent grid showing the original
route over the completed copy of the instruction follower's map. The accuracy
is assessed by counting the number of centimeters squares between the two
routes. The larger the area of deviation between the routes the poorer the

performance. As the raw deviation scores were not normally distributed, the square root of each deviation score was used as the performance measure in subsequent analyses. These transformed data were approximately normally distributed.

How well do aphasics subjects communicate compared to unimpaired speakers? How variable are the levels of communicative performance they achieve? Do they have more difficulty in giving or following instructions?

To answer these questions an Analysis of Variance was performed on the performance data, with Subject Group (Aphasic vs. Controls) as a between subjects grouping factor, Role (instruction givers vs. instruction followers) as a within subjects repeated measure and Map Score (square root of number of squares of difference between routes) as the dependent variable.

The ANOVA showed that on average aphasic subjects had significantly poorer performance scores than their unimpaired peers, $(F(2,44) = 17.04, p < .001)$. There was no main effect or interaction with task role. Both aphasic and age-matched individuals perform equally well or badly as instruction givers and followers.

In general then aphasic subjects communicate less successfully than their unimpaired peers. Given the nature of their linguistic difficulties this is hardly surprising. On average they also cope equally well or badly with giving and following instructions. This is not what might have been predicted. The more dominant communicative role, instruction giving, where the speaker is required to convey critical new information to his partner would seem to be particularly demanding for an aphasic individual. If we look at the aphasic performance data in detail we see that within the overall pattern there are also some surprising individual results. These data are shown in Table 2 (next page). If we consider the performances of subjects in the instruction giver's role we see that over 30% (5/16) of the aphasic subjects produce communication task scores within the range produced by the age-matched control group. Two of these individuals (BA and RS) produce task scores which are as good as that of the average age-matched subjects.

So at least a minority of aphasic individuals communicate surprisingly well on the experimental task. But does this task tap more general communicative abilities? To test this, all our aphasic subjects were assessed by a trained speech therapist who was not a member of the research team and who had known all the aphasic individuals for at least a year, seeing them at least once a week. She based her ratings on the categories of the Revised Edinburgh Functional Communication Profile (Wirz, Skinner and Dean 1990), which requires the rater to assess the communicative abilities of individual clients on a 6 point scale from 0 — no response to interaction, 1 — Acknowledges turn for example by

Table 2. *Map performance scores* for aphasic and age matched subjects*

Aphasic Subjects	Instruction Giver	Instruction Follower	Age-Matched Controls	Instruction Giver	Instruction Follower
AJ	17.1	16.4	LB	6.0	6.5
AM	14.7	16.9	LK	not available	6.2
BA	7.7	6.7	PH	3.1	3.5
CR	11.1	6.2	RG	10.8	10.8
DW	11.0	11.4	RA	7.2	11.4
GM	10.6	6.8	RT	8.0	6.2
HL	12.3	7.7	WA	6.9	5.9
IBG	10.8	10.9	AD	1.7	6.5
IE	17.3	18.1	WA	9.3	10.0
IH	13.6	9.4	RM	7.7	4.6
JM	12.5	8.6	AB	5.6	9.4
JN	10.6	11.0	GD	7.2	6.4
MD	12.1	11.2	DT	8.0	11.1
MS	14.4	11.9	BP	10.4	3.3
RS	7.1	12.6	BH	6.0	7.3
SMCA	Unscorable	10.5	MM	7.3	9.1
Mean	12.1	11.1		7.1	7.4
SD	2.8	3.7		2.4	2.6

*Low numbers indicate good performances.

eye contact but makes no meaningful response up to 5 — conveys complex ideas using speech or a combination of modalities. These Communicative Ability scores were correlated with those from the Map Task. This showed a strong correlation between the two measures, ($r = 0.75$, $p < 0.001$)). So performance on the Map Task does seem to identify those aphasic individuals who can communicate effectively despite their linguistic impairments. But how do these aphasic individuals manage to communicate so successfully? What causes the overall decrement in communicative performance between the aphasic and control groups?

To answer such questions we began a detailed analysis of the way the dialogues were structured, the communicative functions which they contained and the possible role of non-verbal communication in the communicative process.

3.2. Dialogue Analysis

Previous studies of aphasic communication have used different types of dialogue or conversational analysis. Aphasic conversation has been analyzed in terms of the turn taking behavior of the speakers, the speech acts attempted, the completion of adjacency pairs, the repair strategies adopted (Prinz 1980; Ulatowska *et al.* 1992; Milroy and Perkins 1992). Although these approaches have provided valuable information about the nature of aphasic communication, we wished to use a system of analyses which would enable exhaustive coding of all the communicative functions attempted by speakers throughout a dialogue.

The analysis system used here is Conversational Games analysis (Kowtko, Isard and Doherty-Sneddon 1991). In some respects this resembles discourse analyses models such as those proposed by Sinclair and Coulthard (1974) and Traum and Hinkelman (1992). Conversational Games is derived more directly however from the work of Power (1979), and Houghton and Isard (1987), which proposed that a conversation occurs through the accomplishment of speakers' goals and subgoals, these dialogue units being called Conversational Games. For example an instruction is accomplished via an INSTRUCT Game. Conversational Games analysis was developed to detail patterns of pragmatic functions in Map Task dialogues. It provides an exhaustive coding of the dialogues and has been found to capture many different aspects of dialogue structure from developmental differences, Doherty-Sneddon (1993), to the role of intonation in dialogue, Kowtko (1992).

There are two functional levels of analysis within the coding system, which are related hierarchically. The lower level is described in terms of Conversational Moves. The Conversational Move category assigned to an utterance (and there may be more than one move per utterance, or more than one utterance per move), represents the perceived conversational function which the speaker intends to accomplish with that utterance. Coding conversational moves therefore involves taking several sources of information into account: the semantic content of the utterance, the prosody and intonational contour accompanying the utterance, and the utterance location within the dialogue. Non verbal signals can also be used in this interpretive process. The pragmatic function assigned to an utterance will depend upon the collective effect of such variables. Identical lexical strings could be coded differently depending upon the speaker's intonation or the surrounding dialogue context. So an utterance like "Go right" could be coded as functioning for example to instruct, to elicit feedback or to provide feedback depending upon its dialogue context and intonation.

These Conversational Moves are grouped into dialogue units called Conversational Games. Conversational Games are defined by the goal which a sequence of turns serves within the interaction. Games are descriptions of discourse units necessary to ground and accomplish the linguistic and non-linguistic goals of the interlocutors. There are six categories of Games which have been found necessary and sufficient to describe the dialogues studied. An example is an INSTRUCT Game which serves the goal of having the instructee accomplish some task designated by the instructor. This Game in its simplest form may consist of only one Instruct move followed by the action required, but frequently other conversational Games, such as questions, will be embedded within the INSTRUCT Game. So moves are organized into Games, and Games can be imbedded within one another. Extract 2 illustrates the relationship between Moves and Games.

Extract 2

	Game 1	INSTRUCT
Utterance 1	Anne:	Could you put those things in the wash?
		Instruct move
	Game 2	CHECK embedded
Utterance 2	Ian:	All of them?
		Check move
Utterance 3	Anne:	Yes
		Reply-y move
	End Game 2	
Utterance 4	Ian:	Okay *(puts clothes in washing machine)*
		Acknowledge move
	End Game 1	

Two types of Games are illustrated in this short dialogue. Anne's main goal is to get Ian to put on the washing, she therefore uses an INSTRUCT Game to do so. Ian is not sure whether he can accomplish this task as Anne intends (because there is more than one item of clothing around), and so checks his interpretation of her instruction by using a CHECK Game. Notice that it is often necessary, when accomplishing the goal of one Game, to embed other Games with their own subordinate goals. Once the CHECK Game is satisfied the INSTRUCT Game continues with the required action and Ian's acknowledgement of his agreement to carry out the action.

For the communication task investigated in this study (the Map Task) the 6 types of Games, as described by Kowtko *et al.* (1991), are as follows:

INSTRUCT: A direct or indirect request for action or instruction.

CHECK: Listener checks self-understanding of a previous message or instruction from conversational partner, by requesting confirmation that the interpretation is correct.

QUERY-YN: Yes-No question. A request for affirmation or negation regarding new or unmentioned information about some part of the task (not checking an interpretation of a previous message).

QUERY-W: An open-answer Wh-question. Requests more than affirmation or negation regarding new or unmentioned information about some part of the task not checking an interpretation of a previous message).

EXPLAIN: Freely offered information regarding the task, not elicited by co-participant.

ALIGN: Speaker confirms the listener's understanding of a message or accomplishment of some task, also checks attention, agreement, or readiness.

These six games have corresponding moves — that is single utterances which initiate a sequence of one or more utterances or turns which accomplish the conversational game. In addition there are six conversational moves which serve feedback and response functions within conversational games. These are:

CLARIFY: Clarifies or rephrases what has been previously said; usually repeats given or known information; elicited by other person

REPLY-Y, REPLY-N, REPLY-W: An elicited positive, negative or not easily classifiable reply to a **QUERY, CHECK** or **ALIGN** move.

ACKNOWLEDGE: Acknowledgement of having heard or understood, not specifically elicited but often expected before other speaker will continue, announces readiness to hear next move.

READY: Indicates intention to begin a new game and focuses attention on oneself, in preparation for the new move, consists of cue word eg "now" or "right".

Conversational Game coding is particularly useful for analyzing aphasic dialogues as the coder is assigning categories on the basis of the speaker's perceived communicative intentions when producing an utterance. This is judged in the context of the speaker's utterance, its intonation and the coder's knowledge of the dialogue to date, the task being attempted and the information available to each participant at this point in the map task dialogues. This means that partial or inexplicit utterances, of the type often produced by aphasic speakers can be categorized, as can contributions which are partly or fully non-verbal such as hand gestures or head nods. An illustration of how the coding system operates is given in Extract 3, from the start of a dialogues where the aphasic subject is in instruction giving role and his unimpaired partner is the instruction follower.

Extract 3. *Instruction Giver (IG) RS Partner Instruction Follower (IF)*

*E 1 IG Align
IG : Aye right. The sea on the left side?
*M ready align
IF : Mhm
*M reply-y
*E End 1

*E 2 IG Align
IG : There's a river on the ... running through the ... curve
*M align
IF : Yes
*M reply-y
IG : OK
*M acknowledge
*End 2

*E 3 IG Align
IG : < And uh about two inches in from ah the left side and inches one inch um
... above above no ... above ah ... one inch above ... um ... two inches in from
the left de ... and/
*M align
IF : yes
*M reply-y
IG : Down an inch>
*M align-cont
IF : Yes
*M reply-y
IG : Right
* M acknowledge
*E End 3

*E 4 IG Instruct
IG : OK
*M ready
IF : Right
*M acknowledge
IG: Um could you ... down for about two inches
*M instruct
IF : Yes
*M acknowledge

IG : Now the sea and all that ... you ... um ... s- the river and the... Two inches along er right

*M instruct-cont

*E 5 IF Check em

IF : Is that above a gate?

*M check

IG : It's not. No

*M reply-n

* E 6 IG Explain em

IG : It's er below the eh a a pine tree (laughs)

*M explain

IF : Right

*M acknowledge

IG : Eh below the gate

*M clarify

IF : Right

*M acknowledge

3.3. Coding and Reliability

Two trained coders coded the dialogues. In an earlier study interjudge reliability (between relative novices and expert coders) for coding utterances in terms of Conversational Moves was 78% (Kowtko *et al.* 1991). Again in an earlier study the inter-judge agreement of Games as categorized by our two trained coders was measured. Reliability of this agreement was measured using Kappa, a coefficient of agreement for nominal scales described by Cohen (1960). A kappa value of 0.7 was found, ($p < 0.001$), indicating that there was significantly more agreement between the 2 coders, across the 6 types of Games, than would be expected by chance. Indeed this level of agreement is high since kappa is a coefficient which ranges from -1 to 1, with a score of zero indicating no agreement. Seventy-five percent of times where one coder marked the beginning of a Game the second coder agreed both that a new Game had begun and on the type of Game. Many of the mismatches were cause by disagreement about where Games noticeable INSTRUCT Games, began and ended. For example one coder may initiate a new INSTRUCT Game while the other continues a previous Game for another turn before initiating the new INSTRUCT Game. When such disagreements are taken into account the interjudge agreement rose to 90%. For the present study three dialogues from the aphasic group were independently coded by our two trained judges. The interjudge reliability was found to be 85.5% for agreeing on the categorization of Conversational Games, and 87% for Conversational Moves.

3.4. *Results of dialogue analyses*

Our first analyses compared the way that conversational games were distributed across the dialogues and participants.

First we examined the lengths of dialogues. Using the number of turns of speech as our dependent variable we found no significant difference in the lengths of dialogues where aphasic or age-matched controls took the role of instruction givers ($F(1,28) = 1.7$, $p = 0.19$) with the mean number of turns being 180.3 and 137.1 respectively. We thus report the data from the distribution of Conversational Games and Moves with no standardization for length of the dialogues. Analyses which we have conducted on the rate of Conversational Games and Moves per 100 turns show a very similar pattern of results.

In the analyses which follow we will focus on the dialogues where the aphasic and age-matched subjects took the role of the instruction-giver on the Map task. In our first analysis to determine the overall structure of the dialogues involving both types of individuals we totalled the number of Conversational Games in each category initiated by each participant. The ANOVA then had Group (Aphasic vs. Age-Matched Control Dialogues) and Subject (Aphasic/Age Matched vs. Partner) as between dialogue grouping factors and Conversational Game (INSTRUCT, CHECK, QUERY-YN, QUERY-W, EXPLAIN, and ALIGN) as a within-dialogue repeated measure.

In dialogues with Aphasic instruction givers, significantly more of the Conversational Games were initiated by the instruction followers than in dialogues between unimpaired speakers. On average aphasic instruction givers initiate only 32% of the Conversational Games in their dialogues, with their instruction following partners initiating 68% of the Games. In contrast age-matched instruction givers initiate 62% of the Conversational Games in their dialogues with their instruction followers initiating only 38%.

This is shown in the significant interaction between Group and Subject ($F(1,28) = 15.9$, $p < 0.001$). Multiple pairwise planned comparison tests showed that the difference between the behavior of instruction following partners differed significantly ($p < 0.05$). Conversational partners seem to be making an adjustment to the problems of the aphasic individuals by attempting to carry more of the conversational burden, even when the communicative roles are such that the critical information must be supplied by the instruction giver.

The distribution of Conversational Games used by participants also highlighted differences between aphasic and non-aphasic dialogues. Aphasic instruction givers ask their partner fewer questions than do age-matched control subjects. The adjustments made by instruction followers who are partnering an aphasic instruction giver also extend to the kinds of Conversational Games which are used. These instruction followers, explain and volunteer more information, ask more wh-questions and check that they have understood an instruction more often than those who are following the instructions of an unimpaired speaker.

This is shown in the ANOVA by the significant interaction of Group and Game ($F(5,140) = 5.17$, $p < 0.001$) and within the marginal interaction of Group, Subject and Game ($p = 0.07$) planned comparison tests found all these differences to be significant ($p < 0.05$).

This analysis of the distribution of Conversational Games illustrates the general patterns of dialogue structure and content in aphasic dialogues. For a more detailed micro-level analysis of the dialogues we analyse the distribution of the individual Conversational Moves used by different types of speakers.

An ANOVA was conducted on the dialogues where the aphasic and age-matched speakers took the instruction giver's role, with Group (Aphasic vs. Age-Matched Dialogues), Subject (Aphasic/Age-matched vs. Partner) as between dialogue grouping variables and Conversational Move (INSTRUCT, CHECK, QUERY-YN, QUERY-W, EXPLAIN, ALIGN, CLARIFY, REPLY-Y, REPLY-N, REPLY-W, ACKNOWLEDGE and READY) as a within-dialogue repeated measure.

This analysis again showed the partners seemed to adjust to the difficulties of the aphasic instruction-givers. There was a significant interaction between Group and Speaker ($F(1,28) = 6.87$, $p < 0.01$) with an increased number of Conversational Moves from instruction followers partnering an aphasic speaker. Multiple pairwise planned comparison tests however showed that this numerical increase did not reach statistical significance, probably because there was considerable variability in the data particularly from aphasic dialogues.

There was a significant interaction of Group, Speaker and Move ($F(11,308) = 2.94$, $p < 0.001$) Planned comparison tests are not very powerful with this ratio of comparisons to subjects, and only two of the differences were found to be statistically significant. Aphasic instruction givers produce more positive replies than non-aphasics, and their instruction following partners more frequently check they have understood an instruction than those paired with a non-aphasic speaker.

These analyses describe the general patterns in the way dialogues are structured when aphasic individuals take the role of instruction givers in a collaborative problem solving task. In the next set of analyses we explore the relationships between the extent of use of particular conversational moves and overall communicative success. The variability in the data from aphasic dialogues which was problematical for Analyses of Variance may be useful in correlational analyses. Correlation coefficients were calculated between the frequency of use of each conversational move by aphasic instruction givers, their instruction following partners and the overall map score for the corresponding dialogues. Table 3 shows those correlations which were found to be statistically significant. Note that high map scores, represent performances where the completed map route was very different from the original which the instruction giver was attempting to describe. Significant negative correlations then are those which seem to suggest beneficial relationships between frequent use of a particular conversational move and communicative outcome. Positive correlations in contrast show relationships where frequent use of a conversational game co-occurs with a less successful dialogue.

Table 3. *Correlations between Conversational Games and map Score (square root of deviation score) when an Aphasic Speaker is in Instruction Giver's Role*

Move	Speaker	Correlation (Pearson's r)	% Map Score Explained	Helpful?
INSTRUCT	Aphasic IG	−0.308	9%	YES
ALIGN	Aphasic IG	−0.362	13%	YES
QUERY-YN	Aphasic IG	−0.333	11%	YES
REPLY-N	Aphasic IG	0.380	14%	NO
REPLY-WH	Aphasic IG	0.398	16%	NO
ACKNOWLEDGE	Aphasic IG	0.350	12%	NO
CLARIFY	Aphasic IG	−0.472	22%	YES
READY	Aphasic IG	−0.341	11%	YES
EXPLAIN	Partner IF	0.430	18%	NO
QUERY-W	Partner IF	0.364	13%	NO
REPLY-Y	Partner IF	−0.370	14%	YES
READY	Partner IF	−0.337	11%	YES

As can be seen from Table 3 successful dialogues are characterized by aphasic instruction givers who give a relatively high number of instructions, clarify the instructions they have given, ask their partners yes/no questions, check that their partner has understood the instructions given and indicate when the are about to begin a new conversational game. In contrast where the aphasic instruction giver is frequently replying to their partner's questions and acknowledging their partner's contributions, the corresponding dialogues are generally unsuccessful.

If the instruction follower's contributions contain a high frequency of explanations or volunteered information or wh-questions, then again this tends to indicate an unsuccessful dialogue. Where the instruction follower is frequently answering questions and signaling they are ready for the next conversational game, the communication is generally more successful.

Correlational analyses of course can only tell us about patterns of associations between variables and not whether there is any causal relationship between the two. We do not know for example if the apparently detrimental behaviors from instruction followers, are indeed unhelpful. These may indicate a dialogue where the unimpaired conversational partner is dominating the communication process in a way that the aphasic instruction giver finds difficult. Alternatively these behaviors could be responses made by instruction followers to a communication which is not progressing effectively because of the particular linguistic problems of the aphasic speaker. Whilst they may not achieve 'success', the dialogue might have been even less effective had no such adjustments been made. By the end of our research program when we have analyzed dialogues from three phases of testing and can observe the aphasic speakers and partners communicating with different conversational partners, we hope to be able to tease apart these alternative explanations.

When we consider the apparently beneficial behaviors from aphasic instruction givers and their partners, we may be on slightly firmer ground. Again we cannot assume a causal link between any conversational move and task performance. As our aim is to discover how communication is achieved despite linguistic impairments, these analyses may suggest possible explanations.

If we look at individual aphasic instruction givers such as BA who communicates surprisingly effectively, we see that he shows two of the Conversational Move patterns highlighted in the correlational analyses. Extract 1A illustrates BA's dialogue with Conversation Coding. BA's dialogue as an instruction giver shows a high number of Instruct and Clarify Moves. BA uses 43 Instructs where the aphasia group mean is 25.4 with a standard deviation of 17.9. BA uses more Clarify Moves (30) than any other aphasic speaker. Aphasic IG's on average use only 13.2 Clarify Moves, with a standard deviation of 8.

Extract 1A. *BA is the Instruction Giver (IG) his unimpaired partner is the*
            Instruction Follower (IF)
*E indicates the Conversational Game which follows
em indicates an embedded Conversational Game
*M indicates the Conversational Move in the preceding utterance
cont indicates a continuation of a Conversational game or Move

(IG's gestures are shown in brackets)

*E 1 IG Instruct
IG : So start
*M instruct
IF : Mhm
*M acknowledge
IG : Third. One two three third (*Listener Oriented gesture*)
*M instruct cont

*E 2 IF Check em
IF : A third from the top?
*M check
IG : Yes (*Iconic gesture — points left*)
*M reply-y
*M instruct cont

*E 3 IF Check em
IF : Mhm. At the … we're going right
*M check
IG : This (*Iconic gesture — points towards relevant area of map*)
*M clarify
IF : Uh huh. Right.
*M acknowledge

*E 4 IG Explain
IG : Difficult because me and you are different (*Listener oriented gesture*)
*M explain
IF : We're a mirror yes
*M acknowledge
*E End 4
IG : So here (*Iconic gesture — points towards relevant area*)
*M clarify
IF : Uh huh

*M acknowledge
IG : And here *(Iconic gesture — points towards relevant area)*
*M clarify-cont
IF : Uh huh
*M acknowledge
IG : Start *(Speaker oriented gesture)*
*M clarify-cont
IF : Right
*M acknowledge
IG : And eh *(Iconic gesture — points right)*
*M instruct-cont

*E 5 IF Check em
IF : Go to the right?
*M check
IG : Yes *(Listener oriented gesture)*
*M reply-y
IF : Right
*M acknowledge

*E 6 IG Explain em
IG : <And eh/
*M explain

*E 7 IF Query-w em
IF : For how long?
*M query-w
IG : Road. Road. Just here> *(Speaker oriented gesture)*
*M explain-cont
*E End 6

*E 8 IF Check em
IF : Is the road the starting point?
*M check
IG : Yes. Yes *(Listener oriented gesture)*
*M reply-y
IF : Is the road ...?
*M check-cont
Uh huh.
*M acknowledge
So we're starting just below the road?

*M check
IG : Yes
*M reply-y
IF : And going right
*M check-cont
IG : So uh maybe three inches *(Speaker oriented gesture)*
*M reply-w
IF : Mhm
*M acknowledge
IG : That way
*M clarify
IF : Right
*M acknowledge
*End 7

Is there any evidence that his partner adopts patterns of Conversational Moves which contribute to the successful communication? The instruction follower in this dialogue uses a relatively high number of Ready Moves, the highest of any in the aphasic dialogues. This is one of the two helpful IF behaviors shown in Table 3. She also avoids offering frequent explanations, a Conversational Move which may hamper effective dialogues with aphasics. This instruction follower only offers 4 explanations where the group mean is 14.3 with a standard deviation of 9.8.

This instruction follower's most noticeable Conversational Move, illustrated in Extract 1A, is her frequent use of checks on her understanding of the previous contribution from BA. The dialogue contains 45 Checks where the mean is 24 with a standard deviation of 11.8. In general instruction followers check their understanding of a previous utterance from an aphasic speaker more frequently than they do when paired with an unimpaired speaker. This presumably occurs because the instructions which they receive from aphasic speakers are often inexplicit or difficult to interpret. This general adaptation however was not found to correlate significantly with communicative success across the aphasic dialogues as a whole, but it seems it may play a contributory role for this particular pairing.

In contrast RS, the other surprisingly successful aphasic instruction giver uses a different set of 'helpful' Conversational Moves. RS uses a high number of Align Moves, 13 where the mean is 6.3, with a standard deviation of 8.8. This means that he frequently checks or confirms that his partner understands a message or shares his understanding of the current state of the dialogue task. This behavior is clearly illustrated in Extract 3, from the start of RS's dialogue where he wishes to check that his partner shares his orientation to the map. To do this he engages in a sequence of 3 Align Games containing 4 Align Moves before giving any instructions.

RS also uses a considerable number of Ready Moves, 7 where the aphasic group mean is 1.6 with a standard deviation of 3.7. This apparently trivial conversational behavior, where the speaker indicates with a single cue word such as "OK" or "Right" their intention to begin a new game, occurs infrequently in aphasic dialogues and when it does the dialogues are relatively successful. This communicative behavior may indicate a speaker who is sensitive to the interactive aspects of dialogue. Recognizing the need to orientate their listener that a new Conversational Game is about to begin might indicate that these metacognitive skills are unimpaired.

The instruction follower who partners RS also avoids the two apparently unhelpful IF communicative behaviors indicated in Table 3. She rarely offers explanations or asks questions. The dialogue contains only 3 explanations from the instruction follower, aphasia group mean 14.3 with a standard deviation of 9.8, and only 2 wh-queries, group mean 10 with a standard deviation of 9.5. This is the lowest number of such questions from the instruction follower across all the aphasic dialogues. She also shows one of the possibly helpful behaviors in that she produces a lot of positive replies to questions from RS. This general pattern suggests a non-dominant IF who is responding to the communicative behavior of the instruction follower. Again Extract 3 illustrates this pattern in IF's communication.

The patterns of conversational moves and communicative success which we observed across the complete set of aphasic dialogues, also illuminate the compensatory strategies used by the successful aphasic individuals. There appear to be a range of potentially helpful communicative strategies which speakers can consciously or unconsciously adopt. Later we shall see how the different conversational moves used by BA and RS may compensate for their rather different linguistic difficulties. First we examine whether the use of non-verbal communication in dialogue can provide an additional set of compensatory strategies.

4.   Gesture

4.1. *Analysis of Gesture*

The role of gesture in communication in normal and impaired speakers has generated a great deal of research and some controversy, see for example

McNeill (1985), Feyereisen (1987), McNeill (1987). Many different ways of categorizing and coding gestures have been suggested, for a review see Rime and Schiaratura (1991). One distinction has involved whether the gesture conveys a meaning in isolation or only in relation to the accompanying utterance. The meaning bearing gestures have been subdivided by Efron (1941/1972) into deictic, illustrative and symbolic gestures. This tripartite distinction has also been termed indices, icons and symbols following the writings of Peirce (1932/1974). The gestures which are interpreted in terms of the speech they accompany have been subcategorized into batons, which relate to the rhythm of speech and ideographs which describe thought processes (Ekman and Freisen 1969). Feyereisen (1991) describes these various categorization schemes and questions whether all the distinctions might not be as distinct or permanent as the original researchers suggest.

In studies of the role of gesture in aphasic communication various coding schemes have again been used. Cicone *et al.* (1979) coded the part of the body used to gesture and the spatial properties of gestures such as location and direction, in a study of four aphasic speakers in interviews. Behrmann and Penn (1984) had judges rate the function of non-verbal communication such as substituting for verbal content, supporting or interfering with speech production, for eleven aphasic speakers in conversation. Glosser *et al.* (1986) had judges rate the communicative gestures form used in short interviews with ten aphasic speakers. They used a scheme devised by Weiner *et al.* (1972) where gestures were subdivided into four categories, deictics, pantomimics, where the movements mimic some visual or kinesthetic attribute of the referent, semantic modifying gestures which amend or contrast with the verbal content and those gestures of unclear communicative intention. Le May *et al.* (1988) had judges categorize the gestures used to accompany speech according to Ekman and Freisen's classification, of seven aphasic speakers in different communicative tasks.

We wished to know if aphasic speakers could use gesture to assist them in achieving an effective dialogue with their partner. One of the important distinctions which we wished to capture was thus whether the aphasic speaker was consciously gesturing to his partner or whether the gestures were being produced as an unconscious by-product of the communicative process. Our coding scheme was designed to capture this distinction. As we wished to code all 32 aphasic and age-matched dialogues we also needed a simple scheme which could be applied to this substantial data set. Our goal was to produce an objective categorization which coders could use consistently and reliably over a large number of dialogues and which would capture at least some of the most salient distinctions in the communicative impact of the gestures used.

The setting in which the communication task took place was designed to allow us to distinguish those gestures which were made by speakers with the clear intention of signalling to their listener. The two sided sloping table at which participants sat, meant that if speakers wished to gesture to their listener they had to raise their hand slightly above the height of the table. Such communicative gestures were clearly visible from the video tapes of the interactions. We subdivided these gestures into those which had a clear semantic content for which a direct verbal gloss could readily be determined, such as directional pointing, indicating distance by holding up the fingers spaced apart, or drawing shapes in the air. These were categorized as **Iconic Gestures**. This category would include gestures which in other schemes such as Ekman and Freisen or Weiner *et al.* might be classified as deictics, ideographs, pictographs or panto-mimics.

Other gestures which were made clearly in view of the listener but which did not have an obvious semantic gloss we categorized as **Listener Oriented Gestures**. An example of such a gesture would be the speaker circling his hand in the air apparently indicating some kind of general impatience or communicative difficulty. This category would probably include those gestures classified in other schemes as semantic modifiers, illustrative or unclear.

Hand gestures which took place on the speaker's side of the sloping table and thus were not visible to the listener were coded as **Speaker Oriented Gestures**. An example might be if a speaker repeatedly traced the shape of the section of the route he was describing, or pointed at a landmark.

All videotaped interactions were analyzed by a trained coder. A second judge independently coded two dialogues. Interjudge reliability was calculated on these two sets of codings. In 83% of cases both judges agreed that a gestured had occurred and categorized it in the same way.

4.2. *Gesture Coding Results*

Do aphasic speakers use gesture to compensate for their linguistic difficulties? The first analysis was thus to determine if aphasic speakers use gestures more frequently than their unimpaired peers and if certain kinds of gesture are more common than others.

An Analysis of Variance was conducted with Group (Aphasic vs. Age-Matched Control Dialogues), and Subject (Aphasic/Age-Matched vs. Partner) as between dialogue measures and Gesture (Iconic, Listener Oriented and Speaker Oriented) as within-dialogue repeated measure. Here again we concentrate on the dialogues where the aphasic and age-matched subjects take the instruction giver's role.

On average aphasic instruction givers used more than twice as many gestures as their age-matched peers, with a mean of 16.0 gestures per dialogue versus 6.78, respectively. This was shown in the significant interaction between Group and Subject $(F(1,27) = 6.9, p < 0.01)$. Planned comparison tests showed that difference in the number of gestures used by aphasic and age-matched speakers was statistically significant.

There was also a significant interaction of Group and Gesture $(F(2,54) = 5.10, p < 0.01)$ and Subject and Gesture $(F(2,54) = 26.83, p < 0.001)$. The triple interaction of Group, Subject and Gesture was not significant. The mean number of gestures in each category is shown in Table 4.

Table 4. *Mean number of gestures per dialogue used by aphasic and age-matched instruction givers and their partners (standard deviations shown in brackets)*

Speaker	Iconic Gesture	Listener Oriented Gesture	Speaker Oriented Gesture
Aphasic IG	7.7 (9.6)	2.5 (2.9)	37.9 (27.7)
Age-Matched IG	2.0 (2.7)	1.1 (1.6)	17.2 (20.2)
Aphasic's IF	4.0 (5.9)	1.1 (1.1)	9.5 (8.8)
Age-Matched IF	0.4 (0.6)	5.1 (8.4)	3.2 (5.0)

Planned comparison tests showed that there were significantly more Speaker Oriented gestures from aphasic than non-aphasic instruction givers, with an average of 37.9 and 17.2 per dialogue, respectively. There was a numerical difference between the number of Iconic gestures from aphasic and age-matched speakers, 7.7 and 2 per dialogue respectively. This difference did not quite reach the level of statistical significance difference, due to high variability particularly among the data from aphasic dialogues. As can be seen from Table 4, the number of Iconic gestures from aphasic instruction givers varied widely from three dialogues where no such gestures were produced by the aphasic instruction givers, to one dialogue (BA's) where 36 such gestures were produced.

The ANOVA shows the general pattern of gesture use and how this differs between aphasic and unimpaired speakers. To explore the relationship between aphasic speakers' use of gesture and communicative success, we correlated the task performance scores and the frequency of each type of gesture in the dialogues where the aphasic speaker was the instruction giver. The statistically significant correlations are shown in Table 5.

Table 5. *Statistically significant correlations between gesture use and communication succes*

Gesture	Speaker	Correlation (Pearson's *r*)	% Map Score Explained	Helpful?
Iconic	Aphasic IG	−0.485	24%	YES
Listener Oriented	Aphasic IG	−0.343	11%	YES
Iconic	Partner IF	0.477	23%	NO
Listener Oriented	Partner IF	0.390	15%	NO

These data suggest that non-verbal communication, in this case gesture, **can** assist aphasic speakers to communicate successfully. In particular the frequency with which aphasic instruction givers use iconic gestures with a clear semantic content seems to play a role in determining the overall success of the dialogue.

If we turn from these general results on the effects of gesturing on communicative success, to our successful individuals we again see two different patterns of compensatory strategies. In Extract 1 we see clear illustrations of the effective use of iconic gestures. BA overcomes his very limited abilities to give full verbal instructions in part by the judicious and extensive use of gestures. In this extract we see two examples of Instruct moves where all the semantic content is carried by the accompanying gesture. Throughout his dialogue BA uses the highest number (36), of Iconic gestures, and the highest number (10) of Listener Oriented Gestures of any aphasic instruction giver. These figures are also beyond the maximum recorded for any age-matched instruction giver. Some indication of the prevalence of this gesturing behavior can be given by considering that as an instruction giver, BA produces 136 Conversational Moves in a dialogue consisting of 68 Conversational Games, 21 of which are initiated by BA. On average then just over a third of BA's Conversational Moves are accompanied by communicative gestures to his partner and over two thirds of the Conversational Games involve potentially informative gestures from the instruction giver.

RS again presents a different picture. His gesture data are as follows, Iconic Gestures 4, Listener Oriented Gestures 1, Speaker Oriented Gestures, 30. All these figures are below the average values recorded for the aphasic instruction givers and within the range of scores for the age-matched speakers. Even within a single communicative task aphasic speakers differ considerably in their use of gesture. It is not surprising that the results in the literature on the extent of gesturing vary across different tasks and aphasic syndromes. Extensive use of Iconic or Listener Oriented gesture is an additional compensatory strategies which not all aphasic speakers will adopt even within a interactional task where gesture can be a very effective communicative support. In many earlier studies, the communicative context such as an interview, is not one where gesture use might be as helpful in assisting an aphasic speaker to express his communicative intentions.

Our analyses of gestures continue, we plan to explore which kinds of Conversational Moves are typically accompanied by gesture and how frequently, as in these examples, the semantic content is carried by the gesture rather than the verbal content of the move. From later phases of the project data we can determine whether speakers are consistent over time in the extent and character of their gesturing. In addition we have several episodes of story-telling for each speaker and we shall analyze to what extent the rate of gesturing by different speakers such as BA and RS is replicated in a very different communicative context.

In contrast to effective use of gestures from at least some aphasic instruction givers, frequent use of gestures form the instruction following partner co-occurs with less effective dialogues. Is this an example of a mal-adaptive adjustment to the perceived language processing difficulty of the aphasic speaker? Do instruction followers increase their use of gesture when the communication is not progressing well? Do the instruction followers believe that the language production problems of the instruction givers are mirrored by language comprehension difficulties and that by gesturing they will reduce the aphasic speaker's language processing load? Are they consciously or unconsciously gesturing in the hope that their partner will adopt this compensatory communicative strategy? As the intercorrelation between the use of iconic gestures from aphasics and their partners is very low, this last explanation although plausible does not work in our sample dialogues. The absence of a correlation between the use of iconic gesturing also rules out instruction followers gesturing as as unconscious mirroring of the behavior of their aphasic partners.

5.   Discussion

In this chapter we have explored some facets of aphasic communication. In particular we have examined how dialogues between aphasic and unimpaired speakers differ. We are fortunate to have a large enough sample of aphasic speakers to observe both the general patterns which emerge when we compare groups of aphasic speakers and their age-matched peers, and to study individuals within this group. This has proved very valuable in answering questions such as do aphasic individuals communicate better than they speak. The answer to this question depends upon whether we focus on group or individual data. We are able to do both and say that on average aphasic speakers on our communicative task performed significantly less well than unimpaired speakers. Within this general group pattern we were able to identify individuals who did indeed communicate remarkably well despite their linguistic difficulties.

Through the use of Conversational Games and gesture analysis we feel we can illuminate some of the communicative strategies which underpin these impressive communicative achievements. If we compare the two dialogue extracts from BA and RS we can speculate about the way these two different patterns of compensatory strategies might have their beneficial effects. BA's linguistic abilities are more severely impaired, and as the extract illustrates the information content of his individual instructions (Instruct Moves) is fairly minimal. To convey his instructions to his partner he needs to use a large number of these very brief instructions. On many occasions he needs to clarify what he has already said or attempted to say, in response to his partner's checks that she has interpreted an instruction correctly. In addition he also uses iconic and listener oriented gestures to supplement the information content of his instructions. By using this array of compensatory strategies BA achieves a remarkably effective communication despite his severe linguistic limitations.

RS has somewhat less severe linguistic problems. As can be seen from Extract 3, although his utterances are hesitant and not always fully specified, they contain considerably more information content per conversational move than do those of BA. RS is able to produce instructions like that shown in Game 4:

"Um could you ... down for about two inches"

Later in the dialogue he produces other examples of fairly informationally rich instructions:

"Right. Em ... about ... four inches down you should come — go to go ... til you come to the goat."

RS unlike BA then does not have to produce a large number of instructions with a single item of information in each. In fact he produces slightly fewer instructions than the average produced by unimpaired instruction givers. Nor is there as great a need for the instruction follower to check her understanding of such instructions, which in turn reduces the need for clarifications from RS. He makes relatively little use of gesture again presumably because he can verbalize more of the semantic content he is attempting to convey.

RS does have some output difficulties as can be seen in Extract 3. On occasions he has noticeably word finding difficulties and is disfluent when attempting to produce a particular description. These can result in relatively lengthy utterances which are rather hard to interpret such as the opening utterance in Game 3:

"And uh about two inches in from ah the left side and inches one inch um ... above above no ... above ah ... one inch above ... um ... two inches in from the left de ... and"

RS's relatively frequent use of Align Moves, where he checks that his partner shares his view of the current task situation, before giving instructions, may be an attempt to pre-empt the communicative difficulties such disfluencies might cause. RS uses this move more frequently than most aphasic or age-matched instruction givers. Why might the use of Align Moves be useful? When RS uses this move he ensures that he receives feedback that his instruction follower can share his understanding of the state of the task. This feedback confirms both that the IF has understood what RS has said and shares the relevant information about the map which he was attempting to describe. This seems a very useful strategy as the Map Task was designed with some mis-matches of information between the two copies of the maps. These problem points have to be overcome by the participants if they are to achieve a success-ful task outcome. Disfluent instructions which contain references to unknown landmarks seem very likely to cause difficulties to the instruction follower.

In Extract 3 we see RS separating the process of establishing what informa-tion is known to the instruction follower in a fairly lengthy sequence of aligning, before giving instructions at the start of his dialogue. In an earlier study of Map Task Dialogues from unimpaired speakers, Anderson (1995) reported that such a 'top-down' approach to establishing mutual knowledge was uncommon. For RS with his particular linguistic difficulties and communicative strengths this seems an effective strategy with which to begin the dialogue task. Anderson and Boyle (1994) reported a more common analogous process where communicative-ly cautious and successful speakers, ask a brief checking question before using a landmark feature in a subsequent instruction.

RS's use of Align moves, particularly at the start of his dialogue can also be compared to the preliminaries described in conversational openings by Schegloff (1980) in his paper "Can I ask you a question?" An aphasic speaker like RS may exaggerate this normal conversational strategy to compensate for his particular linguistic difficulties. RS is not entirely consistent in his use of Aligns throughout the dialogue, i.e. he does not preface every instruction with such a move. There are however several subsequent occasions when Aligns are used and serve a similar function of prechecking on the listener's knowledge state before a new set of instructions are given. Again what might be thought of as a communicative strategy for conversational openings may be being extended to occur at most of the openings of salient conversational subsections.

The data presented here show that communicative skill seems to be independent of linguistic abilities and to vary among apparently similar individuals. In earlier research we have shown that unimpaired children and adults vary considerably in their communicative ability, and that a simple developmental model of increasing expertise with age does not fit the data we obtain from studying collaborative dialogues (Anderson *et al.* 1994; Anderson and Boyle 1994; Anderson 1995). All the speakers we studied from age 7 upwards commanded the necessary linguistic skills to achieve successful outcomes on our communicative task, but some speakers even among the adult group did not interact effectively enough to achieve a successful dialogue. Conversely some of our youngest speakers showed considerable interactive abilities interacted and produced very good collaborative dialogues. In the aphasic and age-matched dialogues we again see a wide range of communicative abilities. Some of our aphasic speakers achieve considerable task success not through their linguistic abilities but through their grasp of the nature of effective communication and their ability to adapt their available resources to this end. Not all the aphasic speakers demonstrate such abilities, nor indeed do all the unimpaired individuals in our sample.

The data from the Conversational Move and Gesture analyses show that there are a range of possible compensatory communicative strategies which aphasic speakers may adopt. Successful individuals seem to use a subset of these potentially beneficial behaviors. In the two cases we have examined in some detail the communicative strategies adopted seem to mesh very well with the linguistic impairments of the individuals concerned. The adaptations made by the unimpaired conversational partners seem to reflect the precise nature of these difficulties and compensations.

By focusing on the distribution of conversational games and moves we have identified some of the more salient differences which emerge where a linguistically impaired speaker is collaborating with an unimpaired conversational partner. One of the most striking differences which emerged was the difference in how conversational games are initiated. When a speaker takes the instruction giving role in our task, and in non laboratory settings we expect, this speaker has the prime duty to convey information to his partner. This is reflected as we would predict by the majority (62%) of conversational games being initiated by this speaker. In contrast where an aphasic speaker takes this dominant communicative role, they initiate less than a third of the conversational games with their unimpaired partner initiating the great majority of games. This is clear evidence of the conversational partner responding to the problems of her conversational partner and attempting to scaffold the interaction in a manner which seems analogous to that observed when an adult interacts with a linguistically immature child.

This reminder of similar adaptations which have been observed over thirty years of research in Child-Directed Speech (CDS) or 'motherese', sounds some warning bells. There was a period in that research endeavor where each characteristic of CDS was assumed to have a direct benefit in the process of language acquisition. The mother was viewed as providing optimum input in an unconscious attempt to provide the child with a sequence of graded language learning lessons. This view of the omniscient mother is no longer tenable. Many of the special features of CDS are now thought not to be tailored to the child as a language learner but a natural by-product of the communicative context of interaction with a young child of limited linguistic and cognitive abilities, see Snow (1994). Indeed in our own research some of the characteristics of CDS which arose because of the context of parent–child conversations, were found to have surprising and potentially unhelpful aspects when examined in greater detail (Bard and Anderson 1983, 1994).

We must not fall into the same trap in our interpretations of aphasic interactions. We must identify those characteristics of the dialogues which are the unavoidable consequences of the speakers' impaired linguistic abilities and those which are optional communicative strategies which might be used to overcome these limitations. A clear case of an unintended consequence of the communicative situation is the number of instructions used by BA. He does not choose to use a large number of instructions in his dialogue. His linguistic limitations mean that he is unable to produce longer more informative instructions and so has to present the information he is attempting to convey in this way. In contrast when BA raises his hand to gesture to his listener to supplement his verbal instructions and this seems much more likely to be a compensatory strategy which other aphasic individuals might be encouraged to adopt. Other adaptations such as RS's use of alignments and BA's use of clarifications are of less certain status but seem likely to be communicative strategies albeit probably unconscious ones.

We must also identify those adaptations which are in fact beneficial to the communicative process. Again the data we have presented here is useful in this respect because we can see not only what differences emerge when we compare dialogues between aphasic and unimpaired speakers, but also whether those differences appear to help speakers achieve mutual understanding. Some of the adaptations which conversational partners make do not seem to do so. We observed significant negative correlations between many apparently sensible conversational strategies and communicative success, such as offering explanations, asking questions, and gesturing. We are not confident as yet of the explanations for these effects, but they at the least remind us of the dangers of assuming that every conversational adaptation is necessarily beneficial. What do the data presented here tell us about communication in general? They emphasize its deeply collaborative nature. The process of 'grounding' (Clark and Schaeffer 1987) is achieved in these dialogues through considerable efforts on the part of aphasic speakers and their listeners. The linguistic abilities which the aphasic speaker can utilize in support of this process are often very restricted both in terms of syntax and vocabulary. Yet through the way the pragmatic functions are organized by both conversational participants, augmented in some cases by the use of gesture, effective communication is achieved. This success is humbling to those of us who sometimes struggle to communicate our ideas with the whole gamut of linguistic resources at our disposal. This achievement also underlines the flexibility and tenacity of the human communicator. Presented with new communicative challenges by the limitations imposed by disease or injury, many individuals will flexibly and successfully utilize their remaining available resources to reach a shared understanding with their listeners. We have concentrated on the adaptations made by the aphasic speaker but we have also seen the flexibility of unimpaired speakers. They too make a series of adjustments to their usual communicative behavior both verbally and in some cases nonverbally. In the longer term we hope to use the insights we have gained into such strategies and their effects on communicative outcomes, in the therapeutic regimes of aphasic speakers to assist and accelerate beneficial adaptations in a wider range of individuals.

Acknowledgments

This research was supported by the U.K. Economic and Social Research Council funded Human Communication Research Centre and by ESRC Project Grant RC 206120, the authors gratefully acknowledge their support.

References

Anderson, A.H. 1995. "Negotiating Coherence in Dialogue." In *Coherence in Spontaneous Text*, M. Gernsbacher and T. Givón (eds). Amsterdam: John Benjamins.
Anderson, A., M. Bader, E. Bard, E. Boyle, G. Doherty, S. Garrod, S. Isard, J. Kowtko, J. McAllister, J. Miller, C. Sotillo, H. Thompson and R. Weinart. 1991a. "The HCRC Map Task Corpus." *Language and Speech* 34(4),351–366.

Anderson, A. and E. Boyle. 1994. "Forms of Introduction in Dialogues: Their discourse contexts and communicative consequences." *Language and Cognitive Processes* 9(1). 101–122.

Anderson, A., A. Clark and J. Mullin. 1991b. "Introducing Information in Dialogues: Forms of introduction chosen by young speakers and the responses elicited from young listeners." *Journal of Child Language* 18.663–687.

Anderson, A., A. Clark and J. Mullin. 1994. "Interactive Communication between Children: Learning how to make language work in dialogue." *Journal of Child Language* 21.439–463.

Anderson, A., A. Garrod, A. Clark, E. Boyle and J. Mullin. 1992. "The HCRC Dialogue Database." *Journal of Child Language* 19.711–716.

Bard, E.G. and A.H. Anderson. 1983. "The Unintelligibility of Speech to Children." *Journal of Child Language* 10.265–292.

Bard, E.G. and A.H. Anderson. 1995. "The Unintelligibilty of Speech to Children: Effects of referent availability." *Journal of Child Language* 21.623–648.

Beeke, S., E. Dean, K. Kilborn, A. Anderson, A., Robertson and J. Miller. 1994. "The Relationship between Syntactic Processing and Communicative Performance in Aphasia." Paper presented at the International Clinical Phonetics and Linguistics Association Fourth Symposium, New Orleans, Nov. 14–16, 1994. To be published in *Clinical Phonetics and Linguistics.*

Behrmann, M. and C. Penn. 1984. "Non-verbal Communication of Aphasic Patients." *British Journal of Communication Disorders* 19.155–168.

Brown, G., A. Anderson, R. Shillcock and G. Yule. 1984. *Teaching Talk.* Cambridge: Cambridge University Press.

Brulhart, M. 1986. "Foreigner Talk in the ESL Classroom: Interactional adjustments to adult students at two language proficiency levels." *TESL Canada Journal* 1.29–42.

Busch, C., R. Brookshire and L. Nicholas. 1988. "Referential Communication by Aphasic and Nonaphasic Adults." *Journal of Speech and Hearing Disorders* 53.475–482.

Clark, H.H. 1985. "Language Use and Language Users." In *The handbook of Social Psychology*, G. Lindsey and E. Aronson (eds). New York: Harper & Row.

Clark, H.H. and C.R. Marshall 1981. "Definite Reference and Mutual Knowledge." In *Elements of Discourse Understanding*, A.K. Joshi, B.L. Webber and I.A. Sag (eds). Cambridge: Cambridge University Press.

Clark, H.H. and E. Schaeffer. 1987. "Collaborating on Contributions to Conversations." *Language and Cognitive Processes* 2.19–41.

Clark, H.H. and D. Wilkes-Gibbs. 1986. "Referring as a Collaborative Process." *Cognition* 22.1–39.

Cicone, M., W. Wapner, N. Foldi, E. Zurif and H. Gardner. 1979. "The Relations between Gesture and Language in Aphasic Communication." *Brain and Language* 8. 324–349.

Cohen, K. 1960. "A Coefficient of Agreement for Nominal Scales" *Educational and Psychological Measurement* 1.37–46.

Doherty-Sneddon, G. 1993. "Development of Communication Strategies." In *Proceedings of the Child Language Seminar*, J. Clibbens (ed). University of Plymouth.

Efron, G. 1972. *Gesture, Race and Culture.* The Hague: Mouton (originally published in 1941).

Ekman, P. and Freisen, W. 1969. "The Repertoire of Nonverbal Behaviour: Categories, origins, use and coding." *Semiotica* 1.49–98.

Ferguson, C.E. 1975. "Towards a Characterisation of English Foreigner Talk." *Anthropological Linguistics* 17.1–14.

Ferguson, C.E. and C.A. Snow. 1977. *Talking to Children: Language input and acquisition.* Cambridge: Cambridge University Press.

Feyereisen, P. 1987. "Gestures and Speech, Interactions and Separations: A reply to McNeill (1985)." *Psychological Review* 94.493–498.

Feyereisen, P. 1991. "Communicative Behaviour in Aphasia." *Aphasiology* 5(4).323–333.

Feyereisen, P. and J. de Lannoy. 1991. *Gestures and Speech: Psychological investigations.* Cambridge: Cambridge University Press.

Feyereisen, P. and X. Seron. 1982. "Non-verbal Communication and Aphasia: A review. 2. Expression." *Brain and Language* 16.213–236.

Garrod, S. and A. Anderson. 1987. "Saying What You Mean in Dialogue: A study in conceptual and semantic co-ordination." *Cognition* 27.181–218.

Glosser, G., M. Wiener and E. Kaplan. 1986. "Communicative Gestures in Aphasia." *Brain and Language* 27.345–359.

Goodglass, H. and E. Kaplan. 1983. *The Assessment of Aphasia and Related Disorders.* 2nd edition. Philadelphia: Lea & Febiger.

Goodwin, C. 1981. *Conversational Organization: Interactions between speakers and hearers.* New York: Academic Press.

Goodwin, C. 1995. "Negotiating coherence in conversation." In *Coherence in Spontaneous Text*, M. Gernsbacher and T. Givón (eds). Amsterdam: John Benjamins.

Hatch, E., R. Shapira and J. Wagner-Gough. 1978. "Foreigner-talk Discourse." *International Review of Applied Linguistics* 39.39–59.

Holland, A. 1980. *Communicative Abilities in Daily Living.* Baltimore: University Park Press.

Holland, A. 1982. "Observing Functional Communication of Aphasic Adults." *Journal of Speech and Hearing Disorders* 47.50–56.

Houghton, G., and S. Isard. 1987. "Why to Speak, What to Say, and How to Say It." In *Modelling Cognition*, P. Morris (ed.), 249–267. Chicester: John Wiley.

Howard, D. and F.M. Hatfield. 1987. *Aphasia Therapy: Historical and contemporary issues.* Hove and London: Lawrence Erlbaum.

Isaacs, E. and H.H. Chark. 1987. "References in Conversation between Novices and Experts." *Journal of Experimental Psychology: General* 116.26–37.

Keretz, A. 1982. *Western Aphasia Battery.* New York: Grune and Stratton.

Kilborn, K., A.H. Anderson, E. Dean, A. Robertson and S. Beeke. 1995. "Communicative Competence and On-line Processing: Relevance for research and treatment in aphasia." *Brain and Language* 48(1).120–123.

Kowtko, J.C. 1992. "On the Function of Intonation in Discourse: Intonation within the framework of conversational games." In *Proceedings of the Institute of Acoustics, Autumn Conference, Speech and Hearing.* Vol 14: *Part 6,* 65–70, Windermere: UK.

Kowtko, J.C., S. Isard and G. Doherty-Sneddon. 1991. "Conversational Games in Dialogue." *Technical report HCRC publications,* A. Lescardes (ed). University of Edinburgh.

Le May, A., R. David and A. Thomas. 1988. "The Use of Spontaneous Gesture by Aphasic Patients." *Aphasiology* 2(2).137–145.

Manochioping, S., C. Sheard and V. Reed. 1992. "Pragmatic Assessment in Adult Aphasia: A clinical review." *Aphasiology* 6(6).519–533.

McNeill, D. 1985. "So You Think Gestures are Nonverbal?" *Psychological Review* 92. 350–371.

McNeill, D. 1987. "So You Do Think Gestures are Nonverbal! A reply to Feyereisen (1987)." *Psychological Review* 94.499–504.

Merrison, A.J. 1992. "How Aphasics Get from A to B: Total communicative ability and the map task." MSc Dissertation. University of Edinburgh.

Meuse, S. and T. Marquand. 1985. "Communicative Effectiveness in Broca's Aphasia." *Journal of Communication Disorders* 18.21–34.

Milroy, L. and L. Perkins. 1992. "Repair Strategies in Aphasic Discourse: Towards a collaborative model." *Clinical Linguistics and Phonetics* 6.27–40.

Peirce, C. 1974. "Elements of Logic." In *Collected Papers of Sanders Peirce,* C. Hartshorne and P. Weiss (eds). Cambridge: Harvard University Press (originally published in 1932).

Power, R. 1979. "The Organisation of Purposeful Dialogues." *Linguistics* 17.107–152.

Prinz, P.M. 1980. "A Note on Requesting Strategies in Adult Aphasics." *Journal of Communication Disorders* 13.65–73.

Rime, B. and L. Schiaratura. 1991. "Gesture and Speech." In *Fundamentals of Nonverbal Behaviour,* R. Feldman and B. Rime (eds). New York: Cambridge University Press.

Sacks, H., E.A. Schegloff and G. Jefferson. 1974. "A Simplest Systematics for the Organisation of Turn-Taking for Conversation." *Language* 53.361–382.

Sacks, H. and E. Schegloff. 1979. "Two Preferences in the Organization of References to Persons in Conversation and Their Interaction." In *Everyday Language: Studies in ethnomethodology,* G. Psathes (ed.). New York: Irvington.

Schegloff, E. 1980. "Preliminaries to Preliminaries: Can I ask you a question?" *Sociological Inquiry* 50.104–152.

Schober, M.J. and H.H. Clark. 1989. "Understanding by Addresses and Overhearers." *Cognitive Psychology* 21.211–232.

Sinclair, J.M. and R.M. Coulthard. 1975. *Towards an Analysis of Discourse: The English used by teachers and their pupils.* London: Oxford University Press.

Smith, L. 1987. "Nonverbal Competency in Aphasic Stroke Patients' Conversation." *Aphasiology* 1.127–139.

Snow, C.E. 1994. "Beginning from Baby Talk: 20 years of research on input and interaction." In *Input and Interaction in Language Acquisition*, C. Galloway and B. Richards (eds). Cambridge: Cambridge University Press.

Traum, D.R. and E. Hinkelman. 1992. "Conversation Acts in Task-Oriented Spoken Dialogue." *Technical report* 425. Computer Science Dept, University of Rochester.

Ullatowska, H., L. Allard, B. Reyes, J. Ford and S. Chapman. 1992. "Conversational Discourse in Aphasia." *Aphasiology* 6(3).325–331.

Wilkes-Gibbs, D. and H.H. Clark. 1992. "Coordinating Beliefs in Conversation." *Journal of Memory and Language* 31.183–194.

Wirz, S., C. Skinner and E. Dean. 1990. *The Revised Edinburgh Functional Communication Profile.* Tucson, Ariz.: Communication Skill Builders.

Polyphonic Topic Development

Wallace Chafe

University of California, Santa Barbara

Language is a constantly changing process, not a stable object. Because we see so many examples of it in written form, we are apt to think of it as something fixed in time — as we do, for example, when we speak of a "text" as if it were a thing. But once we take the trouble to observe language as it occurs in nature, its dynamic nature becomes immediately apparent. (For further discussion of this and other matters which serve as background to this paper, see Chafe, In press.)

The metaphor of a *stream* of speech is one way of capturing this quality. Actually there are two streams, one consisting of sounds, the other of thoughts that are expressed by the sounds. Both streams proceed in parallel, and of course they are interrelated. What is the force that propels them forward? What makes language move? Evidently it is not the sounds. There is nothing in the nature of sounds themselves that leads one particular sound to be replaced by another particular sound. Rather, language is kept moving by the thoughts, with the sounds keeping pace. The question can thus be narrowed to asking what causes *thoughts* to be continually replaced by other thoughts.

In Chafe (1994:28–35) 1 listed some of the obvious properties of human consciousness, one of them being the inevitable restlessness of focal consciousness. Whether we are speaking or engaged in silent thought, it is easy to observe that our focus of consciousness is constantly shifting from one thought to another. We might, then, answer the question just raised by saying that the constantly changing nature of language results from this restlessness of consciousness. But that cannot be the whole story, for thoughts do not succeed one another randomly. The flow of thought exhibits directionality, and the question can now be rephrased to ask what it is that determines the *direction* in which thoughts move.

One can think of each separate focus of consciousness as contributing to the stream of thought by following from what preceded it and at the same time anticipating something that will come next. The preceding or following context may consist of nothing more than a single focus of consciousness but more often it involves a focus cluster covering an idea that is too large and complex to be brought within a single focus of fully active consciousness. A larger idea of this kind can only be embraced within semiactive consciousness, and can be said to constitute a discourse *topic* (Chafe 1994:120–145). Its extent can vary over a large range, from a minimal subtopic to an extended supertopic. There may, however, be reasons to identify a particular level in this hierarchy as a *basic-level* topic. In what follows we will be examining one such basic-level topic extracted from a much longer conversation.

In a typical situation that arises during a conversation, someone will open a basic-level topic, too big to be in active consciousness all at once, and successive foci will then navigate within it until its content has been judged to have been adequately covered. There are likely to be subtopics and subsubtopics that emerge during this process, but any such hierarchical structure may be subject to modification as the development of the basic-level topic proceeds, sometimes because of changes in plan by the person who introduced the topic, sometimes because other participants in the conversation may change its course in unanticipated ways.

What keeps language moving is, then, essentially the introduction and development of topics. The question to be asked next is what guides the focus of consciousness as it navigates through a topic. What determines its trajectory? In Chafe (1994:120–136) I illustrated two different trajectories of this kind. One was a more or less monologic speaker's reliance on a self-sustaining *schema,* an already familiar pattern of topic development. Typical is the narrative schema in which an initial setting establishes the background for a complicating action, which in turn leads on to a climax, after which a denouement may be followed by a coda that wraps up the topic as a whole. The other trajectory illustrated in that chapter involved an interplay between two interlocutors, their successive foci of consciousness propelled forward by their reactions to what the other had just said. As it happened, one of them repeatedly said things in conflict with the expectations of the other, who in turn expressed surprise and asked questions designed to satisfy his curiosity.

Here I am going to illustrate a mixed trajectory of topic development that was influenced in part by the narrative schema, in part by interactive agreements and disagreements, but also in part by the sometimes simultaneous contributions of two people whose knowledge was similar, just because they had both experienced the incident that provided the subject matter. It was the kind of conversational performance called by Jane Falk (1979, 1980) *dueting,* an appropriate term in the sense that the two speakers were performing a kind of duet to which each contributed more or less equally. Dueting can be thought of as a type of conversational polyphony, as explored further by Coates (1991, 1994, In press, This volume). My purpose here is not just to provide one more example of dueting, however, but to show how a combination of this with other strategies can, in concert, determine the trajectory of the flow of ideas.

Falk (1980:507–508) says that dueters "have mutual knowledge of the topic, ... equivalent authority to express that knowledge, and a sense of camaraderie between them"; furthermore, that "they are addressing in tandem not each other but a mutual audience," and that "they intend it to be understood that each of their contributions counts on both their behalfs." These properties are evident in the example to be discussed here, but with two qualifications. These dueters did not always speak "in tandem," but often simultaneously. And they did not, in Falk's words, "undertake jointly to carry out the communicative task ... in such a way that a written version of their resultant in-sequence text would be indistinguishable from that of a single speaker." Rather, they had different ways of understanding and developing the topic. The effect was analogous to musical counterpoint, with separate voices articulating different melodies at once.

Topics are typically introduced with a spatial, temporal, and often epistemic orientation. In this example speaker A opened a new topic as follows:

(1)   A   Yóu guys won't belíeve [1 what 1] háppened to us in the [2 párking lot 2] of the= máll the other day.

(Transcription conventions are listed at the end of the paper, but it is especially relevant here to point out that the square brackets enclose segments during which another speaker spoke. The numbers provide indices for these overlaps.)

This topic-initial intonation unit was unusual in several ways. In the first place, it was unusually long, its eighteen words contrasting with a mean of approximately five for English conversations. Unusually long intonation units like this are apt to occur at topic beginnings and at the climaxes of narratives. Speaker A succeeded here within a single intonation unit in communicating (1) the people to whom he was speaking (*you guys,* a group composed of the other participants minus his wife); (2) the surprising nature of what he was about to relate (you *won't believe* it); (3) the fact that it was something that *happened to us;* (4) its location in space (*in the parking lot of the mall*); and finally (5) its location in time (*the other day*). All this is something of a challenge to the one-new-idea-per-intonation-unit hypothesis (Chafe 1994:108–119). But it may be that the only truly new idea here was that expressed by the words *in the parking lot of the mall,* the others being either given (*you guys*), presentative (*what happened to us*), or orienting phrases of the sort that do not exact an activation cost (*you won't believe, the other day*). It can be noted, too, that much of (1)

consists of the formulaic collocation *you won't believe what happened to us.*
There is a need for continuing studies of the special properties and environments
of intonation units that are atypically long.

By saying (1), A succeeded in opening and orienting a topic that he must,
at least momentarily, have expected to develop by himself, probably hoping for
an expression of interest by one or more of the others, an interest he intended to
stimulate by promising that the topic would contain something the others
wouldn't believe. There is no way to know how he would have developed it if
he had been left to his own devices, because his wife, speaker B, had also been
present at the incident in question and was equally motivated to tell about it.
She spoke twice while A was saying (1), first showing her immediate recognition of what the topic was:

(2)   B   [1 óh=.1]

and then providing her own spatial orientation, overlapping A's orientation as he
mentioned *the parking lot:*

(3)   B   [2 by the Goodwill store. 2]

A's topic opener anticipated a request from one or more of the other parties that
he proceed with developing his topic, and after a brief pause speaker C obliged
by asking:

(4)   C   (0.2) Whát.

Following a spatial, temporal, and epistemic setting as in (1), the narrative
schema anticipates the idea of some person who will play a major role in the
events to be described. Speaker A conformed perfectly to this expectation:

(5)   A   (0.3) Sóme guy càme óut and he he was ☺

with laughter at the end. The narrative schema typically leads next to the
involvement of this character in a background activity, something he was
engaged in, expressed with an imperfective aspect. Speaker A tried to get started
with such an idea at the end of (5), where the word *was* anticipated a verb form
ending in -*ing*. Probably because of the one-new-idea constraint he was unable
to proceed further within the same intonation unit. Instead, he dissolved
momentarily into laughter, giving his wife a chance to repeat her own interest
in the topic, this time with a higher pitch:

(6)   B   ↑ Óh=. ↑

And now A was able to complete successfully what he wanted to say about the
stranger's background activity:

(7)   A   hé was trying to séll us cológne or [1 something. 1]

So far the development of this topic had followed a trajectory determined by A's adherence to the familiar narrative schema in which an initial orientation is followed by the introduction of a crucial character and then the involvement of that character in a background activity. Speaker B had confirmed her interest in the topic with her *oh* in (2) and (6), as well as her contribution to the spatial orientation in (3). With A's utterance of (7), however, a conflict arose, because what he said was not what she remembered. She expressed her disagreement by saying:

(8) B [1 No 1] he wásn't trying to séll us [2 colò=gne, 2]

Even before she finished – while she was saying the word cologne — A recognized the inaccuracy of (7) and began searching for an appropriate correction:

(9) A [2 Well it 2]

which he was then able to verbalize successfully:

(10) a. A Nò= I guéss he was trying to like lúre us to a,
   b. A (0.2) pláce where they wóuld sèll like,
   c. A (0.3) imitátion cológne?

The narrative schema now dictated a move from the imperfective background activity expressed in (7), (8), and (10) to the introduction of punctual events expressed with a perfective aspect, events that could be anticipated to lead to some sort of surprising climax. The complicating events in this case began with a quoted conversation, which A signaled iconically by rising to a higher level of pitch:

(11) a. A But he said ↑ it's nót imitátion, ↑
   b. A [1 because 1]

He would eventually succeed in completing the *because* clause begun in (11b) but the quote in (11a) stimulated another of the participants, speaker D, to interpolate a stereotyped phrase she associated with hucksters of this kind. Its intended humorous effect was heightened by her use of a hollow voice quality caricaturing the voice of such a person:

(12) D [1 I got 1] [2 a 2] déal you can't [3 refú=se. 3]

With the second of the three overlapping segments in (12), B indicated her acceptance of the way A had reformulated the stranger's intentions in (10):

(13) B [2 Yéah. 2]

It was here that the polyphony began. A's melodic line continued his schematically guided account of how he had interacted with the stranger. Simultaneously B opened and developed a different and independent line, one that expressed the apprehension she had felt because of the stranger's appear-ance. This counterpoint began as an overlap with the word *refuse* at the end of (12), as A took up and completed the *because* clause he had momentarily abandoned in (11b). B began her own subtopic quite independently of what A was saying:

(14) a. A   [3 because it's= 3] [4 máde by the sàme 4] péople,
       b. B   [4 1 mean this kíd was— 4]

As A continued with his quote from the stranger, B continued to develop her description of his appearance:

(15) a. A   [5 but it's pùt in different 5] bóttles?
       b. B   [5 he lóoked like a=, 5]

As the counterpoint went on, A raised his pitch level once again, this time quoting himself while B finished what she had started in (15b)

(16) a. A   [6 And I'm like ↑ whát are you dóin' ↑ 6] out here.
       b. B   [6 kind of a slóppy kind of gúy. 6]

Before he resolved the anticipation he had created by the question in (16a), A rested, allowing B a solo conclusion of her own subtopic:

(17) a. B   (0.5) 1 mean he wásn't—
       b. B   he was dréssed in like,
       c. B   (0.2) óld jéans,
       d. B   and an óld jácket,
       e. B   he just lóoked like,
       f. B   (..) a [1 vágabond. 1]

    The declining prosody toward the end of (17) was a signal to A that B was finishing her solo, allowing him to carry on with his own development, overlap-ping B's last word. His account of his interaction with the stranger continued as follows. The attribution in (18b) of a quote to come was accompanied by laughter:

(18) a. A   [1 He pùlled out 1] this dúffle bà=g,
       b. A   ☺ and I'm like, ☺

    But now the dueting resumed, for B had rested only long enough to allow A to finish (18a), and anticipate a quote with (18b). As A now continued to tell of his interaction with the stranger, again raising his pitch level with the quote from himself in (19a), B followed up on her description of the stranger's appearance by telling of her emotional reaction to the encounter:

(19) a. A   ↑ are you trying to [1 séll us something? 1] ↑
       b. B   [1 And I was like, 1]

(20) a. A [2 And he's like nó, 2]
    b. B [2 Í was ready to 2]

(21) a. A [3 I just want you to sméll it. 3]
    b. B [3 gràb Kévin and rún. 3]

Before this contrapuntal episode had concluded, and in fact simultaneously with all of (21), a third voice, that of speaker D, the person who had inserted her huckster imitation in (12) with *I got a deal you can't refuse,* now interposed an independent suggestion as to what the stranger might have been up to:

(22) a. D [3 I wonder if he'd rìpped it 3] óff in the—
    b. D (0.1) in the stóre.

But A was emphatic in rejecting this suggestion, again with heightened pitch:

(23)   A ↑ Nó=. ↑

His rejection was echoed and then considerably elaborated by B:

(24) a. B No because he w— he wasn't trying to séll it.
    b. B He was just saying does this smell like—
    c. B (0.2) Drakká=r,
    d. B or,
    e. B whatéver,
    f. B (0.3) becàuse,
    g. B (0.8) they're gonna o?—
    h. B try and .. sèe if there's a márket for this stó=re.
    i. B (0.1) That they wanna ópen,
    j. B ♫ dówn the róad, ♫
    k. B (0.1) that [1 sélls, 1]

Speaker B never finished (24k). The basic-level topic had been opened by A in (1), and he had announced it as something the others wouldn't believe. Unlike B, he had a stake in building toward a climax that would impress his interlocutors with the incredibility of this incident. B's explanation of the stranger's purpose in (24) gave him the opening he needed to summarize the stranger's larger function in an unexpected and jocular manner:

(25) A [1 So he's 1] a márketing àgent.

In a different context (25) might not have been judged much of a climax, but as this topic had developed it was perceived as such by the others as evidenced by the strong reactions that followed from all sides. Several participants chimed in with suggestions regarding the stranger's qualifications as a marketing agent, all uttered amid general laughter. It was the explosive kind of reaction a narrator hopes to achieve:

(26) a. B   ☺ He's an MÁ.
      b. E   Óh he's an MÁ.
      c C   MÁ.
      d. A   With an AÁ.
      e. E   And a pretty bad PVÁ.
      f. C   Pretty bad [1 PVA 1]. ☺

(What was meant here by *AA* and *PVA* will have to remain an open question.)

Interspersed with the laughter and speculations in (26) was, however, a different sort of reaction, first articulated by C immediately following (26d), and then seconded by D immediately after (26e):

(27) a. C   Scáry=,
      b. D   Scá=ry=.

These reactions picked up on B's voicing of anxiety in (19) through (21). The return of this motif of fear was now driven home by B's almost literal repetition of what she had said before, presumably triggered by the reactions in (27), and beginning just before the end of (26f):

(28) a. B   [1 Í was like 1] réady to gràb Kévin and rú=n.
      b. B   (0.4) [2 Cause I thought 2] what is this gúy dóing.

The surprising quality of the incident and the fact that it was worth relating — the points being stressed by A — were now confirmed by D, A, and even B in sequence:

(29) a. D   [2 Jee=sh, 2]
      b. D   (0.4) That's wíld.
      c. A   It wás.
      d. B   (0.3) [3 It was wéird. 3]

Segments (26) through (28) formed a jointly constructed denouement to the narrative, with (29) as a final coda. It is therefore not surprising that C decided the topic had reached an adequate conclusion, and that it would now be appropriate for her to open a different topic involving her interest in birthday cards (the gathering was, in fact, a celebration of her birthday). She opened this new topic hesitantly, overlapping B's final evaluation in (29d):

(30) a. C   [3 Mhm, 3]
      b. C   thát,
      c. C   (0.5) Nó more cards,

Not everyone, however, agreed that the preceding topic had been concluded. A, its introducer, having achieved success with the climax articulated in (25), now decided to raise the interestingness of his narrative to a new height by adding a second, fictional climax: a pretense that the stranger's pitch regarding cologne had been a planned distraction concocted to divert his and his wife's attention while a more sinister act was in progress:

(31)   A   And we turned aròund and our cár was gòne.

B reacted with laughter that appropriately disabled the seriousness of A's statement, A did not hesitate to admit that he had invented it, C laughingly acknowledged her understanding of its fictional status, and E contributed more laughter:

(32)   a.   B   (0.7) ☺
         b.   A   (0.1) Júst kídding,
         c.   C   ☺ Yeah really. ☺
         d.   E   [1 ☺ ☺ ☺ 1]

While E was laughing, D cooperated with C by responding to the topic (receiving birthday cards) that C had introduced in (30c):

(33)   D   [1 Nót till 1] Mònday níght.

The joking anticlimax in (31) and the responses to it in (32) provided final closure for the topic opened in (1), and the conversation moved on to matters more closely associated with C's birthday.

What is a Text?

I presented this conversational excerpt in brief segments that captured the constantly changing foci of consciousness verbalized by the several interlocutors. It is of course possible to collect all these segments together into a continuous sequence of the kind that has been called a text. One might even give it a title:

The Cologne Marketing Agent

(34)   A   Yóu guys won't belíeve [1 what 1] háppened to us in the [2 párking lot 2] of the= máll the other day.
         B   [1 Óh=. 1]
         B   [2 by the Goodwíll store. 2]
         C   (0.2) Whát.
         A   (0.3) Sóme guy càme óut and he he was ☺
         B   ↑ Óh=. ↑
         A   hé was trying to séll us coĺogne or [1 something. 1]
         B   [1 No 1] he wásn't trying to séll us [2 colò=gne, 2]
         A   [2 Well it 2]

A Nò= I guéss he was trying to like lúre us to a,

A (0.2) pláce where they wóuld sèll like,

A (0.3) imitátion cológne?

A But he said ↑ it's nót imitátion, ↑

A [1 because 1]

D [1 I got 1] [2 a 2] déal you can't [3 refú=se. 3]

B [2 Yéah. 2]

A [3 because it's= 3] [4 máde by the sàme 4] péople,

B [4 I mean this kíd was— 4]

A [5 but it's pùt in different 5] bóttles?

B [5 he lóoked like a=, 5]

A [6 And I'm like ↑ whát are you dóin' ↑ 6] out here.

B [6 kind of a slóppy kind of gúy. 6]

B (0.5) I mean he wásn't—

B he was dréssed in like,

B (0.2) óld jéans,

B and an óld jácket,

B he just lóoked like,

B (..) a [1 vágabond. 1]

A [1 He pùlled out 1] this dúffle bà=g,

A ☺ and I'm like, ☺

A ↑ are you trying to [1 séll us something? 1] ↑

B [1 And I was like, 1]

A [2 And he's like nó, 2]

B [2 Í was ready to 2]

A [3 I just want you to sméll it. 3]

B [3 gràb Kévin and rún. 3]

D [3 I wonder if he'd rìpped it 3] óff in the—

D (0.1) in the stóre.

A ↑ Nó=. ↑

B No because he w— he wasn't trying to séll it.

B He was just saying does this smell like—

B (0.2) Drakká=r,

B or,

B whatéver,

B (0.3) becàuse,

B (0.8) they're gonna o?—

B try and .. sèe if there's a márket for this stó=re.

B (0.1) That they wanna ópen,

B ♫ dówn the róad, ♫
B (0.1) that [1 sélls, 1]
A [1 So he's 1] a márketing àgent.
B He's an MÁ.
E Óh he's an MÁ.
C MÁ.
A With an AÁ.
E And a pretty bad PVÁ.
C Pretty bad [1 PVA 1].
C Scáry=,
D Scá=ry=.
B [1 Í was like 1] réady to gràb Kévin and rú=n.
B (0.4) [2 Cause I thought 2] what is this gúy dóing.
D [2 Jee=sh, 2]
D (0.4) That's wíld.
A It wás.
B (0.3) [3 It was wéird. 3]
C [3 Mhm, 3]
C thát,
C (0.5) Nó more cárds,
A And we turned aròund and our cár was gòne.
B (0.7) ☺
A (0.1) Júst kídding,
C ☺ Yeah réally. ☺
E [1 ☺ ☺ ☺ 1]
D [1 Nót till 1] Mònday níght.

What sort of object is (34)? Viewed in terms of the on-going processes that were taking place in the minds of the participants in the conversation, its status is certainly questionable. It obviously was not present in the minds of any of these people before these things were said. Nor could it have been present as such in anyone's mind after these things were said. Some or all of the participants may have remembered for a while that A and B talked about a peculiar incident in a parking lot, but they would not have remembered it in the form of (34). Either A or B or both may have had occasion before or since to tell about this incident in different company. What they may have said on such occasions may have borne some partial resemblance to (34), but the resemblance could only have been a partial one. More research on multiple retellings is badly needed, but it is at least clear that things are seldom if ever verbalized in exactly the same way on different occasions (cf. Chafe 1990).

It is instructive to compare "oral literature" — folktales, jokes, rituals, political speeches, and the like — in this respect. In such cases there is a repetition of a content that is relatively the same, though still with partially different language expressing partially different thoughts on each occasion. The relative degrees of permanence and variability in oral literature is another subject in need of further study, but one expects the similarities to be greater than in a typical conversation.

In this light, it is interesting to realize that oral literature has until recently provided the favorite material for text collection, as in the tradition of American Indian folktale collection associated with Franz Boas and many others, a tradition that continues to this day. Although I believe it is a practice whose value would be hard to overemphasize, I also believe it has created an illusion that spoken language has more permanence than it actually does. The conversational materials that are now available to us certainly show a different picture, and it is always important to keep in mind that conversational language reflects the natural workings of the mind more closely than language of any other kind.

To return to the question of what (34) really is, I would suggest that a written transcript is a kind of time machine, invented by linguists and others so that they can examine at their leisure the fluid, constantly changing phenomena that constitute language. This is not to say that there is anything wrong with transcribing and analyzing texts, but only that we need to avoid reifying our transcripts, keeping always in mind that they are an artificial freezing of phenomena which are in constant change. Time machines can be very useful, but they are also unreal.

It is not quite right, either, to think of conversationalists as jointly constructing a text, if by *text* is meant something like (34). It is better, I think, to regard a conversation as a rather wonderful device available to human beings by means of which separate minds are able to influence and be influenced by each other, managing to some extent, but always imperfectly, to bridge the gap that inevitably exists between separate selves. People do not thereby create a static object, but are engaged in a constant interplay of constantly changing ideas.

Transcription conventions

(0.3)	A pause measuring 0.3 seconds
(..)	A pause measuring less than one-tenth of a second
=	Expressive lengthening of the preceding sound
☺	Laughter (either a pulse of laughter, or bracketing words that are accompanied by laughter)
[1 1]	A stretch of speech overlapping with another stretch uttered by a different speaker, indexed when necessary to distinguish several overlaps in close proximity
↑ ↑	A stretch of speech spoken with a higher pitch baseline
♫ ♫	A stretch of speech spoken in a singsong manner

References

Chafe, Wallace. 1990. "Repeated Verbalizations as Evidence for the Organization of Knowledge." In *Proceedings of the XIVth International Congress of Linguists, Berlin 1987,* Werner Bahner (ed.).

Chafe, Wallace. 1994. *Discourse, Consciousness, and Time: The flow and displacement of conscious experience in speaking and writing.* Chicago: The University of Chicago Press.

Chafe, Wallace. In press. "The Flow of Conversation." In *Discourse: Linguistic, Computational, and Philosophical Perspectives,* Daniel L. Everett and Sarah G. Thomason (eds). Pittsburgh: University of Pittsburgh Press, and Konstanz: Universitätsverlag.

Coates, Jennifer. 1991. "Women's Cooperative Talk: A new kind of conversational duet?" In *Proceedings of the Anglistentag 1990 Marburg,* Claus Uhlig and Rüdiger Zimmerman (eds). Tübingen: Max Niemeyer.

Coates, Jennifer. 1994. "No Gaps, Lots of Overlap: Turn-taking patterns in the talk of women friends." In *Researching Language and Literacy in Social Context. Multilingual Matters,* David Graddol, Janet Maybin and Barry Stierer (eds), 177–192.

Coates, Jennifer. In press. *Women Friends Talking.* Oxford: Basil Blackwell.

Coates, Jennifer. This volume. "The Construction of a Collaborative Floor in Women's Friendly Talk."

Falk, Jane. 1979. "The Duet as a Conversational Process." Ph.D. dissertation, Princeton University.

Falk, Jane. 1980. "The Conversational Duet." In *Proceedings of the Sixth Annual Meeting of the Berkeley Linguistics Society,* 507–514.

The Construction of a Collaborative Floor in Women's Friendly Talk

Jennifer Coates
Roehampton Institute London

1. Women and jam sessions

For many years now I've been trying to work out exactly what is different about the talk of women friends. My research is based on a corpus of twenty conversations between women friends and a set of ethnographic interviews with fifteen women about friendship. Overall, what is most noticeable about women's friendly conversation is that the construction of talk is a joint effort: All participants share in the construction of talk in the strong sense that *they don't function as individual speakers*. In other words, the group takes priority over the individual and the women's voices combine to construct a shared text. A good metaphor for talking about this is a musical one: the talk of women friends is a kind of jam session. The dictionary definition of 'jam session' is 'A meeting of musicians for the spontaneous and improvisatory performance of music, especially jazz, usually for their own enjoyment' (Penguin Macquarie Dictionary). The key words here — *spontaneous, improvisatory* and *enjoyment* — are all central to any account of what is going on in the talk of women friends. In fact, we could adapt the definition to read: '*Jam session* — (of speech) A meeting of women friends for the spontaneous and improvisatory performance of talk, for their own enjoyment'.

When women friends meet and talk, they tell each other stories about their own experience and the experience of others (see Coates 1996a, 1996b); these stories normally involve only one speaker, the narrator. All jam sessions — whether of the musical or the conversational kind — include solo as well as ensemble or all-together sections. But the heart of good conversation for women friends is group talk, where speakers are typically 'melding in together', as one of the women I interviewed put it. I will start to pin down exactly what 'melding' entails in linguistic terms by looking at two phenomena characteristic of women friends' talk: jointly constructed utterances and overlapping speech.

2. Jointly constructed utterances

In the conversations I've recorded, two or three or more women friends will work together so that their voices combine to produce a single utterance or utterances.[1] To illustrate the way women friends speak as a single voice. I shall draw on the whole range of conversational material, beginning with some very simple examples where the last word of an utterance is provided by a different speaker:

(1)   [Sue and Liz discuss where they like to talk]

SUE: I mean in someone's house it's easier to talk than=
LIZ: =out/

(2)   [Karen worries that she is overlooked by a neighbour]

KAREN: I mean OK I'm sure he's not=
PAT: =peeping/

(3)   [Helen and Jen speculate on the effect an individual's absence could have on a group]

HELEN: they won't be so=
JEN: =homogeneous/

(4)   [discussion of students fooling around in class]

ANNA: the lecturer doesn't want to say anything though

LIZ: =adults/
ANNA: because they're supposed to be=

These four utterances are all constructed by *two* speakers. They are remarkable because they are identical to utterances produced by a single speaker, in other words, in each case two speakers combine with each other, blend their voices, to produce a single utterance. Below, I present these four examples as single utterances, using the symbol // to indicate a switch of speaker:

1.   I mean in someone's house it's easier to talk than//out
2.   I mean OK I'm sure he's not//peeping
3.   they won't be so//homogeneous
4.   because they're supposed to be//adults

This level of collaboration can only be achieved when speakers pay extremely close attention to each other, at all linguistic levels. For example, in the four examples above, the woman who contributes the last word demonstrates careful monitoring in terms of semantic, syntactic and also prosodic levels.

Jointly constructed utterances may involve more than just the final word of an utterance, as examples (5)–(8) illustrate:

(5)   [discussion of Open Evening at local school]

JEN: they said they kept bumping into all sorts of people=
HELEN: =that they knew/

(6)   [discussion of Christmas play at local primary school]

KAREN: once those cameras start flashing particularly with

KAREN: the infants=
PAT: =it puts them off/

(7)   [discussion of victims and blame]

MEG: women who are victims of rape are often thought to um

MEG: somehow .
MARY: oh have caused the rape/

(8)   [discussion of child abuse]

BEA: I mean in order to accept that idea you're

BEA: having to .
MARY: mhm/ completely review your view of your husband/

In all these examples, two women jointly construct an utterance, negotiating quite complex grammatical constructions. For example, Helen adds a relative clause *that they knew* to the noun *people*; Pat completes the utterance Karen began by replacing *once those cameras start flashing* with the (anaphoric) pronoun *it* and then adding a predicate *puts them [the infants] off*. In example (7), Mary has to deal with difficult tense and aspect choices: she produces *have caused the rape* rather than *cause the rape*, as someone who is a victim must already have been abused or attacked. Example (8) is perhaps most notable for the level of understanding it demonstrates in terms of the meaning of what is being talked about: Bea and Mary here operate very much as one speaker and express the group voice on the position of the mother of an abused child. All these examples demonstrate the way speakers monitor what each other is saying to the extent that the construction of utterances can be shared. Women friends exploit this ability to talk in a more melded way than is typical of other, less intimate, groups of speakers.[2]

2.1. *Joint construction involving simultaneous speech*

A variant on the pattern occurs where two speakers produce part of an utterance *together*, rather than one speaker beginning and another completing the utterance. Examples (9)–(11) below are the most simple kind, where two speakers both say the last words of an utterance.

(9)   [Anna describes her friend Shirley's reaction to her cystitis on their trip to Rome]

ANNA: if she'd been in my position I think I'd have been

ANNA: a bit m⌈ore   sympathetic/
SUE: ⌊more sympathetic/

(10)   [Pat tells Karen about her neighbour's attack of acute indigestion]

PAT: he and his wife obviously thought he'd had a ⌈heart attack/
KAREN: ⌊heart attack/

(11)   [talking about school play]

PAT: and every line they played for a laugh . ⌈got a laugh/
KAREN: ⌊got a laugh/

Saying the same words at the same time may involve more than just the last words of an utterance, as the next example shows. This example comes from a conversation between two women, me and Helen, when we're discussing a local political crisis which we both know about. (Jane Bull was the leader of the local Council at the time of this conversation.)

(12)   [Helen and Jen discuss local political crisis]

```
------------------------------------------------------------
JEN:      and apparently ⌈Jane Bull ((xx))
HELEN:                    ⌊well in fact Jane Bull's very threatened/
------------------------------------------------------------
JEN:                                        ⌈she had this grammar school
HELEN:    because did you- did you hear ⌊she had this grammar school-
------------------------------------------------------------
JEN:      meeting/
HELEN:    yes/
------------------------------------------------------------
```

In this example, I begin to talk about Jane Bull, and Helen picks up this theme to produce *Jane Bull's very threatened*. When Helen begins to say why Jane Bull is threatened, I join in and we say together *she had this grammar school,* an utterance which I complete with the word *meeting*. This is a good example of the extent to which utterances can be jointly constructed. This chunk of talk can not be said to belong to either of us: We are drawing on our shared knowledge of local events to produce talk collaboratively. In this example, it is also quite clear that the main goal of talk is not information exchange, since we both know what the facts are and are aware that each other knows.

2.2. Incomplete utterances

If the potential exists for speakers to share in the construction of utterances, then we would predict that from time to time utterances will be incomplete, since speakers know that others can anticipate what is to come, and others may choose *not* to complete the utterance verbally, but instead may choose to indicate that they understand by nodding or smiling or saying *yes*. This is precisely what we find in conversations between women friends. In the first example here, Meg is summing up a discussion about taking pleasure in others' downfall:

(13)   [schadenfreude]
MEG: funny how . you can be so mean about- it's obviously jealousy isn't it/

Meg doesn't specify exactly what (or who) people are so mean about, but leaves it for her friends to fill in for themselves. Her subsequent tag question — *it's obviously jealousy isn't it* — continues as if the preceding text were perfectly coherent; that is, it assumes her friends have processed the preceding statement successfully. (Note that this tag has falling not rising intonation: Meg does not expect a reply. This is typical of tags occurring in my corpus.)

In the next example, Mary doesn't complete her utterance in the context of a discussion about whether there is ever an occasion when you would not attend a funeral.

(14)   [funeral discussion]

MARY: but if there's no spouse I mean/ <u>and there's very few relatives left/</u>

MARY: <u>it doesn't really seem much of a-</u> ⟨LAUGHING⟩   =mhm/
SALLY: mhm/
JEN: it does seem-   =mhm=
MEG: but it does-

What's extraordinary about this example is that other speakers' comments repeat this lack of completeness: Mary is heard as saying something like 'it (there) doesn't seem much of a point', while my paraphrasing acceptance *it does seem-* presumably means something like 'it does seem pointless'. Meg repeats this, leaving out *seem*, and Mary and I both add minimal responses. The important thing is that all of us clearly understood what is being said, even though not all the words are actually uttered.

In the next example, Pat and Karen continue a discussion of privacy and screening trees which arose from Karen's story of unwittingly seeing her neighbor undress in his living room. Karen mentions that she had recently driven past her old house, where she had planted trees several years earlier:

(15)

KAREN: we drove down Kingshill the other day/ and there's lovely conifers
---
KAREN: up- up in the front/ they've all grown/ [...]

KAREN:
PAT: yeah I think it's worthwhile doing that/ [i.e. planting trees] because as
---
KAREN: that's right/
PAT: you say your neighbor has got um privacy   because of

KAREN: yeah well that
PAT: the trees you planted/ how annoying/

KAREN: doesn't matter does it/ . after all they did pay forty-five
PAT:

KAREN: thousand seven hundred and fifty pounds for the house/ so
PAT:

KAREN: I should think my twelve quids worth of trees- ⟨LAUGHS⟩
PAT: ⟨LAUGHS⟩

Here, Karen's utterance *so I should think my twelve quids worth of trees* is left incomplete. The laughter jointly produced by Karen and Pat immediately after this part-utterance signals their shared understanding of her wry comment. It is an interesting side effect of our capacity to anticipate the conclusion of utterances that we have the option *not* to complete an utterance.

2.3. *Finding the right word*

Nearly all the examples I've given so far have involved only two speakers (though one or two examples have shown other speakers playing a more minor role). I want to look here at three examples which involve more than two speakers. Each of these examples of jointly constructed talk arises in conversation where speakers are struggling to find the right words. In the first example, Kate (aged 16) has just asserted that gay pop groups should be more popular:

(16)   [discussion of gay pop groups]

KATE: I'm gonna go round going "Yes support gay pop groups/

KATE: cos I don't approve of this . raci-" I mean wha- what's

KATE: that thing where [...] if you're g- an- anti-gay/ what's

KATE: ⌈that ((mean))/ ⌈gayist/
GWEN: ⌊gay/   ⌊anti-gay/

KATE: ⌈you're gayist/   =prejudiced/
SARAH: ⌊you're ((xx))- you're prejudiced=
EMILY: =prejudiced= yeah/

Here, after several false starts, the group settles on the word *prejudiced* offered by Sarah, with three of the four friends saying the word in turn. This pattern of repetition (in this case, of an individual word) is another important feature of women's talk.

In the next example, Sue, Liz and Anna are eating and begin to discuss salads of different kinds. Liz and Anna help Sue to find the word she wants:

(17)   [food talk]

SUE:	you know at Tony's dad's they do this lovely salad with

SUE:	parmesan and . you know that traditional Italian- what's

SUE:	the other cheese? parmesan- no ⟨TUTS⟩ soft
ANNA:	Dolcellata?

SUE:	s- no the squidgy stuff that they put on pizzas/
ANNA:	Gorgonzola?

SUE:	=Mozarella/ Mozarella and-
ANNA:	Mozarell⌈a? yeah/
LIZ:	⌊Mozarella= mhm/

SUE:	and it's just the best thing ever/

All three speakers contribute to this chunk of talk, and once the right word has been found their minimal responses (*yeah* and *mhm*) demonstrate that they all take responsibilty for what is said. In this example, the three friends remember the word *mozarella*. In example (18) below, Meg, Bea and I fail to remember the word *schadenfreude* (just as Kate, Sarah and Emily failed to recall the word *homophobic* in example (16) above), but we work together to refine our sense of the concept we are discussing.

(18)

MEG:	Tom [...] says there's a German word to describe that/

MEG:	[...] one of those complicated German nouns which

MEG:	explains the fact that you feel . a perverse displeasure in

MEG:	other people's successes/ [...]

JEN:	oh it's the other way round ((I feel))/ it's sort of pleasure

JEN:	⌈in other people-
BEA:	⌊a perverse pleasure in= =yeah=
MEG:	=in their downfall= =yeah/

These three women friends work together to form the utterance *it's sort of pleasure//a perverse pleasure//in their downfall*. The fact that two of the three add a minimal response — *yeah* — at the end of this co-constructed utterance provides evidence that they are happy both with what is said and with the way it has been said.

Finally, in this section, I want to look at an example involving five speakers, who work together to find the right words in a more extended way. This extract comes from the topic *Apes and language*, which was triggered by my asking whether anyone had seen a TV documentary on this subject the previous evening. The responsibility for singing the main tune is passed from Mary to me, from me to Bea, and from Bea to Meg. Between us we construct an account of what apes are capable of linguistically.

(19) [topic — apes and language]

```
MARY:    I mean they can shuffle words around and
```
```
MARY:    ⌈make a different meaning/
BEA:     ⌊draw up a conclusion
```
```
BEA:     ((xxx))-
JEN:              they put two words together  to form a compound/
MEG:                                        yeah/
```
```
MARY:                                            ⌈that's right=
BEA:                                            ⌊       =mhm
JEN:     to mean something that they didn't have a ⌊lexical item for/
```
```
MARY:    ⌈ that's right/                    for ⌈ a brazilnut/
BEA:     ⌊             a stoneberry for a-  ⌊ a brazilnut/
JEN:     ⌊ which is-
HELEN:                 right/
```
```
JEN:                       ⌈ well th- they can't POSSib⌈ly ⟨HIGH⟩
MEG:     yes/ and ⌈ lotionberry for ⌊ vomit/
HELEN:   mhm/  ⌊ gosh/                                ⌊((was it?))
```
```
BEA:                                =lotionberry for what?
JEN:     be imitating their trainers=
MEG:     yeah/                                        she'd- sh-
```
```
MEG:     she'd- she'd sicked up one morning on yoghurt which
```
```
MEG:     would have had raisins in it/and er she said that ((it
```
```
MEG:     looked)) - they asked her what er- what the vomit was
```
```
MEG:     and she said lotionberry/
BEA:                       ah/
HELEN:                       amazing/
```

Notice how carefully we time our supporting utterances to fit what each other is saying, indicating our continued involvement in the talk and our acceptance of what is being said. This is particularly striking in the opening staves, where the main strand of explication (underlined in the transcript) is voiced in turn by Mary, Jen, Bea and then Meg. This means that speaking turns are shared and everyone participates.

3. Overlapping speech

Overlapping speech is an important feature of women friends' talk, and one that immediately strikes anyone who listens to a recording of women friends' conversation. Women friends combine as speakers so that two or more voices may contribute to talk *at the same time*. This kind of overlapping speech is not seen as competitive, as a way of grabbing a turn, because the various contributions to talk are on the same theme. We've already seen how jointly constructed utterances can involve simultaneous speech, when two women complete an utterance simultaneously. More typically, overlapping speech occurs when two speakers say the same thing but at slightly different times. Here is a fuller version of example (7):

(7′)

BEA:	I mean in order to accept that idea you're

BEA:	having to .	⌈completely
MARY:	mhm . completely review your	⌊view of your

BEA:	change your view of your husband/
MARY:	husband/

Bea overlaps Mary's completion *completely review your view of your husband* with her own completion, which echoes Mary's words, apart from the substitution of *change* for *review*. In other words, two speakers complete the utterance *in order to accept that idea you're having to ...*, but their completions are not produced simultaneously.

Overlap also occurs when two speakers complete an utterance simultaneously but complete it differently (with different words, but saying the same thing):

(20) [talking about aging parents]

LIZ: and I mean it's a really weird situation because all of a

SUE: ⌈you become a parent/yeah/
LIZ: sudden the ⌊roles are all reversed/

(21) [talking about newly painted door]

PAT: it wouldn't be so bad if the door was in the middle of

BARBARA:

PAT: the house/ you know if it ⌈had a window each side/
BARBARA: ⌊yeah so it was balanced/ yeah/

A slightly different kind of overlapping speech occurs when co-participants ask questions while another participant is speaking (see examples 22 and 23 below).

(22) [funeral discussion]

SALLY: well she lived in Brisbane/ ((they were at Brisbane))/

SALLY: so he's going over there- = Australia/ so he's going to
MARY: what   —   Australia?=

SALLY: the funeral/

(23) [talking about Oxford student murder]

LIZ: it was the boyfriend/ yeah she was under the
ANNA: has he

LIZ: floor boards/ =yeah/
ANNA: been charged?=
SUE: =mhm/

In example (22) Mary checks that Sally is talking about Brisbane in Australia, while in (23), Anna's question about whether the boyfriend has been charged overlaps with Liz's account of where the body was found. Overlapping speech

also results when friends comment on what each other is saying. Examples (23)
to (25) illustrate this:

(24)   [discussion of Twin Peaks]

ANNA: it's all about this . you know sort of Canadian border town

ANNA: where ⌈everybody's really sort of respectable and nice
SUE: ⌊I thought it was a nice whodunnit/

ANNA: and that/

(25)   [Becky talks about crying in school]

BECKY: and I cried   not for very long/ j- just sort of . ⌈a few
JESSICA: mhm/   ⌊I hate

BECKY: tears/   =I know/
JESSICA: it when no one notices=

(26)   [mature students at college]

SUE: there's one mature student there/ and she lives in/ ⌈and
ANNA: ⌊oh god/

SUE: they're really quite horrible to her/
ANNA: yeah it must be tough to live in halls/

Comments are often more extensive than these three brief examples, and
can involve other participants in an elaborate descant over the main tune. Here's
a longer example, from a conversation in which Sue is telling a story about a
couple she knows where the wife won't let her husband play his guitar.

(27)   [extract from Obedient Husband story]

SUE: she pushes him to ⌈the abs-
ANNA: ⌊he'll probably stab her with the

SUE: ⌈she pushes him to the limit/   yeah I
LIZ: =yeah grrr ⟨VICIOUS NOISE⟩
ANNA: bread knife one ⌊day=   she'll wake

SUE:	think he will/	I think he'll rebel/
LIZ:	="here you are Ginny" ⟨LAUGHS-----------⟩	
ANNA:	up dead=	⟨LAUGHS-----------⟩

This is a brief extract from a long episode where Liz and Anna embroider on Sue's story. Note how Liz and Anna's contributions, taken in isolation, involve no overlap: Their turns are carefully coordinated to alternate in a continuous commentary on what Sue is saying. Note also how as Sue tells her story she responds to the others' contributions. Her two consecutive utterances *she pushes him to the limit/ yeah I think he will/* are incomprehensible unless we interpret the second as a response to Anna's *he'll probably stab her with the bread knife one day.* I shall return to this extract later.

In the conversations of women friends, the most remarkable examples of overlapping speech occur when speakers pursue a theme simultaneously, saying different but related things at the same time. In the following example, the topic of conversation is Anna's mother. It's agreed that, while she is eccentric, she is a very good cook. Sue and Anna express this in different words simultaneously.

(28) [Anna's eccentric mother]

SUE:	but she cooks nice food=	⌈you know . she cooks
LIZ:	=yeah	
ANNA:		well ⌊she's a- she's a really

SUE:	really inventively/
ANNA:	good cook/

Example (29) is very simple: Anna and Liz are here talking about the same topic — the boy, Dominic. They choose to organize their talk so that their contributions about Dominic overlap rather than occurring in sequence.

(29) [talking about shy boy at piano teacher's]

ANNA:	I make a point of tal⌈king to him every week/
LIZ:	⌊he's just done his grade one/

This example comes from a passage where Anna and Liz are establishing that they both know this boy, a passage that involves several brief overlaps:

(30) [piano lessons]

ANNA:	there's a lovely little boy who goes before me called

ANNA:	Dominic=	[he's got red hair/	[have you seen him?
LIZ:	=Domi[nic yeah/		[he's gorgeous/

ANNA:	he's just [so sweet/ and he's ever so shy/ so I make a
LIZ:	[yeah/

ANNA:	point of tal[king to him every week
LIZ:	[he's just done his grade one as well

ANNA:	[that's right/
LIZ:	has[n't he/

A final example of this pattern will show how carefully speakers are
attuned to each other; this means that a topic can be pursued be two speakers at
the same time.

(31) [discussion of the way history is taught at the local comprehensive
        school]

HELEN:	they ask them really to compare . their life now with

HELEN:	the 19th century/ it's very good sort of introduction
JEN:	yes

HELEN:	[to history itself/	[yes very good/
JEN:	[and they have newspapers and [stuff/

HELEN:	and they went round the park/ and did
JEN:	and ((it's))- and they use ((list))

HELEN:	all sorts of stuff/ I was really impressed by that/
JEN:	primary sources/yes/

In this example, Helen and I are both familiar with the way history is
taught at the local school, and both admire it. We both have things we want to
say which contribute to the topic, and we choose to say them at the same time.
This brief extract shows us making a series of points about the way history is
taught, at the same time as responding to each other's points: for example,
Helen's point that the comparison of life now with life in the 19th century is a
good introduction to history is supported by a *yes* from me, while my point that

they use newspapers is acknowledged by Helen with *yes very good*. This example shows how easily speakers can speak and listen at the same time. Simultaneous talk of this kind does not threaten comprehension, but on the contrary permits a more multi-layered development of topics.

In terms of the jam session metaphor I used at the beginning of this chapter, while jointly constructed utterances can be compared to several instruments playing the same tune, overlapping speech is more like several instruments playing different tunes which fit together harmonically. In the terminology of classical music this latter pattern is called polyphony.[3] All the examples in this section on overlapping speech (examples (19)–(30)) exemplify the pattern of polyphonic talk, where two or more different but mutually reinforcing things are said at the same time.

4. The collaborative floor

I want to looks now at theories of conversational organization. The way speakers cooperate to produce orderly rather than chaotic talk is usually discussed under the heading 'turn-taking'. The goal of those doing research on turn-taking is to work out the underlying rules which can account for the orderly management of talk (see Sacks, Schegloff and, Jefferson 1974; Sacks 1992: passim). After all, most of the conversations we take part in succeed in involving all participants and in producing coherent talk. A key concept is that of the conversational **floor**, that is, the conversational space available to speakers. Carole Edelsky (1981) refines the notion of floor by suggesting that we need to distinguish between two different kinds of floor which she calls the **single** (or singly developed) floor and the **collaborative** (or collaboratively developed) floor. The main characteristic of the single floor is that one speaker speaks at a time. In other words, in a single floor speakers *take turns* to speak. By contrast, the defining characteristic of the collaborative floor is that the floor is thought of as being open to all participants *simultaneously*.

Edelsky's paper arose from her analysis of five university committee meetings involving seven women and four men, some of whom were close friends as well as colleagues. She observed that these meetings fluctuated between talk which was more firmly oriented towards the business they were meant to discuss, and talk which strayed from the agenda. The chief goal of committee meetings is to get through a certain amount of pre-specified business. The kind of talk achieving this goal involves a single floor with one speaker speaking at a time, sometimes at considerable length. But there is another goal at meetings where members of a committee work together on a daily basis and are in some cases friends as well as colleagues: the goal is to maintain good social relations. This more interpersonal goal is achieved through the collaborative floor.

The single floor depends on the notion of the conversational **turn**: Speakers take turns to occupy the conversational floor. We are all of us experienced participants in the single floor, since this is the model of conversation tacitly held by all members of our (English-speaking) culture. As children, we are told not to butt in and to 'wait for our turn'. One of the skills we develop at school is the ability to participate in single-floor talk, since schools also assume a norm of one-speaker-at-a-time.[4] It is probably not surprising that a culture which tends to favour the individual over the community should assume an individualistic model of how conversation works. But this model can only be applied satisfactorily to asymmetrical talk (talk involving speakers who are not equals) such as adult–child, doctor–patient, or to more formal talk (usually in the public domain) such as business meetings. In informal talk between equals, speakers will often develop a collaborative floor, where the individual speaker becomes far less significant and what is said is jointly accomplished by all speakers.

I've shown how women friends make frequent use of jointly constructed utterances and of overlapping speech. These are both classic components of a collaborative floor. Collaborative floors, in Edelsky's account, typically involve shorter turns than single floors, much more overlapping speech, more repetition, and more joking and teasing. But this summary implies that the collaborative floor simply involves more or less of something which is regularly found in a single floor. But it's my contention that the collaborative floor is radically different from the singly-developed floor: It is qualitatively as well as quantitatively different from one-at-a-time turn-taking. This is precisely because the collaborative floor is a shared space, and therefore what is said is construed as being the voice of the group rather than of the individual.

4.1. *Two examples*

To illustrate how a collaborative floor works in practice, we need to look at two longer examples. The first is part of the story *Getting Undressed*, a story jointly told by two friends who use minimal responses, repetition and the shared construction of utterances to maintain a collaborative floor.

```
(32)  KAREN: and I saw him get undressed in his living room/ there's
      PAT:

2     KAREN: no reason why you shouldn't get undressed in your
      PAT:

      KAREN: living room if you want to/      and I thought "My God
      PAT:                          yeah/

4     KAREN:  .  if I can see him"=                and I don't
      PAT:    yeah/                    =he can see you/

      KAREN: always just get undressed in the living room/ ⟨LAUGH⟩
      PAT:

6     KAREN: you know I mean OK I'm sure he's not=      =peeping
      PAT:                              =peeping=

      KAREN: or anything/       but it just-
      PAT:               but he-       you accidentally saw him/

8     KAREN: that's right/
      PAT:               oh I don't blame you/ I think it needs

      PAT:   screening trees round it/
```

This extract involves only two speakers. It is remarkable for the sensitive timing of their contributions: They are able to keep the thread of narrative and evaluation moving without a pause. While Pat allows Karen to tell the narrative core of this story without intervention, once the key narrative clause has been reached — *and I saw him get undressed in his living room* — she joins in. From stave 3 onwards the story is jointly constructed by the two friends, to the extent that Pat completes Karen's *if I can see him,* with *he can see you,* she provides the verb *peeping* to complete Karen's *I'm sure he's not...,* and it is Pat who recapitulates the main point: *you accidentally saw him* in stave 6, and who provides a coda: *oh I don't blame you I think it needs screening trees round it.* This particular example of a collaborative floor does not involve overlapping speech. Overlapping speech is less common in conversations involving only two speakers (but certainly occurs — see example 31).

The second, more extended example I shall focus on in this section involves a great deal of overlapping speech. (It comes from a conversation between six women friends.) This stretch of talk begins with a very brief story told by Janet about her daughter Vicky's performance in a quiz, consisting of one narrative clause: *Vicky drew with Robin Lee last night.* The reason this story is of interest to the assembled friends is that Robin Lee is a teacher at the local comprehensive school where many of the children were pupils. Janet is obviously proud that her 16 year old daughter has managed to equal the score of an adult teacher in a quiz. But the anecdote itself serves mainly as the trigger for a discussion about quizzes in general. Here is the opening section, where Janet tells her story (twice, because she repeats it in the process of clarifying what sort of quiz she is talking about).

```
(33)   JANET:    ooh I must tell you/ Vicky- you know the quiz Vicky

2      JANET:    goes to on Wednesday=      =she drew with Robin
       MEG:                       =mhm=
       MARY:                      ((xx can't guess))

       JANET:    Lee=   =last night ⟨LAUGHS⟩
       MARY:                 ⟨LAUGHS⟩
       HELEN:    =oh=⟨LAUGHS⟩

4      JANET:                                              ((she
       HELEN:    it's quite lucrative this idea as well/ not only is it-
       SALLY:    ⟨LAUGHS⟩ ((xxxxxxxxxxx))
       JEN:                                       what d'you-

       JANET:    got)) two fifty/               it's a-  it's a pub-
       MEG:                                        ⟨CHUCKLE⟩
       HELEN:             in a- in a pub
       JEN:                     what d'you mean it's- it's-

6      JANET:    they have this little quiz/       and apparently Mr
       HELEN:                             ⟨LAUGHS⟩

       JANET:    Lee goes now/ and Vicky was absolutely deLIGHTed/

8      JANET:              she BEAT him/
       HELEN:    ⟨LAUGHS⟩

       JANET:    well she didn't beat him/ ⎡she came-  she drew/
       MEG:                                ⎣you'd love those Jennifer/
```

Once all six friends are clear that the topic of Janet's story is a pub quiz, we launch into talk around this topic, combining factual information about quizzes we have participated in with fantasies about becoming a team ourselves.

```
10   JANET:           yeah/                                    they're
     MEG:      I'm in a  . a qui-⌈quiz league/ we have a marvellous time
     JEN:                        ⌊yes I know/   I was ONCE in one
```
```
     JANET:    starting one at the Talbot apparently tonight=
     MEG:                       mhm/
     JEN:      down-                                      =well the La-
```
```
12   JEN:      don't you remember the Labour Party had one
```
```
     MEG:           =we could put ourselves up
     JEN:      once=          I was in a team
```
```
14   JANET:           =yes we could/ Ox⌈ton Ladies/
     MEG:      as a team=              ⌊the Ladies group/
     MARY:             ⟨SNORTS⟩
     HELEN:            mhm/
     JEN:      with Don Frazer/
```
```
     JANET:    ⟨LAUGHS⟩
     MEG:                yes why not?
     MARY:
     HELEN:                    ⟨LAUGHS⟩
     SALLY:    ⟨LAUGHS⟩
```

In this opening phase of the discussion, notice how some turns occur
simultaneously (but parallel in thematic terms): Meg's *I'm in a quiz league/ we
have a marvellous time/* overlaps with my own *yes I know I was once in one,* and
also with the start of Janet's *they're starting one at the Talbot [pub] apparently
tonight.* Other turns are carefully timed to occur in sequence: Meg's suggestion
we could put ourselves up as a team is followed by Janet's *yes we could/ Oxton
Ladies.* This joke about our title as a putative quiz team is jointly produced by
Janet and Meg, who say *Ladies* at the same time, even though they phrase the
possible title slightly differently. (The evidence that this is accepted as a joke by
all present is reflected in the laughter and snorting of Sally, Helen and Mary as
well as Janet.) At this point, Meg sums up the general view about our future as
a quiz team, while Mary initiates a new phase of talk with a question:

```
16   MEG:      ⌈(((that would be fun wouldn't it))
     MARY:     ⌊what sort of questions do you get asked on these quizzes?
```

In a collaborative floor, speakers can construct talk in this way, rounding off one point while moving on to a new one, *at the same time*. Participants in a collaborative floor are not baffled by this: No one in the conversations I've recorded ever protests at the overlapping talk, and the fact that topics are developed coherently suggests that participants follow this multi-stranded, polyphonic talk with ease. Mary's question leads into a free-for-all, with everyone keen to suggest what sort of questions are typical of quizzes. Here is a brief example:

```
        JANET:    "Where's the biggest pyramid?" was what they had last

18      JANET:    night=                          ="where's the biggest"=
        MARY:           ="What's the biggest pyramid?"=
        SALLY:                          ((shocks xx))

        JANET:              =pyramid/ where/    ⌈ it's in MExico=
        MARY:       = where?=                  in E⌊gypt/
        SALLY:                                  ((is it Ok-xx?))

20      MEG:      =is it?              oh one of those Aztec .    numbers
        MARY:     =oh in Mexico is it?
        SALLY:    =right/                          mhm/

        JEN:      ((xx)) one of those trick ones=
        MARY:                              =god I'd be hopeless at that/
        HELEN:    mhm/                      mhm/
```

The overlapping talk in stave 19 arises as Mary and Sally hazard a guess about where the biggest pyramid is, Janet gives the answer, and then Meg, Mary and Sally react to Janet's answer. The topic is sustained for some time more, with questions on geography and literature being singled out for discussion. This is a fascinating piece of talk because the six speakers (a large number) manage to maintain one floor (rather than splitting into two or more conversations). While the talk may appear anarchic at times, this is clearly a collaborative floor: Speakers are keenly aware of each others' contributions, and all utterances relate to the same topic, with particular points being jointly developed.

4.2. *The test of acceptance*

An important piece of evidence to support the idea of the collaborative floor comes from the fact that no one protests about these patterns of talk. No one ever says, "Let me finish what I'm saying", or "Don't interrupt me". In singly developed floors, where the rule is that one speaker speaks at a time, any overlapping speech or any attempt by a speaker to complete another's utterance will be construed as a bid to seize the floor. But 'interruption' is not an appropriate term for what speakers do in a collaborative floor: The idea of trying to 'seize the floor' becomes redundant, because the floor is already occupied by all speakers. A collaborative floor is a shared floor.

In fact, far from protesting, women friends involved in a collaborative floor explicitly welcome each others' contributions to talk. If we look at fuller versions of some of the earlier examples, what is noticeable is the way friends incorporate each others' contributions into the general stream of talk. This seems to be routine 'melding' work.

(1′)   [Sue and Liz discuss where they like to talk]
- -
SUE: I mean in someone's house it's easier to talk than=   =out/
LIZ: =out=
- -

(2′)   [Karen worries that she is overlooked by a neighbour]
- -
KAREN: I mean OK I'm sure he's not=   =peeping or anything/
PAT: =peeping=
- -

(3′)   [Helen and Jen speculate on the effect an individual's absence could have on a group]
- -
HELEN: they won't be so=   =yes yes/
JEN: =homogeneous=
- -

(5′)   [discussion of Open Evening at local school]
- -
JEN: they said they kept bumping into all sorts of people=
HELEN: =that they
- -
JEN: ⌈they li- they knew and liked/
HELEN: ⌊knew/ yes/
- -

(6′)   [discussion of Christmas play at local primary school]
- -
KAREN: once those cameras start flashing particularly with
- -
KAREN: the infants=   =it puts them off=
PAT: =it puts them off=   =yeah/
- -

In the examples (1'), (2'), and (6'), incorporation is carried out by repeating the collaborative completion, while in example (3') it is carried out by accepting the completion with the agreement token *yes*. In example (5'), I amend *they liked* to the more comples *knew and liked*, incorporating Helen's completion *they knew*. Acceptance of an incorporation is also often overtly signalled with a *yes*, as in (5') and (6').

Speakers also add utterances to each other's utterances, and these are also incorporated into the jointly constructed text:

(34) [novel reading]
- -
SUE: and I kind of skipped to the last chapter/ to make sure that
LIZ: yeah/   yeah/
- -
SUE: I was right=   =and I was/
LIZ: =and you were=
- -

In example 12, when Helen switches from co-constructing the utterance *she had this grammar school meeting*, she signals her continuing involvement in what is being said by her contributions *yes* and *that's right*.

(12')
- -
JEN: ⌈she had this grammar school
HELEN: because did you- did you hear ⌊she had this grammar school-
- -
JEN: meeting= and it was a disaster=
HELEN: yes/   =that's right/   =that's right/
- -

When speakers participate in a collaborative floor, and when the topic under discussion is well known to both speakers, then who says what is unimportant. In example (12), Helen could have said *she had this grammar school meeting* on her own, or she and I could have said the entire chunk together. All that matters is that what is to be said gets said.

4.3. *Minimal responses*

A significant part of a collaborative floor is the use of minimal responses. These brief utterances — *yeah, mhm, that's right* — occur in all forms of talk. But they occur more frequently in collaborative floors than in singly developed floors. This is because, once the floor is construed as occupied by all speakers at all times, speakers have an obligation to signal their continued presence in, and acceptance of, the shared floor. So minimal responses signal that speakers are present and involved. These seemingly minor forms have very important, and very different, functions in these two different floors. When talk is more formal (for example, the vast majority of talk occuring in the public domain), and a singly developed floor is established, then minimal responses say: 'I am listening — and I thus acknowledge your right to hold the floor. I will wait for my turn'. When talk is informal (for example, between friends in private) and a collaborative floor is established, then minimal responses say: 'I am here, this is my floor too, and I am participating in the shared construction of talk'.

We've already noted how important minimal responses are for indicating that speakers accept each others' contributions to talk. Let's look at the full version of example (7) — minimal responses are underlined:

BEA:	I mean in order to accept that idea you're

BEA:	having to .	⌈ completely
JEN:	<u>yes</u>/	
MARY:	<u>mhm</u>/ completely review your	⌊ view of your

BEA:	change ⌉ your view of your husband=	
MARY:	husband⌋=	=<u>that's right</u>/
SALLY:	=<u>yes</u>/	
MEG:	<u>yeah</u>/ <u>mhm</u>/	

This extract comes from a conversation involving five women friends and all five women play their part in this chunk of talk. While Bea and Mary co-construct the 'main tune', the other three women indicate that these words represent their position too. But minimal responses have multiple meanings: For example, my *yes* in the above example is not just supportive — by agreeing with what Bea is saying before she has said it all, I show that, like Mary, I can anticipate what the rest of this utterance might be.

It's been observed by many researchers that women make frequent use of minimal responses (Zimmerman and West 1975; Fishman 1980a). It's also been observed how sensitively women use minimal responses (Fishman 1980b; Coates 1989, 1991).[5] The examples in this paper illustrate how speakers time their responses, as a rule, to come just at the end of a chunk of talk (at the end of a phrase or clause, for example). And this point is so accurately predicted that the rhythm of the 'main tune' is not affected. Examples (35)–(37) below are typical examples of well-placed minimal responses.

(35) [talking about material for sale in local market]

KAREN: it was the prettiest material I've ever seen in my life=
PAT: =mhm/
----

(36) [talking about taping themselves]

LORNA: much better than a diary=
BECKY: =yeah/
----

(37) [discussion of male bias in research]

MARY: it's staggering isn't it=
MEG: =mhm/

Example (36) is a slightly longer extract which demonstrates that minimal
responses are not restricted to clause-final position, but may be used as a sign
of encouragement at other points.

(38) [child abuse]

MEG: you remember that little boy [...] that was um .   carried
SALLY: mhm/

MEG: off=   =and sexually abused=
SALLY: =yes=
BEA: yes/   =yes/

In this instance, Meg hesitates and Sally says *mhm*, at which point Meg
picks up the thread of her utterance. This example also shows how complex
multi-party talk is: Listeners are engaged not only in monitoring, and supporting,
the speaker's turn, but also in monitoring each other's contributions as listeners.
In this example we see Sally and Bea cooperating as active listeners.

When a speaker tells a story, minimal responses occur much less frequently. Story telling gives the speaker a peculiarly priveleged role; listeners normally
listen in silence, with minimal responses only appearing at or near the end of the
story. In conversation, the telling of an anecdote often functions to introduce a
new topic; the utterance of minimal responses signals listeners' acceptance of
the new topic. Typically, all co-participants will join in at this point (whereas,
as in examples (35) to (38), at other points in conversation, one participant's
mhm stands for all participants). In the example below, Becky comes to the end

of her anecdote; her three friends all make a minimal response, which relieves the tension engendered by Becky's self-disclosing story, as well as expressing their support for the new topic she has introduced (feelings about boys).

(39) [Becky confesses her past crush on Damien]

BECKY: and I just suddenly have seen how awful he is and

BECKY: horrible=
CLAIRE: =yeah/
JESSICA: =yeah/
HANNAH: yeah/

Through signaling the active participation of all participants in the conversation, minimal responses play a significant role in the collaborative construction of text and of the maintenance of a collaborative floor.

4.4. *Laughter*

Laughter is a significant component in the talk of women friends. It occurs in response to a variety of different aspects of talk: At the end of self-disclosing and painful stories, at funny or idiotic moments in discussion. Laughter may arise in response to what someone else says, or speakers may laugh at the end of an utterance, or even during an utterance. It can signal amusememnt, surprise, horror, sympathy or catharsis. Example (39) above continues as follows:

BECKY: and I just suddenly have seen how awful he is and

BECKY: horrible=   ⟨SCREAM OF LAUGHTER⟩
CLAIRE: =yeah/ but like um   but
JESSICA: =yeah/   ⟨LAUGHS⟩
HANNAH: yeah/   ⟨LOW CHUCKLE⟩

CLAIRE: they're so stupid right?

Becky's self-disclosure initially triggers supportive minimal responses from her three friends, but when she bursts into a scream of laughter, releasing the tension that has built up during her account of her past infatuation with Damien, Jessica joins in with a matching loud burst of laughter, while Hannah chuckles more meditatively. Claire is left to sum up the reason for Becky's embarassment and the justification for their hilarity: How could you possibly ever 'fancy' one of the boys when they're 'so stupid'?

The opening section of the extract **Quizzes** is full of laughter. This is much more light-hearted than the laughter of Becky and her friends above. As the topic of quizzes is established, laughter signals that this topic is going to be treated as an opportunity to have fun. The main point of Janet's opening anecdote is that the normal pattern has been reversed, with a teacher being held to a draw by a pupil. The overturning of normal expectations is a classic comic theme. In this case, it sets the scene for continued fooling. Key points, such as the suggestion of an Oxton Ladies team, are greeted with laughter, as are moments of mock panic like Mary's *I'd panic at the thought of asking the questions* and Sally's despairing *I heard it tonight* [i.e. a question and answer on Transatlantic Quiz on the radio] *and still didn't know.*

Like minimal responses, laughter plays a special role in the construction of a collaborative floor. It allows participants to signal their continued involvement in what is being said, their continued presence in the collaborative floor. If we assume that a collaborative floor is at all times open to all speakers, then clearly speakers need strategies to signal that they are participating, even when they don't actually produce an utterance. Laughter, like minimal responses, fits this requirement perfectly. It allows people to signal their presence frequently, while not committing them to speak all the time.

In the following extended extract from a conversation between three friends, laughter is extensively used. I've already quoted a very brief part of this extract in the section on Overlapping Speech (example (27)). Even in this brief example, we saw how Liz and Anna laughed together at the climax of their violent fantasizing about what the obedient husband might do to his wife. The overall impression given by the long and complex stretch of talk of which this example was a tiny sample is that all three friends are talking most of the time, but this impression is due in large part to the significant amount of laughter produced by participants simultaneously with each others' utterances.[6] The full extract is interesting from several points of view. It is, firstly, a good example of a collaborative floor. Secondly, it subverts the norms of story-telling, since Sue might expect to tell her story to an attentive audience, but instead, after an initial phase when she recounts the bare bones of the story, she has to contend with a raucous descant from Liz and Anna, who work together to weave a commentary around Sue's account of an 'obedient' husband. Thirdly, it is interesting because there is a constant slippage between narrative (Sue is the only person with access to the facts of the story she is recounting) and discussion (the central point of the story — that the wife forbids the husband to play his guitar — becomes the focus of wide-ranging speculation about what marriage means).

Here's the opening narrative, which Sue tells to Liz and Anna:

Obedient husband

> I told you I went round to a friends who had ((a)) guitar.
> [...]
> The wife right- his wife would not let him have a guitar.
> She said no (*A and L laugh*)
> and he's so obedient.
> She's- she said, "You're not having a guitar",
> so he didn't have one,
> he just didn't play it ever.
> And then for Christmas she allowed him to have a guitar
> as long as he didn't play it in front of her.

This opening narrative provides a variety of themes which all three friends seize on. First, the notion of the wife 'allowing' the husband to have a guitar prompts discussion of power structures in relationships. Secondly, the related theme of 'obedience' is explored, particularly in terms of whether this is an appropriate quality in a husband. Thirdly, the theme of musical instruments is a rich source of talk, as Sue's husband John plays the saxophone, and Sue is known to have mixed feelings about this.

After Sue finishes her introductory narrative, all three friends start to talk, and a collaborative floor is established. (There is no room to give the full transcript of 'Obedient husband': two sections of this episode of talk are reproduced here, to illustrate the way laughter functions in friends' talk.)

Obedient husband (1)

```
1   SUE:     he's just so nice/ he thinks she's wonderful/ and I
    ANNA:
    LIZ:

    SUE:     would be worried if I was her . you know=        to- to push him-
    ANNA:
    LIZ:                                            =what/ that you weren't

3   SUE:     she-        she pushes him to ⌈the abs-
    ANNA:                                  ⌊he'll probably stab her with
    LIZ:     matching up?

    SUE:                        ⌈she pushes him to the limit/ yeah I
    ANNA:    the bread knife one⌊day=                          she'll wake
    LIZ:                             =yeah/ggrrr⟨VICIOUS NOISE⟩
```

---

5   SUE: think he will/ .   I think he'll rebel= ⟨LAUGHS⟩
     ANNA: up dead=   ⟨LAUGHS--------------------------
     LIZ: ="here you are Linny" ⟨LAUGHS-------⟩ =have a s-

     SUE: ⟨LAUGHS⟩ --------------------------------------
     ANNA: --->
     LIZ: have a cut throat ⟨CUTTING NOISE⟩ ⟨LAUGHS⟩--------------------

---

7   SUE: but that- this particular night she let him play the guitar/
     ANNA: ⟨SNORT⟩ ⟨LAUGHS---------------------⟩
     LIZ: --------------------------⟩

     SUE: and it was so nice you know/ and she like she bans him= this
     ANNA:
     LIZ: ⟨LAUGHS--⟩ =⟨CACKLES⟩

---

9   SUE: is what I f-=
     ANNA: =I wouldn't put up with it I'm sorry
     LIZ: =he'll probably pick it up one day and go

     SUE: =I wouldn't/ no/ but you've got to see it to
     ANNA: though/ would you?=
     LIZ: [ckxxx] ⟨MIMICS BREAKING NOISE⟩

---

11 SUE: believe it because he's just . obedient/ and she-⎡and she
     ANNA: ⎣
     LIZ: !why did

     SUE: just-   ⎡what/ obedient?
     ANNA:
     LIZ: you use that word/ that's a dreadful ⎣word/   obedient/

---

13 SUE: yes ((x))   yes but he is/ that's what
     ANNA:
     LIZ: makes him sound like a pet rabbit/

     SUE: he's like/ he's obedient/ ⎡he just does as she says/
     ANNA: ⎣oh how aaww-ffuull/
     LIZ:

At the climax of this extract (staves 5–6), all three women are laughing at once. Sue establishes that Rob is 'nice', that he adores his wife — *he thinks she's wonderful* — and that she forbids him to play the guitar. Anna and Liz, clearly appalled by this scenario, begin to fantasize about what the husband might do if he were to rebel. Their laughter expresses many things: Their amusement at the cartoon-like violence they conjure up with their scenario of the husband stabbing the wife, their sense of the unlikelihood of this fantasy, given Sue's assertion that Rob is like a pet rabbit, and perhaps also a sense of their own daring at expressing such violent ideas. (It's interesting how they use sound effects to great effect in this part of their conversation, though skill with sound effects is widely recognized as a feature of boys' talk, and is not usually associated with the talk of adult women. See Coates 1986; Smith 1983.)

As collaborative talk, this extract is very interesting. The three speakers construct a collaborative floor where Sue plays the main tune, while Liz and Anna either jointly construct a commentary on what Sue is saying, or take it in turns to comment. Their laughter increases the impression of all three friends participating all the time. In the extract above, there are 14 staves: of these, 9 (64%) involve two or more speakers speaking at the same time; 13 (93%) involve two or more speakers speaking or laughing or adding sound effects at the same time. Laughter seems to be an intrinsic component of friendly talk among women. This being the case, the impression given by this chunk of conversation of extremely involved participation from all three speakers is accurate.

To demonstrate that this is not an isolated example, here is another extract from this same stretch of conversation. The three friends have begun to consider more seriously the suggestion that the husband can't be as obedient as he seems to outsiders. Sue tells Liz and Anna what her husband, John, thinks:

Obedient husband (2)

```
1  SUE:   ⌈John  says  at  home   he must-   he must rebel/ he ⌈must/
   LIZ:   ⌊there's a limit-     yeah  must be/              ⌊yeah he must/
```

```
   sue:             John can't bear to think-
   ANNA:                             ⌈John probably wants to help him
   LIZ:   ((cos)) John-  ⟨LAUGHING⟩  ⌊John can't  bear-
```

```
3  SUE:                                           ⌈d'you know what
   ANNA:   rebel/ "Come ⌈round for lessons in rebelling"⌋
   LIZ:               ⌊he gives him- yeah          ⌊give him-
```

```
   SUE:   the funny thing is-                         yeah/
   LIZ:                "Buy a saxophone — I'll give you the number
```

```
5   SUE:                        ⎡yeah/      he would/ he's got this twi- he's got this
    LIZ:        where you ⎣buy one"/
```

```
    SUE:        nervous twitch/                                    exactly/ he's got this
    ANNA:                       ⎡I'm not surprised/ ⟨LAUGHS----------------------------
    LIZ:                        ⎣oh/ ⟨LAUGHS----------------------------------------
```

```
7   SUE:        nervous t- ⟨LAUGHS⟩ he's got this real nervous twitch/ and John says
    ANNA:       -------------------------------⟩
    LIZ:        --------------------------------------------⟩
```

```
    SUE:        "I'm going to ask him about it"/
    ANNA:                                                           ⟨LAUGHS⟩
    LIZ:                                            ⟨SHRIEKS OF LAUGHTER⟩
```

This example is made up of 8 staves — all of these, apart from the last one, involve two or three speakers talking and laughing at the same time. In the first stave, Sue and Liz talk polyphonically on the theme that the husband must rebel at home, but timing their utterances so that the key word *must* is uttered simultaneously. But with this theme established, Liz and Anna again cooperate to fantasize on the nature of this rebellion, taking turns to imagine John in the role of agent provocateur, while Sue continues with her (factual) account, bringing in the new point that the husband has a nervous twitch. This brings the house down, especially when Sue weaves the theme of John as agent provacateur into this new theme.

4.5. *Talk as play*

These brief extracts from a conversation between Sue, Liz and Anna on the topic of an obedient husband show us three women having enormous fun. They use the topic as an excuse to play with ideas about marriage and obedience, and also to play with words and with their skill at collaborative talk.

In the interviews, women friends tended to deny that they 'do' much together, since they don't class talk as 'doing'. Research on men's friendships emphasizes the importance men place on shared activity such as playing football or pool, going to watch a match, going to the pub (Johnson and Aries 1983a, 1983b; Pleck 1975; Miller 1983; O'Connor 1992; Seidler 1989). When we were children, we called these sorts of activities 'play', and playing was what we did with friends. It seems that men's 'play' is activity-oriented, while women's 'play' centres on talk. I want to argue here that women's melding talk takes the shape it does *precisely* because it *is* play. Talk-as-play is inevitably structured differently from talk-as-serious-business. To begin with, the main goal of talk-as-play is the construction and maintenance of good social relations, not the exchange of information (though this will also be one of the functions of friendly talk, as there in an informational component to all interaction). The second goal of talk-as-play is that participants should enjoy themselves. The fun of talk arises as much from *how* things are said as from *what* is said.

This exposition of the functions of women's friendly talk brings us back to the idea of talk as a kind of jam session. Women friends arrive at each others' houses and, after a brief warm-up over a glass of wine or a cup of tea, start playing. Solo passages alternate with all-in-together ensemble passages. We improvise on each others' themes, share painful and funny experiences, laugh at ourselves and with each other. The construction of a collaborative floor symbolizes what friendship means to us: As we create utterances together, as we say parallel things on the same theme at the same time, we are demonstrating in a concrete way the value we place on sharing and on collaboration. Our individual voices merge and blend in a joint performance. Laughter occurs frequently not just because people say funny or shocking things, but because we take huge pleasure in the talk we create and in our skill at 'melding in together', our skill at constructing and maintaining a collaborative floor.

Transcription Conventions

The transcription conventions used for the conversational data are as follows:
1.   a slash (/) indicates the end of a tone group or chunk of talk, e.g.:
       she pushes him to the limit/
2.   a question mark indicates the end of a chunk of talk which I am analyzing as a question, e.g.:
       do you know anyone who's pregnant?
3.   a hyphen indicates an incomplete word or utterance, e.g.:
       he's got this twi- he's got this nervous twitch/
       I was- I was- I was stopped by a train/
4.   pauses are indicated by a full stop (short pause — less than 0.5 seconds) or a dash (long pause), e.g.:
       he sort of . sat and read the newspaper/
5.   horizontal broken lines mark the beginnings and ends of staves; the lines enclosed by the lines are to be read simultaneously (like a musical score), e.g.:

     A: *the squidgy stuff that they put on pizzas/*

     B: *Mozarell⌈a/*

     C: ⌊*Mozarella/*

----

6. an extended square bracket indicates the start of overlap between utterances, e.g.:

     A: *and they have newspapers and* ⌈ *stuff/*

     B: ⌊ *yes very good/*

7. an equals sign at the end of one speaker's utterance and at the start of the next utterance indicates the absence of a discernible gap, e.g.:

     A: *because they're supposed to be=*

     B: *=adults/*

8. double round parentheses indicate that there is doubt about the accuracy of the transcription, e.g.:

     what's that ((mean))/ gayist/

9. where material is impossible to make out, it is represented as follows, ((xx)), e.g.:.

     you're ((xx))- you're prejudiced/

10. angled brackets give clarificatory information about the preceding chunk of talk, e.g.:

     I don't always just get undressed in the living room/ ⟨*LAUGH*⟩

and also about preceding underlined material, e.g.:

     why doesn't that creep — <u>start to go wild</u>/ ⟨*LAUGHING*⟩

     <u>I can't help it</u> ⟨*WHINEY VOICE*⟩

11. capital letters are used for words/syllables uttered with emphasis:

     it's in MExico/

12. the symbol % encloses words or phrases that are spoken very quietly, e.g.:

     %bloody hell%

13. the symbol .hh indicates that the speaker takes a sharp intake of breath:

     .hh <u>I wish I'd got a camera</u>/ ⟨*LAUGHING*⟩

14. the symbol [...] indicates that material has been omitted, e.g.:

     Tom [...] says there's a German word to describe that/

Acknowledgments

This paper is based on chapter 6 of my book *Women Talk: Conversation between Women Friends*.

Notes

1. The phenomenon I am calling 'jointly constructed utterances' has been variously described as 'utterance completion' (Sacks 1992:647); 'collaborative completion' (Rae 1990) and 'mutual sentential completion' (Diaz 1994). Harvey Sacks discussed the phenomenon at several points in his lectures, for example, in Lecture 3, Fall 1965, Lecture of March 2, 1967; Lecture 4 Fall 1967 (see Sacks 1992:144–149, 523–534, 647–655). For further discussion of this phenomenon in all-female talk, see my 1994 paper, 'No gap, lots of overlap: turn-taking patterns in the talk of women friends'.

2. Married couples also talk in a more melded way — see Falk (1980), Johnson (In press) — as do friends in mixed groups — see Bublitz (1989), Edelsky (1981). There is no research evidence of all-male groups talking in this way: what little evidence there is suggests men friends prefer a one-at-a-time floor (Coates 1997).

3. POLYPHONY: '[MUSIC] The simultaneous combination of a number of parts, each forming an individual melody, and harmonizing with the others' (Shorter Oxford English Dictionary). This metaphor is also used by Wallace Chafe to describe talk where there are 'separate voices articulating different melodies at once' (this volume, page 43). See also Chafe (1994:120–136).

4. The assumption that *all* talk involves a single floor (perhaps more accurately, the lack of knowledge about collaborative floors) means that examiners in the newly established oral component of public examinations in English have problems rewarding girls who use conversational strategies typical of a collaborative floor. See Cheshire and Jenkins (1991), Jenkins and Cheshire (1990), Wareing (1994).

5. Zimmerman and West (1975) argue that male speakers sometimes delay — that is, deliberately mis-time — minimal responses in order to signal lack of interest in what is being said.

6. I am grateful to participants at the postgraduate seminar on Gender and Discourse Analysis, Schloss Munchenwiler, Switzerland, November 1993 (especially Jenny Cheshire and Peter Trudgill), who refined my understanding of the role of laughter in this particular piece of talk.

References

Bublitz, Wolfram. 1989. *Supportive Fellow-Speakers and Cooperative Conversations*. Amsterdam: John Benjamins.

Chafe, Wallace. 1994. *Discourse, Consciousness and Time: The flow and displacement of conscious experience in speaking and writing*. Chicago: The University of Chicago Press.

Chafe, Wallace. This volume. "Polyphonic Topic Development."

Cheshire, Jenny and Nancy Jenkins. 1991. "Gender Issues in the GCSE Oral English Examination: Part 2", *Language and Education* 5(1).1–22.

Coates, Jennifer. 1986. *Women, Men and Language*. 1st edition. London: Longman.

Coates, Jennifer. 1989. "Gossip Revisited: Language in all-female groups." In *Women in Their Speech Communities*, Jennifer Coates and Deborah Cameron (eds), 94–122. London: Longman.

Coates, Jennifer. 1991. "Women's Cooperative Talk: A new kind of conversational duet?" In *Proceedings of the Anglistentag 1990 Marburg*, Claus Uhlig & Rudiger Zimmermann (eds), 196–311, Tubingen: Max Niemeyer.

Coates, Jennifer. 1994. "No Gap, Lots of Overlap: Turn-taking patterns in the talk of women friends" In *Researching Language and Literacy in Social Context,* David Graddol, Janet Maybin & Barry Stierer (eds) 177–192. Clevedon: Multilingual Matters.

Coates, Jennifer. 1996a. *Women Talk: Conversation between Women Friends.* Oxford: Basil Blackwell.

Coates, Jennifer. 1996b. "Women's Stories: The role of narrative in friendly talk." Inaugural Lecture, Roehampton Institute London.

Coates, Jennifer. 1997. "One-at-a-time: The organisation of men's talk." In *Language and Masculinity*, Sally Johnson & Ulrike Meinhof (eds) 107–129. Oxford: Basil Blackwell.

Edelsky, Carole. 1981. "Who's Got the Floor?" *Language in Society* 10(3).383–421 (reprinted in Deborah Tannen (ed.) (1993) *Gender and Conversational Interaction.* Oxford: Oxford University Press).

Falk, Jane. 1980. "The Conversational Duet." *Proceedings of the 6th Annual Meeting of the Berkeley Linguistics Society*. Vol. 6, 507–514.

Fishman, Pamela. 1980a. "Conversational Insecurity." In *Language: Social psychological perspectives*, Howard Giles, Peter Robinson and Philip Smith (eds), 127–132. Oxford: Pergamon Press.

Fishman, Pamela. 1980b. "Interactional Shitwork." *Heresies* 2.99–101.

Haas, Adelaide. 1978. "Sex-associated Features of Spoken Language by Four-, Eight- and Twelve-year-old Boys and Girls." Paper given at the 9th World Congress of Sociology, Uppsala, Sweden, August 14–19.

Jenkins, Nancy and Jenny Cheshire. 1990. "Gender Issues in the GCSE Oral English Examination: Part 1." *Language and Education* 4.261–292.

Johnson, Anthony. In press. *Couples Talking.* London: Longman.

Johnson, Fern and Elizabeth Aries. 1983a. "The Talk of Women Friends." *Women's Studies International Forum* 6(4).353–361.

Johnson, Fern and Elizabeth Aries. 1983b. "Conversational Patterns among Same-sex Pairs of Late-adolescent Close Friends." *Journal of Genetic Psychology* 142.225–238.

Miller, Stuart. 1983. *Men and Friendship.* San Leandro, Calif.: Gateway.

O'Connor, Pat. 1992. *Friendships between Women: A critical review*. London: Harvester Wheatsheaf.

Pleck, Joseph. 1975. "Man to Man: Is brotherhood possible?" In *Old Family, New Family*, N. Glazer-Malbin (ed.). New York: Van Nostrand.

Sacks, Harvey. 1992. *Lectures on Conversation*. Vol 1. Oxford: Basil Blackwell.

Sacks, Harvey, Emanuel A. Schegloff and Gail Jefferson 1974. "A Simplest Systematics for the Organisation of Turn-taking in Conversation." *Language* 50.696–735.

Seidler, Victor. 1989. *Rediscovering Masculinity*. London: Routledge.

Wareing, Shan. 1994. "Cooperative and Competitive Talk: The assessment of discussion at Standard Grade." Unpublished Ph.D. Thesis, University of Strathclyde.

Zimmerman, Don and Candace West 1975. "Sex Roles: Interruptions and silences in conversation." In *Language and Sex: Difference and dominance.* Barrie Thorne and Nancy Henley (eds), 105–129. Rowley, Mass.: Newbury House.

Memory and Conversation

Toward an Experimental Paradigm

Connie Dickinson and T. Givón

University of Oregon

1. Background

During face-to-face communication, speakers–hearers are engaged simultaneously in a great number of tasks, most prominent among them are the management of **cooperative interaction** between the interlocutors, and the processing of coherent **information-flow.** It seems altogether reasonable that the two tasks are not totally divorced from each other. But the methodological approaches that emerged earlier on in discourse studies have often tended to split the study of these two aspects of human communication. The first approach, conversational analysis, has focused primarily on the study of face-to-face communication, and within it primarily on the organization of the **turn-taking** system and the linguistic and paralinguistic cues used to regulate it (see e.g. Sachs, Schegloff and Jefferson 1974; Goodwin 1982; among many others). The second approach, focusing primarily on information flow and the role of grammatical cues in regulating it, has concentrated primarily on the study of monologic discourse (e.g. Chafe 1979, 1980 ed. 1987, 1994; Givón 1979 ed. 1983 ed. 1985 ed. 1988, 1992, 1994; DuBois 1987; Tomlin 1985, 1987, 1987 ed., 1991; among others).

One would be remiss not to observe that an integrated approach to the study of discourse has been around for just as long, most prominently among researchers of early child language acquisition (Ervin-Tripp 1970, 1976; Dore 1973; Keenan 1975, 1977; Ochs and Shieffelin eds 1976; Scollon 1976; Guo 1992; among others). These studies have focused, from the very start, on the social nature of early child communication, where information-flow itself is highly collaborative. More recently this approach has been extended to face-to-face communication among adults, where collaboration between interlocutors has been shown to play an important role in building a coherent information-flow (e.g. Clark and Wilkes-Gibbs 1986; Clark and Schaefer 1987; Goodwin 1988, in press, 1995; Wilkes-Gibbs 1986, 1994; Wilkes-Gibbs and Clark 1992; Anderson 1995; among many others). What these studies suggested to us is that to quite an extent the dichotomy between discourse as interaction and discourse as information-flow is an artificial one, reflecting accidents of history and methodology, as well as perhaps pre-empirical philosophical or ideological perspectives.

In parallel with the initial dichotomy between interactional and information-flow studies, the two extreme methodological paradigms have also diverged, often implicitly, in their attitude toward **mental models** of language processing. The conversational-analysis paradigm has tended to de-emphasize cognition and mental models, focusing on the **situated social context** of face-to-face communication. Such an emphasis is often characterized by the mantra "it is all in the social situation".

Information-flow research, on the other hand, has tended to express its generalization in frameworks increasingly couched in cognitive terms (e.g. van Dijk and Kintsch 1983; Chafe 1987, 1994; Anderson, Garrod and Sanford 1993; Givón 1992, 1994, 1995; Tomlin 1991; Gernsbacher 1990; among others). At the same time, cognitively oriented studies have often tended to ignore the interactional aspects of discourse, and thus the seminal position of face-to-face communication in shaping human language and its attendant cognitive and neural mechanisms.

That face-to-face communication is the most fundamental mode of human language hardly requires belaboring. It is phylogenetically prior in language evolution. It is ontogenetically prior in child language acquisition. And it is distributionally most frequent in every-day human communication, excepting perhaps the highly specialized genres practiced by academics.

There is something both unnecessary and undesirable about the intellectual segregation between the two sub-fields of discourse studies. To begin with, the episodic memory system that makes coherent multi-clausal (or multi-turn) communication possible is the very same cognitive–neurological system, supporting the production and comprehension of monologue and conversation alike. The attentional systems deployed in both types of communication are undoubtedly the same. And the working memory sub-systems supporting both are, most likely, the very same.

Further, the attentional and memory systems that support face-to-face communication probably support, simultaneously, both the interactional and informational aspects of discourse.

Finally, the social–situational aspect of face-to-face communication is not an objective, external entity. Much like other kinds of information available to the organism, the current speech situation must be selectively extracted from the "external" situation, and converted into a mental representation. It is only this **on-going mental model** of the speech situation that is relevant to the process of face-to-face communication. Fundamentally, then, the dichotomy between "situational" and "cognitive" is false.

The work we report here has been motivated by a growing conviction that the mental representation of the speech situation, on the one hand, and of episodic information, on the other, demand an integrated approach. Before outlining the goals and methodology of our first experimental study, it would be useful to survey the little that we assume to be known about the memory systems that are most relevant to discourse production and comprehension.

2.   Relevant cognitive systems

2.1. *Shared information as mental models*

Human communication is founded on the assumption of shared background information. Only on the foundations of this assumption can human communication as we know it proceed. The information that speakers can assume hearers share with them falls into three major categories.

(a)   The **shared cultural world-view,** as coded primarily in the shared conceptual lexicon. As a mental model, this is, rather transparently, the psychologists' **permanent semantic memory.**

(b)   The shared **current speech situation.** As a mental model, this is, as we will argue here, the psychologist's **working memory** or current focus of attention.

(c)   The shared **current discourse.** As a mental model, this is, again rather transparently, the psychologists' **episodic memory.**

The first two mental models, and their systematic use in social communication, pre-date humans. They are just as fundamental to pre-human as to human communication. The third is a distinct evolutionary development in humans, although its evolutionary precursors can be found in the hippocampus-based visual episodic memory system of pre-human mammals. The adaptive value of stored — mentally modeled — prior discourse for both learning from experience and planning for the future is too obvious to require further comment.

2.2. *Episodic memory*

The cognitive and neurological literature suggests that the early episodic memory system, based in the sub-cortical hippocampus and medial-temporal cortical structures adjacent to it, is the system that represents episodic ('specific', 'declarative') information coming in from both visual processing and verbal communication (Squire 1987; Squire and Zola-Morgan 1991; Mishkin 1978; Mishkin *et al.* 1984; Mishkin and Petri 1994). This memory system is thus not modality-specific; so that both verbal and non-verbal input, via either the visual, auditory or tactile modality, finds its way into the same processing and represen-tation system.

The more salient characteristics of the hippocampus-based episodic memory system are, briefly (following Squire and Zola-Morgan 1991; *inter alia*):

(a)   It is extremely malleable and involves further processing, reprocessing and reorganization of stored information (Loftus 1980).

(b)   It is a limited-capacity processor in which storage space and processing activity still compete.

(c)   It is emptied periodically into a more permanent episodic memory system, and thus remains available for the processing of in-coming new information.

(d)   It is thus a crucial intermediary between the short-capacity working memory (see below) and longer-term episodic storage, located most likely in the frontal or pre-frontal neo-cortex.

(e)   Impairment in episodic recall due to hippocampus lesions is dissociated from both procedural and lexical-semantic knowledge.

(f)   Hippocampus lesions do not impair the recall of old, long-established episodic knowledge, presumably because of the latter's frontal localization.

(g)   Surface grammatical information that is preserved in some perceptual form in working memory may not survive into episodic representation. Put another way, grammatical clues are stripped away from the episodic representation of speech (Gernsbacher 1985).

2.3. *Working memory*

Information entering early episodic memory must pass via some modality-specific **working memory** "buffer", with or without the participation of the central, cross-modal **executive attention.** All working memory sub-modules are fundamentally **attentional activation** processors with limited capacity and thus short duration.

The modality-specific working-memory processors are described by some as an "auditory loop" and a "visual scratch-pad" that rehearse and keep alive an "echoic" perceptual representation of short input segments, before further processing may convert them into more durable ("cognitive") episodic mental representations (Baddeley 1986; Squire 1987; Gathercole and Baddeley 1993; Carpenter and Just 1988; Gernsbacher 1985; *inter alia*).

Some of those who identify working memory as an attentional system view it as a processor capable of considerable analysis and even inference (Bowers and Morrow 1990; Just and Carpenter 1992; Posner, in personal communication). A recent review even attributes longer duration to this cognitive capacity (Ericsson and Kintsch 1995).

A schematic representation of the relationship between working memory and episodic memory is given in Figure 1 below.

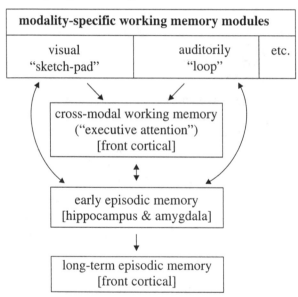

Figure 1.   *Relationship between modality-specific working memory, cross-modal "executive attention", early episodic memory and long-term episodic memory (integrated from Shallice 1988; Baddeley 1986; Gathercole and Baddeley 1993; Squire and Zola-Morgan 1991)*

3.   Mental representation of the current speech situation

In this section we survey the linguistic facts that bring us to believe that dynamic, on-going ('on-line') mental representation of the current speech situation must reside in one of the three memory capacities discussed above, more specifically — if tentatively — in working memory. We argue that a **running mental model** of the current speech situation must be activated in the mind of speakers–hearers during communication, if we are to understand the facts of communicative behavior.

3.1. *Spatial-temporal deixis*

The existence of an ongoing mental representation of the current speech situation must be assumed if one is to explain even the most rudimentary facts of the grammar of spatial deixis. In particular, the presumption of definiteness, thus accessibility, of deictic referents depends on their spatial position relative to the speaker (or hearer). Consider first:

(1)	**Pronouns:**	I, you, we, y'all
	Demonstratives:	this, that
	Locative adverbs:	here, there, yon
	Deictic verbs:	go, come, bring, take

It would be impossible to understand the systematic communicative use of the linguistic expressions in (1) without assuming that both interlocutors have constant access to a running mental model of their respective spatial position *vis-à-vis* each other, as well as a running model of who is speaking ('I') and who is listening ('you').

Likewise, the temporal deixis seen in the use of temporal adverbs and tense compels us to assume that the temporal aspects of the current speech situation are also part of the running mental model of the current speech situation.

(2)   **temporal adverbs:** now, then, today, yesterday, tomorrow, last week, a week ago
       tense: worked, have worked, is working, will work

Since our putative mental model must represent the speech situation *at the very time of speech*, and since in face-to-face communication the speaker may change constantly, the mental representation of the current speech situation is not necessarily relevant to what speaker need to be preserved in longer-term episodic memory for future access. Portions of the activated information about the current speech situation may indeed reach longer-term episodic storage, and can then be accessible to later retrieval. In this respect, our putative running mental model may be akin to Ericsson and Kintsch's (1995) "long term working memory" (LTWM).

The running mental model of the current speech situation displays many of the salient characteristics of **working memory.** Like working memory, it is a necessary but not sufficient condition for longer-term episodic storage. Indeed, the evidence from people's memory — and subsequent reports — of past conversations strongly suggests that *some* representation of *past* speech situations must reach longer-term episodic memory, at least under some conditions. This information is often explicitly associated with specific portions of the "propositional contents" of the communication. This assumption is absolutely necessary in order to account for our ability to interpret, as a matter of course, reported communications such as (the hypothetical):

(3)   So **then** he told **me**:
        "**I** want **you** to take **this** chair right **now** and put it
        there next to **you**".
        And boy, I tell **you,** he's got the nerve! So **I** told him:
        "**That** chair is **yours,** so **I** don't see why **you'**d want it
        here next to **me**".
        Now, **you** might think...

Consider the following three examples of natural communication. They represent, in order, the transcript of a conversation recorded in one of our recent experiments (4), and the transcripts of the subsequent verbal report about that conversation by the two participants, (5) and (6):

(4)   **Conversation between Lori and Vicky:**
        VICKY: [...] first what was the guy wearing?
        LORI: He was wearing, uh, red shorts and a white T-shirt.
                 No shoes ...
        V: No shoes?
        L: No shoes.
        V: My guy was wearing [foot...] or something...
        L: OK... Now, first [...] the guy came in carrying three long
            tools and a.. uh, hatchet... and, uh, he walked over to a
            tree, set them down, they fell down once and he brought...
            and then... he picked them up..
        V: OK, mine... I'd, you know I didn't really count... I think
            mine had two...
        L: Yeah.
        V: And, they dropped and he picked them back up.
        L: OK. And then what did he do?
        V: And he had, uh... a hatchet.
        L: Yeah

V: And he went over to the wood pile, ove' to where the wood was... and he started chopping, it was rather ineffective, but he was chopping, and...

L: Pieces of wood? [OL]

V: Yeah they were about... boy, maybe, two inches in diameter...

L: Yeah... [OL]

V: three... pieces about... foot-and-a-half long...

L: OK

V: And...uh he would... chop them and throw them over the side... uh there're maybe seven or eight...of them...

L: There may have been more, I think [...] more [...]

V: [...] my guess is there were four or five... Umm... and then the woman came in, she's wearing uh a pink skirt and, a white... blouse, a light shirt with color... she was wearing red shoes... That the same?

L: Umm, all th't I really remember 'bout the dress there was a dress... I think it was a skirt and a blouse...

V: OK.

L: And the blouse was white, or was a light color... it was half color...

V: OK... uh... what did she do?

L: Well, they talked, they conversed... and... ummm... it sounded to me like she was telling him... you know "Right [...] enough with the wood..." you know, "go... go hoe..." you know, the... the field or whatever...

V: "I'll take care of the fire..."

L: Yes... and so she collects the wood, and she goes over to like, one of those little umm... lean-to, or shed... and... she, collects some... uh... some kindling, or some little twigs... OK, what's up?

V: My lady she went over and kinda yelled at him for... sounded like she yelled at him for doing whatever... and then she took, his, pile of wood and went over to a big... uh... kind of a little mountain of brush... she was hauling to around... and she... too out about a dozen a took them and broke them... and collected them all in a bundle...

In the two transcripts of the two subsequent reports on the conversation, we italicize the parts that are not about the contents of the conversation (4), but rather about the dynamics of the interaction itself.

(4)   **Subsequent report by Lori:**
...The conversation I had with Vicky. First of all she started out by saying, saying what the man was wearing, and that he was carrying three farming utensils plus a hatchet, and, *actually, no, she started out asking me* what he was wearing. *And I said that* he was wearing red shorts and a white T-shirt and no thongs or anything. *And she said that* he was wearing red shorts and a white T-sirt, but that he had flop flops on. *She said that and then she said that* he had three... He had three, uh, um, farming utensils and, um... *I said, well I think I saw* two, *and that was one difference that we, that we had in the film. And then she said, then she said that* he went over to... *uh, no then I said that* he went over to some wood and he started chopping the wood. *And I said that* the wood was probably about two inches in diameter. And *maybe* it was about a foot and a half long the pieces, and *that* he was chopping, but rather ineffectively, and *that* he was throwing the pieces of wood over to the side. *And I said* he chopped seven or eight pieces, *and then she said that* he chopped four, three to five, something like that. And then, what happened next... *and then I think that she said that* the woman came in *and then she described* the woman's outfit, *that* it was a white blouse with a collar that was buttoned up. And it was a pink skirt? ... *Then I said, well, I couldn't remember what she was wearing exactly, that maybe* it was a white blouse and a skirt, and it was like a pastel color. And... and *that*, um, they went over and they had some sort of an argument, *and I said that to me it sounded like* she was telling him *you know* "why are you cutting this wood? I can take care of the fire wood. You go and, and you know, hoe the field". And so he went and hoed the field. He picked up his utensils. *I, we didn't talk about that...*

Subsequent report by Vicky:
Oh boy. I wasn't thinking about that. I forgot. Um, okay. We were trying to decide whether we had the same video or not. Um, first I asked Lori what the guy was wearing. *Um she said* he was wearing a white T-shirt or white shirt and red shorts and no shoes. *And I said that* my guy was wearing flip-flops, *I thought* it sounded like flip-flops. *Um... then I said that... um... the video started with* the guy coming in, he walked across the field carrying three tools

and a hatchet. He went over to a tree, he put/leaned them up against the tree and they fell down and he put them back up... *and I asked Lori if that was the same thing that happened in hers, and she said "yes", and she said that* he took the hatchet and went over to the wood pile and started chopping up wood kind of very ineffectively. *Um, we discussed* the size of the wood, about 2 inches in diameter, about a foot and a half long. *And, um, she said that* he'd made about seven or eight cuts, or seven or eight pieces of wood, *and I said that I thought, mine was, my video had* a few less, four, five or six, *um, and then I said that* the woman came in. She was wearing a white shirt with a collar and a pink shirt and red shoes. *Um, she said she wasn't paying a whole lot of attention, but she knew that she thought* the lady was wearing a white shirt and some, *oh, she said* the lady was wearing a dress. *And then she thought about it longer and said* probably a white shirt and some sort of pastel light colored... *um then I think that Lori said that* she went over, *yeah, Lori said that* she went over to the guy and kind of talked with him, *and then she said* she was kind of yelling at him in a way for, um, messing with the wood when he should be out hoeing his fiel, field. *So, she, Lori told me that* she, she then went over to a lean-to and started chopping up wood. Um, or not chopping up wood but gathering brush, something like that. *And I interrupted and said that* my lady didn't go over to a lean-to, that she took his pile of wood then went over to kind of a small mountain of brush and started collecting stuff.

Language users are clearly capable of transferring at least some portions of the running mental model of the current speech situations into longer-term episodic storage. But the representation of *past* speech situations appears, at least in the conversation reported in (5), (6) above, to be integrated with the representation of the contents of the conversation.

3.2. *Mental representation of the hearer's current belief-and-intention states*

The spatio-temporal aspects of the current speech situation and the identity of speaker and hearer is only one aspect of the information that must be activated in the mind of interlocutors during communication, perhaps even the simplest aspect. A more thorny issue concerns the representation, in the mind of the speaker, of the hearer's current belief-and-intention states.

Consider first the conventional use of declarative, interrogative and manipulative **speech-acts** (Grice 1968/1975 *inter alia*). This use is inconceivable without assuming that speakers construct and carry a running mental model of hearers' current beliefs and intentions. Such a mental model must be extremely dynamic, and must shift constantly between one clause uttered by the speaker and the next. Consider, for example, the hypothetical exchange:

(7) a. So she got up and left.
  b. You didn't stop her?
  c. Would you?
  d. I don't know. Where was she sitting?
  e. Why?
  f. Never mind, just tell me.

Let us assume that (7a–f) is a multiple-turn conversation between two inter-locutors, A (turns (7a, c, e)), and B (turns 7b, d, f)). During each turn, the speaker activates a different representation of the hearer's belief-and-intention states, those that are relevant for a declarative clause (7a), a yes/no question (7b, c), a negative (7d), a WH question (7d, e), and an imperative (7f). This running assessment of the hearer's current mental states shifts constantly, since the hearer's beliefs and intentions accrue and shift as the conversation progresses. Without assuming that such a running mental model is available 'on line' during communication, it would be impossible to explain how communications such as (7) can ever be coherent and successful.

But the running mental model of the hearer's intention-and-belief states that was presumably activated during conversation (7) seldom if ever survives into the episodic trace of the conversation. In scores of pages of our transcripts of recalled immediate-past conversations, we find no single reference to such representation. Unlike the deictic elements, which are well represented in episodic accounts such as (5), (6) above, we have never seen accounts such as (8) below of. Account (8) would have been, as far as one can imagine, the episodic report of conversation (7) in which the speakers report their shifting mental model of the hearer's belief-and-intention states at each turn of (7a–f):

(8) a. So I told him then, *knowing that he didn't know it, and knowing that he wanted to hear about it from me:* "So she got up and left".
  b. So I asked him, *knowing that it was likely that he knew the an-swer, and that he knew I didn't know it, and believing that it was socially proper for me to ask him, and that he was well dispoed toward sharing this knowledge with me:* "You didn't stop her?"
  c. So I asked him, *knowing that he was likely to know, and that he knew I didn't know, and believing that he was well disposed toward giving me the answer:* "Would you?"

d. So I told him, *knowing he had considered the possibility that I would indeed stop her, and thus intending to disabuse him of his mistaken belief:* "I don't know". And then I asked him, *suspecting he knew the answer, and knowing that the woman had been sitting somewhere else, and knowing he knew I didn't know the answer, and believing he was well disposed toward telling it to me:* "Where was she sitting?"

e. So I asked him, *knowing that he knew his own motives for asking me where she was sitting, and believing he was amenable to sharing his motives with me, and that he knew I didn't know the answer:* "Why?"

f. So I told him, *knowing he knew I had the right to address him in such a peremptory manner, and suspecting he wasn't going to resent me for it, and knowing he was capable of successfully complying with my demands:* "Never mind, just tell me".

This is not to say that upon reflection, under some condition, and with specific retrieval cues, speakers/hearers who would readily remember and explicitly report conversations such as (7) could not also reconstruct some of what must have been going on in their own mind concerning their interlocutor's shifting belief-and-intention states. But such information is, most likely, not as readily available in their episodic trace of the conversation as were the deictic aspects of the speech situation.

There are good adaptive reasons why traces of the shifting mental model belief-and-intention states of the interlocutor are not stored as efficiently in episodic memory as other aspects of conversation. First, this portion of the running mental model is supremely **irrelevant** at any other time except during on-line processing of a particular clause or turn. Second, the information involved is highly conventionalized, rule-governed and highly **predictable.** As such, it is of scant interest to the hearer.

Finally, the manner of·activation of this information during conversation may be of a different kind — **unattended** or **unconscious.** And this may contrast with the attended, conscious activation of information about the propositional contents, the speech situation or the identity of the speaker. A broadly similar interaction between the attended vs. unattended status of visual information during initial activation (working-memory) and the explicit vs. implicit episodic recall of visual information have been reported by Treisman (1995).

3.3. *Other mental models relevant to the use of grammar*

The entire grammar of referential coherence, definiteness, modality and evidentiality, foregrounding and backgrounding, presupposition and assertion, clause chaining and adverbials, etc. etc., would be utterly nonsensical without assuming the existence, in the speaker's mind, of a dynamic mental representation of the hearer's belief-and-intention states (see Chafe 1994; Givón 1994; *inter alia*). This representation shifts constantly during communication — be it conversation or monologue — in much the same way as it does for speech-acts, and for the same reasons. The interlocutor's beliefs and intents can shift with every clause or turn.

Consider, for example, the referent introduced for the first time as indefinite in (9a) below, and thus at that point assumed to be inaccessible to the hearer, given his/her then-current belief state. In the next clause (9b) that referent is assumed to be both accessible and currently active, and for that reason is coded as a definite anaphoric pronoun:

(9)   a. There was *a man* there sitting at the bar.
      b. The waitress had taken *his* order, *he* wanted a beer.
      c. But the place was so crowded, another man got served first, then another, then a whole bunch. It just went on and on.
      d. Finally, the man *sitting at the bar* got up and left.

Likewise, the assertion in (9a) is presumed to be new to the hearer and thus still challengeable at that point. Left unchallenged, it is soon converted into a presupposition in (9d), coded as a restrictive REL-clause, and assumed **accessible** to the hearer and **unchallengeable** — at that point.

Again, there are scant grounds for believing that the running model of the interlocutor's belief-and-intention states survives into longer-term episodic memory. Narrative (10) below would be an explicit if unlikely episodic account of (9):

(10) a. So I told him, *knowing he didn't have a way of knowing which man I was talking about:* "There was a man sitting at the bar"
      b. And, *knowing that now he could identify that man easily,* I then added: "the waittress had taken his order, he wanted a beer" ...
      d. ...Then, *knowing that he already knew about where the man was sitting,* I told him: "Finally the man sitting at the bar got up and left..."

Consider finally example (11) and the information that must be activated for the successful use of modality and evidentiality during communication.

(11) a. It *would* be nice if you *could* do this for me
      b. She's back in town, *I hear*
      c. *I'm afraid* she's not coming
      d. He's not going to do it, *y'know*

An explicit episodic trace of examples (11a–d), as in (12) below, would look indeed bizarre if it incorporated the speaker's dynamic assessment of the hearer's shifting mental states during the conversation. And this is in spite of the fact that such information was indispensable at the time conversations (11) were taking place.

(12) a. So I told him, *knowing he probably wasn't feeling obligated, but trying to be nice and maybe he'd consent:* "It would be nice if you could do this for me".
      b. So I told him, *suspecting that he'd prefer that I didn't represent hearsay information as solid fact:* "She's back in town, I hear".
      c. So I told him, *knowing he would be disappointed:* "She's not coming".
      d. So I told him, *sensing he was not particularly friendly, and that he was going to be disappointed and maybe blame me:* "He's not going to do it, y'know".

In suggesting that *all* communication depends on a running mental model of the interlocutor's mind, one must lay to rest the curious piece of fiction that some forms of human discourse are not hearer-oriented. As Morti Gernsbacher (in personal communication) has noted, during the production of non-face-to-face discourse, the intended audience's epistemic and intentional states are simply anticipated. And this anticipation shifts and is updated constantly during discourse production. In a very real sense then, narrative text has never been anything but an — admittedly impoverished and feedback-deprived — dialogic enterprise.

4.   Methodology

4.1. *Overall design*

Five experimental conditions were created in the phase of the study reported here. The first three (I, II, III) serve as controls for all subsequent conditions, creating a base-level of episodic recall to which all subsequent conditions are then compared. The last two conditions (IV, V) assess the effect of two types of face-to-face interaction, taking place between input and its episodic recall:

In all conditions, subjects viewed the same short video film. The viewing was followed by various interventions, following which the subjects were asked to verbally recall the events of the film. Their verbal recollections, as well as the verbal interaction preceding it in conditions IV, V, were recorded and transcribed. This section deals with the methodology common to all five experimental conditions. Procedures specific to the individual conditions will be discussed in subsequent sections.

4.2. *Text elicitation*

A short, 6.25 minute long video was used. This video had been developed previously for use in another experimental project (Givón 1991). The following is a brief summary of the story:

SYNOPSIS OF CHICKEN STORY:
A man walks toward a tree, leans his farming implements on it and goes on to chop wood with an axe. A woman appears and walks to him. After some conversation, she takes the wood, moves aside and collects some more wood, then carries it all away. The man quits his chopping, collects his tools and walks off toward a grove. The scene shifts to the woman coming around a small shed. She unloads her wood, lights a fire, fetches water from a barrel and sets a pot of water to boil. She disappears behind the shed and comes back carrying a chicken. She tries to slaughter it with a knife, but clumsily bungles the job and the chicken escapes. After some perfunctory chasing, the woman goes back to the house, brings out some bread and cheese, makes a sandwich, wraps it up and leaves with it. The scene shifts to the man hoeing in the field. The woman arrives and offers him the package. They sit down, the man unwraps the food, rejects it, throws it back at the woman, then chases her around the tree with his hoe. (Givón 1991, pp. 143–144)

The Chicken Story film does not have a prototypical western plot-line or structure. The subjects cannot rely on western cultural norms to understand, contextualize, and infer meaning. The actors spoke Swahili and thus the subjects could not understand the language, and received no overt language input. The video was also designed to present many simple, active and transitive events. The camera changes location twice, resulting in three basic locales, or episodes. The camera, for the most part, simply follows the movement of the characters.

4.3. *Subjects*

The subjects were sixty University of Oregon undergraduates who were offered extra credit in an introductory linguistics course in exchange for their participation. All spoke English as their native language and were accustomed to watching videos.

4.4. *Computing a base-line control for recalled information*

In order to have a standard for comparing the subjects' recollection of the video, it was necessary to create a base-line control for the "information contents" of the elicitation film. Most studies of text rely on the experimenter's intuitive judgements as to what is the 'gist' — most salient, important, indispensable — information in an elicitation text. In this study we create the information base-line from subjects' own on-line descriptions of the film — during viewing. Under this on-line condition (I), ten subjects watched the film and were instructed to describe the events as they watched them. Their on-line verbal descriptions were tape-recorded and transcribed. All event clauses mentioned by at least *seven out of ten* subjects were included in the baseline. This cutoff point — 7 and above — was determined by computing the mean (4) and standard deviation (3) of the number of subjects that mentioned those clauses. We thus included in the base-line all clauses above one standard deviation from the mean. Although this cutoff point is somewhat arbitrary, the measure pulls in the clauses most likely to be noticed by all subjects. A total of fifty-eight base-line clauses were identified (see Appendix).

4.5. *Semantic considerations*

The problem of deciding what constitutes "the same event" (or "the same state") in the subjects' on-line verbal descriptions is far from trivial. The detailed grammatical form of the event-clause was not taken into consideration. Thus, relative clauses, adverbial clauses and independent clauses were considered on a par. In examples (13) below, the italicized verbs were considered to indicate separate event-clauses.

(13) a. **REL-clause followed by main clause:**
          a man *carying* tools *walked* over to some trees
    b. **Main clause followed by ADV-clause:**
          he *picked up* the axe *to chop* some wood
    c. **Main clause followed by REL-clause:**
          she *walked* over to the man who was *hoeing* the ground
    d. **Main clause followed by REL-clause:**
          a woman *came* over *wearing* a white blouse and a peach skirt

Verbal complement clauses pose somewhat of a problem. We found no perception, utterance, cognition or manipulation verb complement in our transcripts. But modality-verb complements were common. Such complements share their temporal, spatial and subject-NP reference with the main clauses. They also tend to be highly integrated syntactically with their main clause (Givón 1990, ch. 13). We decided then to consider such verbs and their complements as single clauses, as in:

(14) **Modality verbs and their complements:**
  a. she *started to make* a fire
  b. she *tried to cut off* his head
  c. she *began breaking* branches
  d. he *started chasing* her around

How does one determine when two different verbs in the transcripts of two different subjects refer to the same event in the film? Most verbs in our transcripts depict physical motion and/or physical manipulation of objects. We divided verbs initially into four sub-groups: simple transitive, motion, stative, and complement-taking verbs. Deciding whether two (or more) verbs referred to the same event was based first on the verbs falling into the same general category; second on whether their arguments referred to the same participants (entities); and third on the identity of the case-roles of the participants (Fillmore 1968; Givón 1984, ch. 4).

Motion verbs presented somewhat of a problem in that some are syntactically transitive ('enter', 'leave', 'approach'); some have ablative or allative directional senses ('come', 'go'). Others incorporate manner into their meaning ('walk', 'run'). Because the directional sense of some motion verbs depends on the perspective taken by the speaker, and is not necessarily part of the event itself, we ignored subtle differences resulting from variation in perspective. Both transitive and manner-incorporating motion verbs were counted as simple motion verbs that require a locative argument. For example, clauses (15a–d) below were counted as representing the same event, while clauses (16a–c) were not. 'Approach' (15c) is syntactically a transitive verb, but was considered as encoding the same event as the other verbs in (15), since it has the same locative argument ('the fireplace'). 'Carry' in (16c), on the other hand, does not encode the same event as clauses (16a, b) because it has an additional argument ('the wood').

(15) **'Same event' judgement:**
  a. She *came* back over to the fireplace
  b. She *went* back over to the fireplace
  c. She *approached* the fireplace
  d. She *walked* over to the fireplace

(16) **'Different event' judgement:**
- a. She *came* back over to the fireplace
- b. She *walked* quickly
- c. She *carried* the wood over to the fireplace

Our procedures sometimes led to the exclusion of verbs which intuitively seem to encode the same events. However such stringent requirements allow for consistency based on our three criteria:

(a) **Verb class:** motion, transitive, complement taking, stative
(b) **Type and number of semantic arguments:** agent, patient, locative, dative, beneficiary, instrumental, manner, etc.
(c) **Reference to same entities:** man, woman, chicken, pot, fire, woods, wood, axe, matches, etc.

Self-referring interjections by the speaker such as "I think", "then I saw", "I thought" were not counted. Given our criteria, we found very few cases where inclusion or exclusion was problematic. Some of the variations in the choice of verbs to represent base-line clauses can be found in the Appendix.

4.6. *General experimental procedures*

All subjects watched the film on a large overhead video projection screen. They were told that after viewing they would be asked to recount, with as much detail as possible, what happened in the film. Directly after viewing, they were asked to perform various intervening tasks (see sections 4, 5, 6, below). After viewing, all subjects were then asked to describe what they remember of the film, starting at the beginning and proceeding in order. They were explicitly enjoined from adding personal evaluations or comments, but asked to merely "tell us what happened" from beginning to end, with as much detail as possible. Their narrations were recorded and transcribed. Their correspondence to the information base-line (Appendix) was then computed by the criteria described above.

4.7. *Control conditions I, II, III*

The first three experimental conditions, used as controls for the final two conditions, involved three different variants of obtaining a base-level of recall performance:

CONDITION I: on-line verbalization during viewing;
                                       a distractor task between viewing and recall
CONDITION II: no on-line verbalization during viewing;
                                       no time delay between viewing and recall

CONDITION III: no on-line verbalization during viewing;
                   a distractor task between viewing and recall

The choice of each control condition was motivated by specific considerations. It has been reported in a previous study (Givón 1991) that the on-line
descriptions of the film were on the average twice as long and more detailed
than the post-viewing recalled descriptions. We chose condition I to assess
whether previous verbalization during viewing affects the amount or fidelity of
recalled information.

Since the hippocampus-based episodic memory system depends on time for
consolidation (Squire 1987; Squire and Zola-Morgan 1991), we wanted to make
sure that it was the effect of conversational intervention (conditions IV, V),
rather than the effect of time delay *per se,* which was responsible for any
differences in recall following conversational intervention. Conditions II and III
were chosen to provide a control on the independent effect of time delay, by
contrasting them with each other.

In choosing an intervening distractor task for conditions I and II, we
followed Baddeley's (1992) observation that tasks which differ greatly from
each other, functionally or cognitively, produce less interference effects. We thus
chose as distractor task a verbal arithmetic manipulation (see below).

5.   Conditions I, II, III

5.1. *Procedures*

5.1.1. *Condition I*
In condition I, ten subjects were asked to verbally describe the video as they
wached it. They were encouraged to keep talking and to report only what they
saw happening on the screen rather than indulge in evaluation or reflections.
Their on-line descriptions were tape-recorded. Directly following the film
presentation, the subjects performed a distractor task, counting backwards from
400 by threes for four minutes. They were then asked to recall the video.
Subjects were discouraged from evaluation and asked to simply tell what happened
in the video, starting at the beginning and continuing sequentially to the end.

The recorded on-line description was transcribed and used to create the
base-line of salient events. The recall description was transcribed and compared
with the base-line. The procedures outlined in section 3.5. above were used to
determine which clauses in the recall matched those in the base-line. The total
number of clauses produced by each subject was also computed.

5.1.2. *Conditions II, III*

In Condition II, ten subjects watched the film in silence, and then immediately produced their verbal recall. Their descriptions were tape-recorded, transcribed and compared with the base-line. The total number of clauses for each subject was also recorded.

In Condition III, ten subjects watched the film in silence, then performed for four minutes the same distractor task as in condition I (see above). They then gave their verbal recollections of the film, and those were recorded, transcribed and analyzed in the same manner as in conditions I, II.

5.2. *Results*

The narration produced by each subject was recorded, transcribed, and then compared with the base-line produced by the subjects in Condition I (see Appendix). As noted earlier, this base-line consisted of 58 clauses mentioned on-line by at least seven of the subjects of condition I (see Appendix). The total number of clauses produced in the recalled description were also counted for each subject. Means and standard deviations for each condition were calculated. The results pertaining to base-line events recalled in conditions I, II, III are given in Table 1 below.

Table 1. *Mean number and standard deviations for number*
of base-line clauses recalled

condition	# of subjects	mean # base-line clauses recalled	st. deviation
I	10	38.1	6.59
II	10	37.4	4.99
III	10	36.1	5.36

The results reported in Table 1 were subjected to a one-way ANOVA analysis. No significant difference was found between the three conditions ($F(2,27) = 0.32$, $p < 0.7302$). Neither on-line verbalization (condition I) nor time delay and distractor task (condition III) produced any significant effect on the number of base-line events recalled. This is particularly surprising in that the subjects in condition I created the baseline; yet their recall of base-line events did not differ significantly from that of the subjects in conditions II and III.

It is of interest to see whether some differences between the three conditions may exist but somehow are not captured by the base-line measure. To assess this possibility, we also recorded the total number of clauses produced by the subjects under each condition. Means and standard deviations were then computed for each condition, and the results are given in Table 2 below.

Table 2. *Means and standard deviations for the total number*
        of clauses produced

condition	# of subjects	mean # base-line clauses recalled	st. deviation
I	10	107.1	19.1
II	10	99.0	**38.76**
III	10	96.2	23.95

These results were also subjected to a one-way ANOVA. No significant difference was found between the three conditions ($F(2,27) = 0.39$, $p < 0.6817$). However the standard deviation in condition II is quite large due to a single subject who produced 200 clauses. Subjects in condition I, while more consistent (their standard deviation was smaller), produced on the average only slightly more clauses than those in conditions II and III.

5.3. *Further analysis*

As noted above, we found no statistically significant differences between the three conditions in terms of the number of base-line clauses or the total number of clauses produced. But we wondered to what extent the subjects in condition I matched the verbal material they themselves produced on-line. Did their general pattern of recall differ significantly from the subjects in the other two conditions? To evaluate this, we compared the number of condition-I subjects who mentioned a specific base-line clause in the on-line task with the number of those who mentioned that clause in the recalled text. The base-line itself was made out of the clauses mentioned by seven or more subjects in the on-line description in condition I. So each one of the 58 base-line clauses has a specific value of how many subjects mention it — 7, 8, 9 or 10. And a clause that was mentioned by an x number of subjects in the on-line task might be mentioned by either more or less subjects in the recall task (see Appendix).

We now examined the percent distribution of clauses in the recall task that were mentioned more often, less often, or the same number of times as in the base-line — for all three conditions. Our initial assumption was that most of the clauses would be mentioned less often in the recall task than in the base-line, given memory decay. But did subjects in condition I mention any of the clauses more often in their recalled text than in the base-line? If this were the case, it would suggest that perhaps they were not relying in their recall primarily on their previous verbalization. This conclusion would be true especially if the proportions of more-mentioned, less-mentioned, and same-number-mentioned in condition I differed from conditions II and III. The results of this analysis are given in Table 3 below.

Table 3.   *Proportions of clauses mentioned more, less and the same*
            number of times as in the base-line

Condition	clauses mentioned more often		clauses mentioned less often		clauses mentioned same #		total	
	#	%	#	%	#	%	#	%
I	11	18.97	36	62.06	11	18.97	58	100.00
II	12	20.69	37	63.79	9	15.52	58	100.00
III	13	22.42	36	62.06	9	15.52	58	100.00

These results were subjected to a One-way ANOVA analysis. No significant differences were found between the conditions ($F(2,173) = 0.03$, $p < 0.9733$). It appears that the resources which subjects in all three conditions were drawing upon in the recall task were similar, and that on-line verbalization (condition I) did not help the subjects in their subsequent recall task. Nearly 19% of the clauses recalled in condition I were mentioned by more subjects than in the on-line production. So apparently some subjects recalled clauses that did not appear in their on-line verbalization.

5.4. *Interim discussion: Conditions I, II, III*

Both in terms of the number of recalled base-line events and the total number of narrated events, we found no significant differences between the three conditions. Condition I revealed no advantage of on-line verbalization during viewing. Several past studies (Paivio 1969; Yuille and Paivio 1971; Schnorr and Atkinson 1969) have reported the advantage of visual imagery when added to verbal rehearsal; but the converse does not appear to hold in our study. We found no significant difference between condition II and III. The distractor task with its associate time delay produced no effect on either the number of base-line clauses or the total number of clauses recalled. The lack of effect of the distractor task was perhaps to be expected. Recent work on memory indicates that different types of tasks and different modalities used to perform them may draw on different cognitive resources (Baddeley 1992). Whatever differences we find between the interactive conditions IV, V and the three control conditions must be due to the effect of the intervening conversational interaction itself, rather than to the presence of an on-line verbalization, the time delay, or the distractor task.

6. Condition IV

6.1. *General considerations*

The purpose of condition IV was to study the effect on recall of contradictory information. Many previous studies have shown that new information presented to a subject between observation time and recall time can alter or supplement the recall of previously acquired information (Loftus 1975, 1980; Loftus *et al.* 1978). However, Loftus (1980) found that there are limits, in terms of plausibility, on the type of misinformation that is likely to be integrated. If the misinformation is presented first and blatantly contradicts a clearly perceived feature of an important object in an event, subjects tend to reject the misinformation, and further, tend to be more resistant to other, more subtle, forms of misinformation. However, if more subtle misinformation is presented first, and the more blatantly contradictory misinformation is presented later, the subtle misinformation is still likely to be incorporated into the subjects' recall, even when the subsequently presented more blatant misinformation is rejected.

Loftus' work suggests that new information is not automatically integrated. Subjects can compare the new information with their initial mental representation and either accept (and integrate) or reject it. Pre-existing information that is less central to the event or episode is more easily modified than information about more central features, presumably because central features receive stronger — more distinct, durable or retrievable — memory representation.

In this study, we were not so much interested in whether *specific* pieces of misinformation would or would not be integrated into the recall of the video, but rather in the overall effect of contradictory information on recall. Our hypothesis regarding condition IV was that the effort needed to make sense of contradictory information and either reject or integrate it into a pre-existing memory representation of the film would result in fewer event-clauses recalled.

6.2. *Procedures*

Each of the ten subjects was asked to watch the film with another "student". They were told that they would later be asked to discuss the video with that "student", and will be then asked to recall the film. The "student" was actually a volunteer posing as a student. After viewing the video, this volunteer discussed the video with the subject. The volunteer encouraged the subject to be aggressive and produce most of the discussion. During the discussion, the volunteer provided contradictory information about four events in the film:

(16)   **Contradictory information supplied by volunteer:**
1. The woman was initially chopping wood
2. The chicken was killed
3. The woman brought the man water as well as food
4. The man became angry when the woman spilled the water

In the film, the man, not the woman is initially chopping wood; the chicken escapes; the woman does not bring water; and she does not spill the non-existent water. The first two false bits of information can be considered "blatantly" contradictory. The wood-chopping scene is fairly long and detailed; and the chicken obviously did escape. The final two bits are somewhat more "subtle" and plausible. The woman did fetch some water, although she did not take it to the man. And the man did become angry in the final scene, although not because the woman spilled the water.

The volunteer did not attempt to push the bits of contradictory information on the subjects, but simply presented them as her version of the story. If the subject objected, the volunteer simply stated that that's what she thought happened, and then moved on to the next topic. We did not expect the subjects to "swallow" the distortions. We simply wanted to see the effect of contradictory information on their overall episodic recall.

As in the first three conditions, the subjects were asked to describe what happened in the video from beginning to end, avoiding evaluative comments. The narrations were recorded, transcribed and analyzed via the same protocol as in conditions I, II, III.

6.3. *Results*

The mean number and standard deviation of base-line clauses recalled under condition IV is given in Table 4 below together with those of control conditions I, II, III.

Table 4. *Mean number and standard deviation for recalled*
        base-line events (4 conditions)

Condition	# of subjects	mean # base-line clauses recalled	st. deviation
I	10	38.1	6.59
II	10	37.4	4.99
III	10	36.1	5.36
IV	10	**29.9**	5.34

A clear difference appears between the number of base-line events recalled in condition IV and those recalled in the control conditions I, II, III. These results were subjected to a One-way ANOVA analysis. A significant difference was found between condition IV and conditions I, II, III $(F(3,39) = 4.46$, $p < 0.0092)$. Subjects in condition IV recalled approximately 17% less of the base-line clauses than did the subjects in the control conditions.

We were again interested in comparing the total number of clauses produced, and here again a clear difference emerged between condition IV and the three control conditions. The results are given in Table 5 below.

Table 5. *Mean and standard deviation for the total number of clauses produced*

Condition	# of subjects	mean # clauses recalled	st. deviation
I	10	107.1	19.1
II	10	99.0	38.76
III	10	96.2	23.95
IV	10	**60.1**	17.88

The results were subjected to a One-way ANOVA analysis, revealing a significant difference between condition IV and the three control conditions. $(F(3,36) = 6.23$, $p < 0.0016)$. Subjects in condition IV produced on the average 30% less clauses in their recalled narration than those in the control conditions. However the number of base-line events recalled in condition IV (29.9, Table 4) is approximately half that of the total number of clauses recalled (60.1, Table 5). In other words half of the clauses recalled by the subjects in condition IV were base-line clauses. In contrast, in the three control conditions only about 30% of the recalled clauses were base-line clauses. To express this difference more explicitly, we took the average number of base-line clauses recalled in each condition and divided it by the average total number of clauses recalled. The results of this computation are given in Table 6 below.

Table 6. *Percent of base-line clauses recalled out of total # of clauses recalled*

Condition	# of subjects	mean % of base-line out of total # of clauses	st. deviation
I	10	35.96	6.09
II	10	40.21	7.79
III	10	38.92	7.86
IV	10	**51.28**	7.56

These results were subjected to a One-way ANOVA analysis. A significant difference was found between conditions I, II, III and condition IV ($F(3,36) = 8.83, < 0.0002$). Condition I had the *lowest* ratio, 35.96%; while condition IV had the highest, 51.28%. As one may recall, the subjects in condition I created the base-line. Yet base-line clauses constituted a smaller number of their total production. What appears to have happened is that while the subjects in condition IV recalled less, what they did recall are the more salient base-line events. In contrast, subjects in condition I, who recalled more base-line clauses, also produced a proportionately larger body of "elaborative", non-base-line events. Such clauses depict events that are perhaps less central and thus less salient, as compared to the base-line events.

In sum, the deliberately planted misinformation indeed creates an uncertainty and reduced recall. But the impact of this uncertainty hits unevenly — more in the elaborative portion of recalled information than in the base-line of "core" information. By comparison, on-line verbalization (condition I) did not significantly affect the recall of base-line events, but rather stimulated the production of more elaborative, "non-core" descriptions.

6.4. *Cross-subject individual variation*

We next turn to analyzing the output of individual subjects in condition IV. Six of the ten subjects produced less than thirty of the base-line clauses. Only two out of the thirty subjects in the other three conditions produced less than thirty base-line clauses. We decided to evaluate the subjects of condition IV according to how strongly the misinformation was represented in their recall of the base-line events. To do this, we scored the effect on each subject of the four false bits of information. If the subject reproduced the inaccuracy, he was given a score of 1. That is, if the subject stated that the woman killed the chicken he would receive a score of 1 for that bit of false information. If the subject stated that the woman killed the chicken but expressed some uncertainty, i.e. added statements or adverbs expressing doubt such as "I thought", "maybe", or "it seemed like", the subject was given a score of 0.5. If the subject reproduced an accurate report, i.e. "the woman didn't kill the chicken" or "the chicken got away", they received a score of 0. Finally, if they reproduced an accurate report but it was coded with uncertainty, i.e. "I didn't think she killed it, but maybe she did", they again received a score of 0.5. The coding system is reproduced in (18) below.

(18) **Scoring schema:**
  a. accurate report with no uncertainty   =   0
  b. accurate report with uncertainty   =   0.5
  c. inaccurate report with uncertainty   =   0.5
  d. inaccurate report with no uncertainty   =   1.0

A sample of this scoring is given in (19) below.

(19) **Examples of scoring:**

It looks like she's about to cut it's head off but
it got free and ran away   = 0

She doesn't succeed in killing it   = 0

I guess she had a jug of water, although
I don't remember really   = 0.5

But she's just gonna take care of it
[the chicken] then and there and,
I guess I didn't think that she did   = 0.5

... and then the lady was chopping wood...
and then ... the man was chopping wood
with an ax   = 1.0

She spilt over the bucket of water   = 1.0

An overall score of 4 would indicate that a subject accepted all four false bits without uncertainty. A score of 0 indicates that they rejected all four false bits without uncertainty. The results of this analysis are given in Table 7 below, where the reaction to false information is placed, for each subject, against the number of base-line clauses recalled.

A Pearson Correlation Test addressed the relationship between the number of base-line clauses produced in condition IV ($M = 29.9$) and degree of acceptance of false information ($M = 0.6$). The correlation turns out to be statistically significant, $r(8) = 0.71047$, indicating that these two variables are inversely related. However, only three of the subjects expressed doubt or "swallowed" the false statements. Subject #1 reproduced all but one of the false claims. This subject stated that the woman was chopping wood first, she brought the man water, and she spilled the water, but expressed doubt as to whether the chicken was killed or not. This subject produced the lowest number of base-line clauses. Subject #5 expressed doubt concerning all four of the false statements, and Subject #6 expressed doubt as to whether the woman brought the man water.

Subjects #9 and #10 produced the largest number of recalled base-line clauses. These two subjects also expressed a large degree of doubt about the false informa-

Table 7. *Degree of acceptance of false claims compared to number of base-line clauses produced*

subject	degree of acceptance of false claim	# of base-line clauses recalled by each subject
#1	3.5	22
#5	2.5	24
#6	0.5	27
#3	0.0	28
#4	0.0	29
#7	0.0	29
#8	0.0	31
#2	0.0	34
#10	0.0	35
#9	0.0	40

tion given by the volunteer. Both asked the volunteer if she had seen the same movie they had. Both strongly rejected the volunteer's misinformation during the conversation. The number of clauses produced by these two subjects is similar to the average number of clauses produced in the three control conditions.

6.5. *Interim discussion of condition IV*

Loftus (1975, 1980) has reported the effect of misinformation on subjects' later recall of events. However, her studies assessed the effect of misinformation on specific details. Our results seem to indicate that false claims can have a global depressing effect on the number of event clauses recalled. The more the subject accepts the misinformation, it seems, fewer events are recalled; and the loss seems to target more specifically elaborative detail than base-line events.

One may wish to argue that the causal chain may have been the reverse: The subjects who accepted the false information did so *because* their memory representation was weaker to begin with. However, there is a statistically significant difference between subjects in this condition and those in the other three conditions. It may be that, by sheer chance, the subject group in this condition included more subjects with poorer memory capacity. But the consistency of recall of base-line events among the thirty subjects in the three control conditions makes this possibility unlikely.

7. Condition V

7.1. *General considerations*

In the next experiment, we tried to create a more natural conversational situation. We were interested in the effect on episodic memory of trying to explain the events of the video to someone who had not seen the film. In the three control conditions, subjects were told to recall the film events in sequence. Likewise in condition IV, the volunteer and the subject were told to discuss the film in sequential order. In the intervening task in condition V, between viewing and recalling, the subjects were required to answer questions about the film from another person who did not see it. The subjects thus had to **make thematic sense** of the events while recalling them to the other person. Their recall during the interaction may be out of linear order, but their aim is nevertheless to make the story coherent to a person who did not see the film.

We expected that such an intervening task would demand — and thus result in — a more elaborate mental representation of the story in the mind of the narrator, and a higher-level understanding, as compared to the more simple control tasks of sequential recall. The task facing the subjects under condition V presumably demanded of the subjects a more precise identification of referents, locations and other more local details.

After the intervening conversation, both subjects were instructed to individually narrate the events of the film. The narration from the subjects who did *not* watch the film was not analyzed in this study.

7.2. *Procedures*

Twenty subjects participated in this condition, ten who watched the film, ten who didn't. After viewing, each subject who watched the film was paired with one who didn't. The subject who did not see the film was instructed to ask questions about it. Both subjects were told that they would have to narrate the story later.

Subjects who watched the film were told that they would be asked questions about it by a person who did not see it. They were told not to elaborate, but to simply answer all questions. These subjects had a hard time following this instruction and often volunteered information about events when not asked to. After approximately four minutes of verbal interaction, both subjects were asked to immediately recall the story, starting at the beginning and providing as much detail as possible.

The conversations between the subjects as well as the subsequent individual narrations were recorded and transcribed. The conversations and the narrations by subjects who did see the film were compared to the base-line. The total number of event-clauses produced was also counted.

7.3. Results

The mean number of base-line clauses recalled by the subjects who saw the film, as well as the standard deviations, are given in Table 8 below, where they are compared with the results of the preceding four conditions.

Table 8. *Mean numbers and standard deviations for recalled base-line clauses (5 conditions)*

Condition	# of subjects	mean % of base-line out of total # of clauses	st. deviation
I	10	38.1	6.59
II	10	37.4	4.99
III	10	36.1	5.36
IV	10	**29.9**	5.34
V	10	**29.1**	**9.43**

Much like in condition IV, the total number of base-line clauses recalled in condition V was lower than that of the three control conditions. But what stands out in particular was the large cross-subject variation in condition V. Subjects in this condition produced both the largest (46) and the smallest (17) number of base-line clauses. Seven subjects produced less than thirty clauses, two produced over forty, and only one produced an amount close to the mean of the three control conditions (33). The standard deviation for condition V tells the story, being almost twice that of the other four conditions. We will return to this further below.

The results given in Table 8 were subjected to a One-way ANOVA analysis, comparing the mean number of base-line clauses recalled for all five conditions. A significant difference was found between conditions ($F(4,45) = 4.28$, $p < 0.0051$). A Duncan's Multiple Range Test indicated that the means for conditions I (38.1), II (37.4), and III (36.1) were significantly larger than the means for conditions IV (29.9) and V (29.1). But the differences between the means of conditions I (38.1), II (37.4), and III (36.1) were not significant. The means of conditions IV (29.9) and condition V (29.1) did not differ significantly either.

The total number of clauses produced was also counted and compared with the other three conditions. The results are given in Table 9. below.

Table 9. *Means and standard deviations for the total number of clauses produced (5 conditions)*

Condition	# of subjects	mean # clauses recalled	st. deviation
I	10	107.1	19.1
II	10	99.0	38.76
III	10	96.2	23.95
IV	10	60.1	17.88
V	10	73.0	**25.65**

The subjects in condition V produced more clauses than in condition IV, but still less than in the three control conditions.

These results were subjected to a One-way ANOVA analysis, comparing the mean number of total clauses produced for all five conditions. A significant difference was found between some of the conditions ($F(4,45)$, $p < 0.0009$). A Duncan's Multiple Range Test indicated that the means for conditions I (107.1), II (99.0) and III (96.2) did not differ significantly. The means for conditions IV (60.1) and V (73.0) also did not differ significantly between them. But the means of the three control conditions I (107.1), II (99.0) and III (96.2), when taken together, are significantly larger than the means of conditions IV (60.1) and V (73.0). When the means of conditions III (96.2) and V (73.0) are compared separately, however, the difference between them is not significant.

The statistical analysis thus identifies three groups whose members differ significantly across groups but not within groups:

(a) Conditions I, II, III
(b) Conditions IV and V
(c) Conditions III and V

As with condition IV, we also computed the ratios of base-line clauses recalled over the total number of clauses produced. The results are given in Table 10 below.

Condition V had only a slightly higher ratio of base-line clauses over total clauses than the three control conditions, while Condition IV had a clearly higher ratio. These results were also subjected to a One-way ANOVA analysis, comparing the percent of base-line clauses out of the total clauses aross all five conditions. The difference between conditions was significant, ($F(4,45)$, $p < 0.0008$). A Duncan's Multiple Range Test indicated that the mean of condition IV (51.28) was significantly higher than the means for conditions I (35.958), II (40.212), III (38.92) and V (41.201).

Although subjects in condition V produced almost the same number of base-line events as those in condition IV, the ratio of base-line events to total

Table 10. *Percentage of base-line clauses recalled out of*
            total # of clauses produced (5 conditions)

Condition	# of subjects	mean % of base-line clauses out of total number of clauses	std. deviation
I	10	35.96	6.09
II	10	40.21	7.79
III	10	38.92	7.86
IV	10	**51.28**	7.56
V	10	41.20	**11.30**

number of events produced in this condition resembled more the ratio in the
three control conditions. Also, condition V did not differ significantly from
condition III in terms of total number of clauses produced; although it did differ
significantly in that respect from conditions I and II.

7.4. *Analysis of individual variation*

The large cross-subject variability in the number of base-line clauses recalled in
condition V begs for further exploration. In an attempt to account for this large
variation, we counted the number of questions asked by the subjects who did not
see the film, as well as the number of base-line events mentioned during the
conversation between the two subjects. The results are given in Table 11 below.
    A correlation was found between the number of questions asked during the
conversation and the number of base-line events recalled later by the subject
who saw the film. There was also a correlation between the number of base-line
events mentioned during the conversation and the number of base-line clauses
produced later by the subject who saw the film.
    The results in Table 11 were subjected to a Pearson Correlation Test,
addressing the relationship between number of base-line clauses mentioned
during the conversation $(M = 18.6))$ and number of base-line clauses later
recalled by the viewing subject $(M = 29.1)$. A significant positive correlation
between the two variables was revealed $(r(8) = .80113, p < 0.0053)$.
    A Pearson Correlation Test was also applied to the relationship between
number of questions asked during the conversation. $(M = 38.1)$ and number of
base-line clauses recalled later by the viewing subject $(M = 29.1)$. A significant
positive correlation between these two variables was also found $(r(8) = .69133, p < 0.0268)$.

Table 11. *Number of base-line clauses recalled by each subject compared with the number of base-line clauses produced during conversation and number of questions asked during conversation (cond. V)*

subject	# of base-line events recalled	# of base-line events produced in conversation	# of questions asked during conversation
1	17	8	15
2	21	16	47
3	24	12	23
4	24	18	51
5	26	7	21
6	27	26	13
7	29	6	37
8	33	24	18
9	44	35	90
10	46	34	66

A Pearson Correlation Test also revealed a statistically significant correlation between the number of questions asked during the conversation ($M = 38.1$) and the number of base-line clauses mentioned during the conversation ($M = 18.6$), ($r(8) = .61354$, $p < 0.0592$)

7.5. *Interim discussion*

The results of condition V indicate that the conversation which intervened between the viewing and recalled narration strongly affected recall. The wide cross-subject variation in condition V turns out to be directly related to specific features of the conversation.

The more base-line clauses were mentioned during the intervening conversation, the more base-line clauses were recalled during subsequent narration. Conversely, a paucity of mentioned base-line clauses during the conversation yielded a corresponding paucity in their subsequent recall. This effect is not due to the mere presence or absence of previous verbal encoding of events, since in condition I subjects produced an on-line verbalization during viewing and before recalling. And the comparison of condition I to conditions II, III showed that previous verbalization did *not* affect later recall. On the other hand, the verbalization of events during the intervening conversation in condition V significantly enhances later recall. It thus appears that verbally rehashing base-line events during a conversation — i.e. *interactive* rather than monologic verbalization — is what enhanced later recall.

The number of questions asked during the interaction also affected the number of base-line clauses recalled later. This correlation was somewhat weaker than the one between number of base-line clauses mentioned in conversation and later base-line recall. The contents of these questions was apparently a factor. While the number of questions asked correlated significantly with the number of base-line clauses produced during the interaction, the questions did not always pertain to base-line events. Thus for example, one subject who recalled only 21 base-line clauses later on, was asked 47 questions during the conversation. But during that conversation, only 16 base-line clauses were mentioned. And further, 32 of the 47 questions — 68% — concerned details which were not part of the base-line (the weather, the ages of the actors, what clothes they were wearing, etc.). Thus, it appears that both the number and content of the questions seem to affect recall. One may wish to argue that condition V differs from condition I in that it provides the opportunity for additional rehearsal. But so does condition IV, where the intervening verbalization did not enhance recall — presumably due to the presence of contradictory information. Thus, neither previous verbalization (condition I) nor previous rehearsal (condition IV) enhanced recall.

The results of condition V clearly suggest that it was the quality of verbal interaction itself that was responsible for the effect. When a **cooperative interaction** was not achieved, i.e. when the conversation did not produce many coherent questions and relevant responses, subsequent episodic recall of the film suffered. In condition IV, episodic recall suffered due to the presence of non-cooperative misinformation. But when the interaction was more cooperative, with many pertinent questions and answers and no contradictory information, i.e. in instances of condition V, recall benefitted.

8.   Discussion

8.1.   *Conversational cooperation and episodic recall*

We have shown that interposing conversational interaction between the presentation of visual information and its subsequent episodic recall has two possible effects on the recalled information. When the interlocutor is uncooperative and introduces misleading, contradictory information (condition IV), the amount of episodic information recalled later goes down. On the other hand, when the verbal interaction is cooperative, involving a greater amount of coherent questions and responses (condition V), the amount of episodic information recalled later goes up. This effect goes beyond the effect of mere prior verbalization (I), and probably reflects the salutary effect of the need to re-organize the information more coherently during cooperative interaction. The quality of the intervening verbal interaction (condition V) during the consolidation of episodic information, rather than the mere quantity of rehearsed verbalization (conditions I, IV), appears to make the real difference.

8.2. *Integration of episodic and situational memory*

The five experimental conditions we report here, taken together, can be considered as controls for a series of ongoing and future experiments. Thus far, we have only measured the effect of various interactional conditions on the recall of *episodic* information. But as noted in the introduction, there are good grounds for suspecting that at least some *interactional* information must be integrated into episodic memory. The conditions under which the two types of information processed during conversation, episodic and interactional, interact and are either integrated or not integrated in episodic memory, remain our current preoccupation. The two conditions we are trying to test now are:

CONDITION VI:
Two subjects who saw the same Chicken Story film are told to tell each other in detail about the film, after being told that they saw similar but not identical films. Their recall of their conversation is then solicited and recorded.

CONDITION VII:
Two subjects who saw two different movies (one of them the Chicken Story) are told to tell each other in detail about the film they saw. As in condition VI, both are told they saw the similar but not identical films. Their recall of their conversation is likewise solicited and recorded; but only the data from the subjects who saw the Chicken Story film are analyzed.

We are interested, first, in the relative balance in the recalled conversations between recall of interactional detail vs. recall of episodic information about the Chicken Story. We are also interested in the degree to which the interactional and the episodic positions of the information is integrated into a coherent, unified representation. Finally and perhaps most crucially, we are interested in the way specific features of the conversation — cooperative (condition VI) vs. non-cooperative (condition VII) interaction, explicit agreement, contradiction — affects various aspects of the subjects' recall, of both the interactional and episodic information.

Appendix: **Baseline clauses and number of subjects contributing each*)**

		#1	#2	#3	#4	#5	TOT
				conditions			
1.	there's a man/guy (7)	5	7	5	4	3	24
2.	a man/guy/he walking (7)	7	10	6	6	6	35
3.	person/he carrying tools/shovels/ax (8)	6	7	8	4	7	32
4.	he's wearing a white t-shirt and white shorts (7)	0	5	4	1	5	15
5.	he's putting/setting leaning them/shovels + prep. (7)	8	8	10	8	7	41
6.	he takes/picks up/has an ax/hatchet (7)	9	8	10	4	5	36
7.	he's walking/going + preposition (8)	9	8	7	2	4	30
8.	he chops/cuts/hits/breaks wood/kindling/it/ branches/sticks (10)	10	10	10	9	10	49
9.	someone else/a person/ a woman/she coming/walking + preposition (8)	9	10	10	10	10	49
10.	they're talking (7)	6	3	4	4	2	19
11.	she's asking/wondering/questions/something/what (7)	3	6	6	3	7	25
12.	he speaks/talks/responds/answers (7)	3	2	2	0	2	9
13.	she's taking/picking up/collecting/grabbing/ gathering wood/kindling/sticks (10)	9	10	8	9	7	43
14.	she's walking/wandering + locative (9)	7	10	8	9	5	39
15.	she puts/sets/lays wood/pieces/sticks/kindling + locative (8)	1	1	3	2	0	7
16.	she's getting/picking up/collecting/grabbing/ gathering/taking them/kindling/firewood/shurbs/ sticks (9)	6	7	4	3	4	24
17.	she breaks/cuts/snaps branches/twigs/shrubs/ones/ pieces/sticks/them (9)	7	8	9	9	5	38

*) The number in parenthesis is the number of subjects in Condition I who mentioned the clause in their on-line verbalization during viewing.

	conditions					
	#1	#2	#3	#4	#5	TOT
18. she picks up/grabs/gathers the bundle/stuff/pile/ sticks/branches/them (8)	5	5	8	6	4	28
19. she walks/goes/wanders + locative (7)	4	3	5	4	5	21
20. man/guy walks/goes/wanders + loc (8)	2	4	4	1	2	13
21. he picks up/takes/gets/grabs/gathers tools/them (10)	2	8	4	1	3	18
22. he's walking/wandering + loc. (9)	1	8	4	2	4	19
23. she/the woman comes/walks/goes + loc (10)	8	9	7	3	6	33
24. she holds/carries/brings/takes the wood/sticks/ bundle/kindling/branches (9)	3	2	1	0	3	9
25. she sets/puts/drops sticks/it/wood/them/bundle/ bunch + loc (10)	7	5	7	2	3	24
26. she walks/wanders/goes + loc (7)	2	1	2	0	0	5
27. she picks up something (7)	4	2	2	2	1	11
28. she starts/makes/builds/lights a fire (10)	10	10	10	10	9	49
29. she puts/adds them/kindling/sticks/pieces/wood/ branches/shrubs/twigs + prep. (10)	8	3	3	1	2	17
30. she picks up/takes/grabs/gets a pot/pail/bowl/ bucket (9)	9	7	8	8	6	38
31. she walks/goes/wanders + loc (8)	7	10	9	8	5	39
32. she's putting/pouring/getting/tipping water/liquid + prep. (9)	9	10	9	8	7	43
33. she's walking/coming + locative (8)	5	6	2	3	4	20
34. she sets/puts pan/pail/it/pot on the fire/block (8)	10	9	9	9	6	43
35. she adds/puts leaves/wood/them/shrubs/fuel + prep. (7)	3	1	2	1	1	8
36. she walks/goes back/to/towards outhouse/shed (10)	10	9	7	10	8	44
37. she's carrying/getting/has something (7)	7	9	8	8	10	42
38. she walks back to/toward the fire (7)	2	5	2	4	3	16

		#1	#2	#3	#4	#5	TOT
39.	it is/looks like a chicken/animal (9)	5	1	2	1	0	9
40.	she has/picks up/grabs a knife (7)	10	6	8	6	3	33
41.	she's slaughtering/killing/sacrificing/decapitating/ cutting the chicken/chicken's head (10)	9	10	10	9	10	48
42.	the rooster/chicken/it gets/runs away (10)	10	8	8	9	9	44
43.	she forgets/gives up it/the chase (8)	7	6	9	6	5	33
44.	she goes/walks back to/towards the shed/building/ shack (8)	10	10	10	10	9	49
45.	she takes/grabs/carries/pulls out something (7)	10	10	10	10	7	47
46.	she walks/comes back to/toward the fire (7)	5	5	3	5	6	24
47.	she unwraps/takes out/opens/unfolds it/something/ package (8)	8	4	6	5	4	27
48.	she picks up/grabs/has/gets the knife (7)	4	2	2	0	1	9
49.	she cuts/slices it/the food/something/them/pieces (10)	9	10	9	7	8	43
50.	she puts something/everything/it in/into bag/cloth/ wrapping/sack/bundle (8)	4	2	0	2	1	9
51.	she rolls/rewraps/wraps it/the cloth/all/everything up (10)	8	8	8	8	6	38
52.	she walks/goes back + loc (7)	9	4	5	7	7	32
53.	he/the man is turning/wacking/hitting/hoeing the earth/ground/garden (8)	9	4	9	5	4	31
54.	the woman enters/comes/walks + loc.	8	5	4	2	2	21
55.	she/calls/talks/speaks (7)	6	4	4	2	3	19
56.	she gives/hands him the package/bundle/food (7)	9	8	7	7	6	37
57.	he is angry/mad/disgusted/pissed/upset/not happy/ not pleased	3	7	9	3	6	28
58.	he's chasing/running after her	10	10	10	10	10	50

conditions

References

Anderson, A.S. 1995. "Negotiating Coherence in Dialog." In M.A. Gernsbacher and T. Givón (eds) 1995.

Anderson, A.S., S. Garrod and A. Sanford. 1983. "The Accessibility of Pronominal Antecedents as a Function of Episodic Shift in Narrative Text." *Quarterly Journal of Experimental Psychology* 35A.

Baddely, A.D. 1986. *Working Memory.* Oxford: Oxford University Press.

Baddely, A.D. 1992. "Working Memory: The interface between memory and cognition." *Journal of Cognitive Neuroscience* 4(3).281–288.

Carpenter, P.A. and M.A. Just. 1988. "The Role of Working Memory in Language Comprehension." In *Complex Information Processing: The impact of Herbert Simon,* D. Klar and K. Kotovsky (eds). Hillsdale, N.J.: Lawrence Erlbaum.

Chafe, W. 1979. "The Flow of Thought and the Flow of Language." In T. Givón (ed.) 1979.

Chafe, W. (ed.). 1980. *The Pear Stories: Cognitive, cultural and linguistics aspects of narrative production.* Norwood, N.J.: Ablex.

Chafe, W. 1987. "Cognitive Constraints on Information Flow." In R. Tomlin (ed.) 1987.

Chafe, W. 1994. *Discourse, Consciousness and Time.* Chicago: The University of Chicago Press.

Clark, H. and E.F. Schaefer. 1987. "Collaborating on Contributions to Conversation." *Language and Cognitive Processes* 2.

Clark, H. and D. Wilkes-Gibbs. 1986. "Referring as a collaborative process." *Cognition* 22.

Dik, S. 1978. *Functional Grammar.* Amsterdam: North Holland.

Dore, J. 1973. "The Development of Speech Acts." Ph.D. Dissertation, City University of New York.

DuBois, J. 1987. "The Discourse Basis of Ergativity." *Language* 63.

Ericsson, K.A. and W. Kintsch. 1995. "Long-term working memory." In *Psychological Review* 102.2.

Ervin-Tripp, S. 1970. "Discourse Agreement: How children answer questions." In *Cognition and the Development of Language,* J. Hayes (ed.). New York: Wiley.

Ervin-Tripp, S. 1976. "Some Features of Early Child–Adult Dialogues." *Language and Society* 7.

Fillmore, C. 1968. "The Case for Case." In *Universals of Linguistics Theory,* E. Bach and R.T. Harms (eds). New York: Holt, Rinehart and Winston.

Foley, W. and R. Van Valin, Jr. 1984. *Functional Syntax and Universal Grammar.* Cambridge: Cambridge University Press.

Gathercole, S.E. and A.D. Baddeley. 1993. *Working Memory and Language.* Hillsdale, N.J.: Lawrence Erlbaum.

Gernsbacher, M.A. 1990. *Language Comprehension as Structure Building.* Hillsdale, N.J.: Lawrence Erlbaum.

Gernsbacher, M.A. and T. Givón (eds). 1995. *Coherence in Spontaneous Text*. Amsterdam: John Benjamins [TSL, 31].

Givón, T. 1979. *On Understanding Grammar.* New York: Academic Press.

Givón, T. (ed.). 1979. *Discourse and Syntax*. New York: Academic Press [Syntax & Semantics, 12].

Givón, T. (ed.). 1983. *Topic Continuity in Discourse: A quantitative text-based study*. Amsterdam: John Benjamins [TSL, 3].

Givón, T. 1984. *Syntax: A functional-typological introduction*. Vol. 1. Amsterdam: John Benjamins.

Givón, T. (ed.). 1985. *Quantified Studies in Discourse. Text* 5(1/2).

Givón, T. 1988. "The Pragmatics of Word-Order: Predictability, importance and attention." In *Studies in Syntactic Typology*, M. Hammond, E. Moravcsik and J. Wirth (eds). Amsterdam: John Benjamins [TSL, 17].

Givón, T. 1990. *Syntax: A functional-typological introduction*. Vol. 2. Amsterdam: John Benjamins.

Givón, T. 1991. "Some Substantive Issues Concerning Verb Serialization: Grammatical vs. cognitive packaging." In *Serial Verbs: Grammatical, comparative, and cognitive approaches*, C. Lefebvre (ed.). Amsterdam: John Benjamins.

Givón, T. 1992. "The Grammar of Referential Coherence as Mental Processing Instructions." *Linguistics* 30.

Givón, T. 1994. "Coherence in Text, Coherence in Mind." In *Pragmatics and Cognition* 1(2).

Goodwin, C. 1982. *Conversational Organization*. New York: Academic Press.

Goodwin, C. 1988. "Embedded Context." Paper read at the *AAA Annual Meeting*, Phoenix, Arizona, Nov. 1988.

Goodwin, C. In press. "Sentence Construction within Interaction." In *Aspects of Oral Communication*, U. Quastoff (ed.).

Goodwin, C. 1995. "The Negatiation of Coherence within Conversation." In M.A. Gernsbacher and T. Givón (eds 1995).

Grice, H.P. 1968/1975. "Logic and Conversation." In *Speech Acts*, P. Cole and J. Sadock (eds). New York: Academic Press [Syntax and Semantics, 3].

Guo, J.-S. 1992. "The Interaction of Structure and Meaning: Children's use and development of the Mandarin model *neng* (can)." *Symposium on Mood and Modality*, UNM, Albuquerque (MS).

Just, M.A. and P.A. Carpenter. 1992. "A Capacity Theory of Comprehension: Individual differences in working memory." *Psychological Review* 99(1).

Keenan, E. Ochs. 1975. "Again and Again: The Pragmatics of Imitation in Child Language." *Pragmatics Microfiche*.

Keenan, E. Ochs. 1977. "Making it Last: Uses of repetition in children's discourse." In *Child Discourse*, S. Ervin-Tripp and C. Mitchell-Kernan (eds). New York: Academic Press.

Loftus, E.F. 1975. "Leading Questions and the Eyewitness Report." *Cognitive Psychology* 7.560–572.

Loftus, E.F. 1980. *Eyewitness Testimony.* Cambridge: Cambridge University Press.

Loftus, E.F., D.G. Miller and H.J. Burns. 1978. "Semantic Integration of verbal Information into a Visual Memory." *Journal of Experimental Psychology: Human learning and memory* 4. 19–31.

Mishkin, M. 1978. "Memory in Monkeys Severely Impaired by Combined but not Separate Removal of Amygdala and Hippocampus." *Nature* 273.

Mishkin, M., B. Malamut and C. Bechevalier. 1984. "Memories and Habits: Two neural systems." In *Neurobiology of Learning and Memory,* G. Lynch and J.L. McGaugh (eds). New York: Guilford Press.

Mishkin, M. and H.L. Petri. 1994. "Memories and Habits: Some implications for the analysis of learning and retention." In *Neuropsychology of Memory,* N. Butters and L.R. Squire (eds). New York: Guilford Press.

Ochs, E. and B.B. Schieffelin (eds). 1979. *Development Pragmatics.* New York: Academic Press.

Paivio, A. 1969. "Mental Imagery in Associative Learning and Memory." *Psychological Review* 76.241–263.

Paivio, A. 1971. *Imagery and Verbal Processes.* New York: Holt.

Sachs, H., E. Schegloff and G. Jefferson. 1974. "A Simple Systematic for the Organization of Turn-taking for Conversation." *Language* 50.

Schnorr, J.A. and R.C. Atkinson. 1969. "Repetition versus Imagery Instructions in the Short- and Long-term Retention of Paired Associates." *Psychonomic Science* 15.183–184.

Scollon, R. 1976. *Conversations with a One-Year-Old Child.* Honolulu: University of Hawaii Press.

Shallice, T. 1988. *From Neuropsychology to Mental Structure.* Cambridge: Cambridge University Press.

Squire, L.R. 1987. *Memory and Brain.* Oxford University Press.

Squire, L.R. 1991. "Declarative and Non-declarative Memory: Multiple brain systems supporting learning and memory." In *Journal of Cognitive Neuroscience* 4(3).222–241.

Squire, L.R. 1992. "Memory and the Hippocampus: A synthesis from findings with rats, monkeys, and humans." *Psychological Review* 99(2).195–221.

Squire, L.R. and S. Zola-Morgan. 1991. "The Medial-temporal Lobe Memory System." *Science* 253.

Tomlin, R. 1985. "Foreground-background information and the Syntax of Subordination." In T. Givón (ed.) 1985.

Tomlin, R. 1987. "Linguistics Reflections of Cognitive Events." In R. Tomlin (ed.) 1987.

Tomlin, R. (ed.) 1987. *Coherence and Grounding in Discourse.* Amsterdam: John Benjamins [TSL, 11].

Tomlin, R. 1991. "Focal Attention, Voice and Word-order: An experimental cross-linguistic study." *TR 91–10,* Institute of Cognitive and Decision Sciences, University of Oregon.

Treisman, A. 1995. "Object Tokens, Attention and Visual Memory." *Attneave Memorial Lecture,* University of Oregon, Eugene, April 10, 1995.

van Dijk, T. and W. Kintsch. 1983. *Strategies of Discourse Comprehension.* New York: Academic Press.

Wilkes-Gibbs, D. 1986. "Collaborative Processes in Language Use in Conversation." Ph.D. Dissertation, Stanford University (MS).

Wilkes-Gibbs, D. 1995. "Coherence in Collaboration: Some examples from conversation." In M.A. Gernsbacher and T. Givón (eds 1995).

Wilkes-Gibbs, D. and H. Clark. 1992. "Coordinating Beliefs in Conversation." *Journal of Memory and Language* 31.

Yuille, J.C. and A. Paivio. 1967. "Latency of Imaginal and Verbal Mediators as a Function of Stimulus and Response Concreteness-imagery." *Journal of Experimental Psychology* 75.540–544.

The Occasioning and Structure of Conversational Stories

Susan M. Ervin-Tripp and Aylin Küntay[1]
University of California, Berkeley

1. Orientation

What do we mean by a story? Recent usage has turned almost everything, even the non-verbal, into a narrative.[2] For example, Ochs and Capps (1996) have a remarkably inclusive definition of narratives of personal experience as "verbalized, visualized, and/or embodied framings of a sequence of actual and possible life events." The absence of a common guiding framework has led to the blossoming of criteria used by different narrative researchers for identifying their respective units of study. When one looks for personal experience stories in natural conversations, the most striking fact is that they are not always clearly recognizable by traditional narrative-internal criteria such as the presence of a protagonist and events creating conflict, reference to events in the past, presence of a climactic complicating action, or closure of the storyline with a resolution. Further, the onset of conversational stories does not always clearly demarcate the narrative segment from the preceding talk. Some stories are explicitly introduced into the ongoing conversation with a preface like "do you remember when ..." or "did I tell you about ...," or are elicited by instructions to tell a story. But in children's talk or talk between adults, there are many marginal cases.

Our focus is on identifying a conversational story and how it is occasioned. Given that the story is part of discourse and the storyteller a participant in an interaction, some of the structural organization of the story is directed to its function in a particular conversation. "Narrators linguistically shape their tellings to accommodate circumstances such as the setting as well as the knowledge, stance, and status of those in their midst" (Ochs and Capps 1996). We intend to examine how the embedding contexts of telling alter the internal structure and features of conversational narratives, attending to some issues raised by Jefferson in her classic study of the conversational embedding of stories (1978).

2.　Narrative genre vs. narrative production

Now that we have the video and audio technology to look at conversational sequences, we have the possibility of two different levels of analysis in the study of talk. One level is the live interaction, negotiated on the spot in dialogue or through listener response. Another level is that of talk about talk using genre and speech act vocabulary, that is, classification by speakers and listeners or even by coders, and reference during talk to something said before or about to be said: "she told a story about …", "he told me to …", "he asked me to …" This is what Hymes referred to in his development of an ethnography of communication (1972) or what is sometimes called metapragmatics. This level includes our category and prototype system for talk. There is a similar distinction in the study of speech acts like requests. What happens in real-time circumstances can differ from what is retrospectively recognized, remembered, reported, or judged, and therefore from what enters into speech act theories — the recollection of speech acts in tranquillity (Ervin-Tripp, Strage, Lampert and Bell 1987).

There are thus two forms we could call a story. One is the social genre that has prototypes and ideal forms and provides a model for what we expect when we ask "Tell me that story about when …" The genre is talked about and has a cultural existence in member instruction and evaluation. The second is whatever happens when people talk about the past, the future, or recurrent events or practices in ordinary conversation. When we look at conversational events in a transcript, we do not know how much notions of prototypic genres affected performance, or even whether the speaker considered what was said to be a story. Very little work has addressed the relation between talk about talk and the interactional events such talk refers to. One exception is the work of Bauman (1993), who examined a speaker's "metanarrational comments" and "disclaimers of performance on the grounds of insufficient knowledge" (p. 188) as an indicator of the speaker's construction of genre conventions. However, although Bauman emphasized the relevance of such metapragmatic comments to the analysis of the features of narratives that embed them, he did not attempt to relate speakers' notions of prototypic narratives to what gets said in ongoing talk. It seems obvious that interactional events as remembered have some bearing on talk about talk. But do the prototypes and genre classifications have any effect on ongoing talk? When we cannot interview the tellers we have to make inferences from the narrative features, evaluations, and changes under conditions of evaluative monitoring.

Some theoretical approaches[3] view narrative genre as a "dynamic expressive resource, in which the conventional expectations and associations that attach to generically marked stylistic features are available for further combination and recombination in the production of varying forms and meanings" (Bauman, 1992:127). In short, the two notions of narrative — narrative as a recognizable social genre or norm and narrative as a spontaneous, often ambiguous conversational event — may converge or diverge from one another, depending on the occasioning conditions which influence narrative features.

3. Standard narrative

The standard characterization of personal narratives in social science research grew out of the Labov and Waletzky analysis (1967). Labov's first elicited stories came from his "danger of death" sociolinguistic survey question, which was designed to produce style shifts toward the vernacular variety of the speakers, in the heat of emotional recall. Eventually more than 600 American east coast adolescents and adults were posed the standard question "were you ever in a situation where you thought you were in serious danger of getting killed?" As a result, Labov elicited stories of near-death experiences that got rendered in fully formed narrative structures, upon which Labov and Waletzky later built their theory. They proposed that it is only spontaneous accounts of past personal experience, "not the products of expert storytellers that have been re-told many times" (p. 12), which could provide a window on the most fundamental forms of narrative structure. However, the methodology they used in order to obtain narratives is not appropriate for either spontaneous or first-time narratives. On the contrary, danger of death stories are likely to be retold, to be seen as attention-grabbing and entertaining to listeners, and to be thought appropriate for prototypic performance occasions. A human protagonist is at the center, and usually there is some kind of conflict and suspense even in brief telling. Thus, what Labov and Waletzky pursued in personal experience narratives, that is, first telling of thematically dramatic experiences, involves a contradiction in terms; the inherent ever-present conversational relevance of such stories makes them amenable to repetition and stabilizes their structures. In spite of the specificity of the so-called "invariant structural units that are represented by a variety of superficial forms" (p. 1) to this very limited genre of danger of death stories, the internal features that Labov and Waletzky (1967) found have been taken as fundamental in most narrative research since. Labov (1972) defined narrative as "one method of recapitulating past experience by matching a verbal sequence of clauses to a sequence of events which (it is inferred) actually occurred. ... We can define a minimal narrative as a sequence of two clauses which are temporally ordered. ... There is temporal juncture between the two clauses, and a minimal narrative is defined as one containing a single temporal juncture" (pp. 360–361). The narrative clauses, he pointed out, had to be coordinate, not subordinate or conditional, as are clauses used in representations of practices or recurrent events, or in backgrounding of information. The Labov and Waletzky narrative can be taken as typical of a certain culturally defined type of narrative that optimally occurs under elicitation.

Peterson and McCabe, beginning their study of narrative development in 1974, also opted for eliciting spontaneous personal narratives (summarized in McCabe, In press). Their strategy for collecting narratives is to have a familiar interviewer engage the child subject in a conversation. During those informal conversations, the experimenters use what they call a conversational map, a series of short, deliberately unevaluated narratives about things that supposedly happened to themselves and could possibly have happened to the child (e.g., getting a bee sting). Such a methodology carries considerable ecological validity since it is the naturally occurring conversation, at least from the perspective of the child participants in the study, that occasions the topics of narration. However, adults could push their agenda of obtaining data quite strongly in such elicitation contexts, sometimes not giving children enough chance to select or expand on their own favorite topics. As a result, it becomes difficult to strip off the effects of heavy narrative scaffolding from the outcome structure.

The elicitation method, which is employed most commonly to obtain comparable narratives from different subjects in developmental studies, folklore, and sociolinguistic interviews, demonstrates that stories are cultural constructs. If we are asked for stories, we know what is meant, and we are able to identify good stories and good story-tellers. Most research on narratives has relied on elicited stories or prefaced stories, those most likely to be identified by both speakers and audiences as fitting the cultural prototype.[4]

4. A boundary case

As opposed to elicited stories, stories occasioned in the conversational situation often do not exhibit many of the prototypical narrative genre cues that are thought to be embedded in the structure of a story. The example below illustrates a marginal case of classification that occurs in conversation when stories are spontaneous, not elicited. After the Loma Prieta earthquake, a student taped a conversation that included two brothers and other student friends. He had received an assignment to tape and analyze about an hour of naturally occurring interaction.

(1) Earthquake story[5]

Albert and Ned are two brothers. Olga is Ned's friend, Cynthia her roommate. All are college students.

53 Al: you know that-
54   that *nice *glass *china *display case in our *dining room?
55 Ned: =in the *dining room=
56 Cyn: =o-o-oh=
57 Al: **trashed/
58 Cyn: =forget it/=
59 Ned: =*absolutely= trashed/
60 Al: whole thing a=bsolutely..yeah =
61 Ned: =*every *single bit= of *glass and
62   *pottery in th-
63 Olg: and *crystal?
64 Ned: *all the crystal..*trashed/
65 Al: crystal
66 Ned: *everything ..*trashed/
67 Cyn: =o-o-oh my go-o-o-d=
68 Al: =oh a er *antiques *genuine= *antiques
69 Ned: =and the *amount of *money= we have lost
70   is going to be **astronomical/
(UCDisclab:QUAKE)

Features. This example does not meet the usual criteria of narrative. There is (a) no animate protagonist, (b) no sequence of events, (c) no temporal juncture, (d) no temporal connectives, (e) no conflict. Why does this seem to people who hear it to be a story? There is the introduction of the "protagonist," a piece of furniture, by a "common ground" preface (53). There has already been an event in time, an earthquake, so the story is about an implicit temporal sequence, an earthquake followed by the outcomes of the earthquake. Most important, the rhythm of the telling, the alternation between ellipsis and expansion, the lexical and syntactic repetitions, the evaluation by the listeners (56, 67) and by the tellers (68–70) and the probing by participants (63) is appropriate to the excitement of a dramatic story, so it seems to listeners to be a story.

Context of telling. Example (1) occurred in a spontaneous conversation, in a series of *rounds* about different facets of the earthquake experience. To have restated the obvious, to have given a temporal, causal sequence such as "we were in the classroom and suddenly it shook" would have made no sense because everyone present already had experienced the beginning. The highly salient experience of the earthquake established the common ground for the round participants to reveal their individual observations in the immediate aftermath of the shared disaster.

Stories of disasters recently experienced by everyone in the room probably have these common properties — they often occur in rounds, and they are both semantically and syntactically elliptical, building on common knowledge and conversational sequences leading up to the story. As told later when the common knowledge is forgotten, or to audiences who don't share the same history, the stories must be reshaped to provide both orientation and temporal sequences to fill in what is not shared.[6] In fact, when Luebs (1992) interviewed 14 people two months after the Loma Prieta quake, the speakers provided extensive orientation and full-fledged narrative structures. Moreover, since the narratives were not part of naturalistic conversation, but were elicited by the researcher, most of them included codas, that is, verbal or nonverbal ways of showing that a narrative is over. Luebs' data confirm that elicited narratives move closer to the prototype.

4.1. *Databases for study*

Adult data. The UC Disclab adult data consist of 180 transcripts collected in a variety of contexts, but primarily from informal natural groups taped in natural settings by students[7] in California, with 500 lines of transcription archived using the Gumperz and Berenz (1993) notation.

American school data. We created a non-task waiting room context for best friends of seven and ten to tape natural sociable conversation in a California public school, where the children were varied ethnically and some were bilingual. These ten dyads and triads are in the UCDisclab archive.

Family data. The Ervin-Tripp family data consist of 38 transcripts from 8 multi-child California families with at least one child 3 years old. Some families were videotaped over a period of 18 months in their homes. We observed meals or child free play with siblings and a visiting peer, with the goal of differentiating the social marking features in children's speech with peers, siblings, and adults.

Turkish preschool data. We obtained child–adult conversations at preschool sites[8] in Istanbul, Turkey. Both of the preschools had 3-to-5-year-olds, providing around 40 children from whom we taped different kinds of elicited and spontaneous extended discourse. The informal preschool system provided multiple settings such as classroom environments, various organized and spontaneous play groups, and casual chats to search out the early deployment of narrative skills. For the examples included in this paper, we analyzed around 60 hours of audiotaped talk.

4.2. *Locating narratives in transcripts*

To identify candidate instances of narrative segments, we employed several methods: computerized search for specific linguistic markers such as temporal connectives, reading over the datasets for larger-level indicators of narrative such as reference to irrealis events or past events, prefaces by narrators, prompting by audiences, or audience evaluations. No single method is adequate by itself for identifying all the segments of talk that are of interest. This problem brings us back to the definitional problem we discussed in the beginning of the paper. If we have to determine what constitutes stories, we are probably better off in considering the narrative genre as a continuous cline, consisting of many subgenres, each of which may need differential research treatment. Since there currently exists no single model that includes criteria encompassing all the range of oral narrative forms, we need to approach the problem employing different tools.

Once we identified narratives, the next step was to look back at the antecedent context to find how the narratives were situated, and how they were occasioned by what was said before. We were surprised at how often this context changed the interpretation of the narrative.

5.   Observed features and contexts of conversational narratives

We found that using judges to identify proto-narratives in the family transcripts produced a wide variety of short descriptive utterances like "when I was little I lived in San Francisco." When we looked for *temporal connectives* that identi-fied temporal junctures in the family and the adult data, we found projections of future events, fantasies, descriptions of regularities, reports of conversations, and reports of events that have occurred — including dreams. It was important in the case of young children to use a linguistic criterion for choosing text materials, so as not to impose categories that are not in the system of the child. If we used temporal connectives as a search criterion — such as *when, while, after, before*, and *and then* — we found that they first appeared in child speech in commands and in planning for future coordinated action, rather than in experience or fantasy narratives (Ervin-Tripp and Bocaz 1989). In other words, planning displays some narrative qualities in child usage. The temporal clause in such sequences defines the relation between two activities of a single actor or between two actors' activities.

"I'm going to make a garbage can when I'm all through with the train lid." (3.0)[9]

Temporal clauses occurred both in reference to *simultaneous events* such as "you listen while I read" (3.3), and to *successive events*, as in "can I have your worm when you get finished" (3.1).

Young children describe sequences of actions in elaborate future plans, including directorial planning of complex dramatic play with coordinated scenarios that are temporally detailed. There is especially rich past and future reference whether the child plays the director planning the actions, or an actor undertaking the script. Outside of dramatic play, young children talk less often about the past than adults do. Among the narrative-like sequences we found were generic descriptions of scripted events, describing what happens on a regular basis, or if you do something, what results.

The following dramatic play enactment illustrates an occasioning of talk about the past. The actor playing the patient is preparing a command to operate on her leg, but describes a personal experience in the past to account for the injury. We see from other child texts (see **3** below) that injuries are usually asked about and are explained by a story of what happened. The child inserts this common type of topic sequence into dramatic play.

(2) Doctor–patient play of 4–5 year olds
  1 Kit: pretend there's something wrong with my leg. my leg–
  2   let's pretend that I tell you that my leg's–um–
  3   let's pretend I tell you– first, you operate on it.
  4   um, but before you operate on it,
  5   let me tell you something, okay nurse?
  6 Jill: um, 'kay.
  7 Kit: um, when I was walking down the street,
  8   I saw this piece of glass and I picked it up,
  9   then I didn't see too well, then it goes way up to here.
  10   see now. it's–now it's over there.
  11   can you–can you operate on it, nurse?
  12 Andy: I can.
  13 Kit: can you not–I said–um–
  14   somebody has to operate on- on- on it.
  (Ervin-Tripp Family Transcripts: Bowyer5)

This segment begins in the directorial voice (1–3) which switches without any marking into enactment in the patient's voice (5). Kit starts with a request for the floor (4,5) which Jill acknowledges (6), and Kit then begins the story with a subordinate backgrounding clause (7) establishing the place of the event and the protagonist's activity at the time of an action (8) by the protagonist, reported by a telic verb. Gestures showed the injury (9,10). There is a sequence of narrative events (9). The story provides the explanation of an injury needing repair in the dramatic medical scenario planned at the beginning (1–3), so it is an inserted elaboration before the medical scenario unfolds (11).

We made similar form-based searches in our extensive database of adult materials, looking for markers of temporal juncture[10] as a way to locate story sequences. We found relatively few extended stories. Those referring to the past often were brief, as in the examples to follow. They were stimulated by the sight of objects, pictures, people or television. While the children relied often on the setting as a source for talk, in the adults, we found more stories that continued prior talk, either in story rounds, or in stories to support or challenge conversational claims. There were scripts, that is stories about customary events, and stories that reported dialogue only. The focus of much of the students' social talk was on character, on the implications of events rather than on the events themselves, and on daily problems that they could not solve. In the last type of interaction, the discussions of problems, we can expect some of the kinds of sequencing that Jefferson (1988) has reported for troubles talk.

Unlike Labov and Waletzky's narrators, our tellers of spontaneous stories did not take a long time to build to a high point. It was rare that stories involved drama or suspense. The character anecdotes usually presented a brief event, and the problem situations began with a single event to initiate a topic, with interchanges about alternative outcomes. These stories in young adults are analogous to the stories Ochs, Smith and Taylor (1989) have found in American families, which propose problems and alternative outcomes. These speakers did not seize the floor for a long performance of a story with suspense.

5.1. *Elicited/prefaced narratives*

It is elicited or prefaced stories that best demonstrate that the structure of stories is strongly related to the circumstances of their telling. They are likely to fit some paradigm of a good story, since the prototype is evoked for tellers. The elicitation signals that the respondent has to undertake a performance. The preface signals that the teller is willing to identify what is to be said as a story. They are, in some sense, accountable to the public standards for a story.

While adults may preface or volunteer stories to entertain, in many of the examples we found there was questioning from the audience to prompt the teller, and to give the teller the floor. But a question can focus a reply on a narrow issue rather than on a full story, thus altering the temporal ordering in the story relative to the order in the events being reported. The following reply to a question illustrates such a shift in narrative ordering.

(3)   Broken foot elicitation

       Melody is 4;7, Lisa is 2. Dave and Georgette are researchers in the home of the children making a videotape. There is an overlapping hosting conversation by the father which interweaves the two sets of speakers.

4	Dav:	OK. in the course of the next months,	
5	:	we hope to be out here a few more times.	
6	Geo:	what happened to your foot, Lisa?	Fa: =would= you like any-
7	Mel:	=um= [to G] she, she =cut it=	thing to eat or drink?
8		in the wheel.	D: =not me= [to Fa]
9		she cut.	Fa:=Georgette do you?=
10		=when.when=, =when the=	G: =no thank you=
11		friend was next door, then, then	
12:		then, then, then, then she was pushing her on the bike,	
13		and it got caught in the spoke or the wheel.	
14	G:	oh boy	
15	M:	and she broke a bone.	
16	G:	oh boy.	
17	L:	a bone. (Melody) I broke this	
18	:	=(it go slip) = [to G]	Fa: =what kind of= sandwich would
19	:	(the bone slipped)	you like to eat, Melody?
20			M: Uh, um what kind do you have?

       (Ervin-Tripp Family Transcripts: Fleurs11)

The focus of Melody's reply was specifically selected by a narrow "what happened to your foot?" question, which prompts Melody first to a summary (7) and then backwards in time to the circumstances that brought this result (10–13). As a story, it gets audience reaction (14, 16). The disruption of the real time temporal order in the story results from the specificity of the eliciting question.

Most children observed in the Turkish nursery schools by Aylin Küntay did not produce stories for other children, who gave them no prompts. It was adults who often supported children's elicited stories with prompts to get started and to continue. In the following example, Emre has been talking to the adult researcher (Ad) about a children's entertainment center that he visited over the weekend:

(4) Alligator game prompting [Translated from Turkish] (Age: 4;11)
1. Emre: there is a scoreboard, shows our score
2. > Ad: is that so? how did you– did you make a lot of points?
3. Emre: (I) did
4.   *but* once I won a lot of things
5.   that alligator-shooting game did not give us
6.   because some part of it was broken
7. > Ad: is that so? what happened?
8. Emre: got broken
9.   we had won a lot of shillings
10.   at that time it got broken
11. Ad: my gosh!
12. Emre: *but then– but* at that time then you know
13.   those people who are at Piramit {entertainment center}–
14.   those people who control Piramit– they fixed that
15.   and *then* we got all that shilling.
(Aylin Küntay: Eryavuz preschool)

This story has a classic construction with a high point and resolution, but the temporal marking appears to be affected by the adult prompting. The adult question (2) takes the child from a description to a specific event. In answering the question, the child begins by a short reply to the question, yet the *but* signals a newsworthy issue or violation of expectation (4), even as the story is beginning, marked with *once*. The story then begins. The resolution does not immediately follow the complicating action, but the adult question interrupts the flow (7). At this point the child repeats and moves back in time to recapitulate the sequence of winning before the equipment broke, even using a pluperfect affix to mark anteriority before the time evoked by the question, and then points out the problem resolution with a *but then* marker. While *eliciting* seems to bring out prototypic stories, *prompting* can alter the temporal sequence by its focusing effect.

5.2. *Rounds of stories*

In many conversational settings, stories implicitly invite related stories from other participants. Goffman (1974) states that "an illustrative story by one participant provides a ticket another participant can use to allow the matching of that experience with a story from his repertoire" (p. 510). Adults, in their interactions characterized by a series of stories, pick out some features from previous stories and work them into their ongoing story without bothering to frame each story anew (Ryave 1978), much as speakers in sequential self-introductions use the same frame repeatedly. Umiker-Sebeok (1979), analyzing preschool children's narratives produced spontaneously within natural conversation with other children, found that the most common response to a narrative was similar narrative. At age three, response narratives in Umiker-Sebeok's data did not seem to advance the conversation "as a conjoint elaboration of a conversational topic" (p. 107), but appeared as "dangling narratives" that generally concerned the same general topic.

In the following Turkish preschool example, Can initiates the series of narrative contributions by establishing the theme to be visits to the doctor's office. Single statement initiations that do not go beyond minimal event representations are very common in this younger age. The children await the teacher's interested reaction before building upon their original one-line narratives. In this particular example, the teacher demonstrates interest by saying "is that so, dear?" (2), setting up the topic of visits to the doctor as interesting for all the children.

(5)   Visits to the doctor
      Beril (4;0) is one of the two girls in a seven student class. Osman is 4;0. Can is 3;7. It is breakfast time, and all of the children are sitting around a table, with their Teacher (Teach) and the researcher (Res) present.

   1 Can: my mother took me to the doctor
   2 Teach: is that so, dear?
   3 Beril: my mother took me to the doctor, too
   4 Can: shall I say what *(he/she)* said
   5 Can: *(he/she)* said let him eat waffles a bit later
   6 Teach: said let him not eat too much waffles, right?
   7 Can: said let him bite in teeny-weeny bites with his teeth
   8   and then also pickles..
   9 Teach: did you get a shot Can?
  10   no:
  11 Can: *(I)* don't really like
  12 Teach: let him eat little
  13   little by little
  14   let him not eat much
  15   xxx would you like biscuits? {to Res}
  16 Res: no, thanks
  17 Beril: Teacher, the doctor told me don't eat anything
  18 Teach: the doctor?

19		but if we don't eat we can't grow
20	Beril:	no *(he/she)* said have breakfast but
21		don't eat those that your mother brings
22	Teach:	is that so?
23	Osman:	my mother did not take me to the doctor's
24	Teach:	because you aren't sick, right?
25		don't get sick, ideally

(Aylin Küntay: Ubaruz preschool)

Beril, after replicating Can's one-liner in line (3), follows on Can's subtopic about his doctor's nutritional advice. Aside from demonstrating thematic continuity, Beril's story features formal similarities to Can's, such as employing quoted speech of a doctor. Osman then contributes (23) by reporting non-occurrence of the topical event in his life. In Turkish children's rounds like the above, second narrators frequently claimed to have exactly the same experience as first narrators, down to the same details.

Since the overarching motivation for rounds of Turkish children in class-room settings seems to be to gain the teacher's interest, they usually try to top other children's stories with their own versions. If an initiation story attracts the attention of the teacher, other children select out of the thematic possibilities of the original story to construct their own. Usually, some of the thematic content gets replicated in the following stories. As Cortazzi (1993) suggests, usually "later narratives are highly pre-specified, showing marked parallels of topic, theme, character of events with preceding narratives" (p. 32–33).

Rounds allow for the ellipsis of presupposed information or allusion to information from earlier stories. The highly elliptical Earthquake narrative (1) occurred in a series of rounds with successively changed protagonists. Students began by telling where they were when the earthquake happened, and what they and people around them did. They added second-hand stories about what other people did. Then they began talking about what happened to their pets and then to their houses and apartments. The protagonists thus descended on an animacy hierarchy. After a discussion about the behavior of their dogs, Cynthia said that nothing of hers fell down, turning the topic to inanimate objects, including the immediate cues in the room in which the taping occurred.

(6)	Earthquake round	
1	Cyn:	==yeah our room our room looks like nothing happened at all,
2	Dom:	== I was I was worried about this [pointing at empty beer
3		bottles on shelves] i-i-it's like coming home to find a big
4		pile of lads. [lads refers to empty bottles]
5	Ned:	this is the first this is the first indication

> 6   that this was something
> 7   because the last one that happened was like a six
> 8   [referring to Richter scale] in Los Gatos and I was sitting
> ....
> 16 Ned: and then Al and I come back and we are just all *oh my
> 17   =*god there it is tilted nearly fallen off just hanging=
> 18 Al: =yeah.. instant hand up supporting them because they are just-=

The three who were present here co-produce a description of the state of the beer bottles. At this point Dom continues a round of reports on each person's room, including non-effects.

> 34 Al: nothing happened in my room.
> 35 Cyn: ==things were moved.
> 36 Ned: [to A] yeah funny thing Al=your room is a m-=
> 37 Geo: =you couldn't tell=
> 38   if something happened to your room.

There is an acceleration (39) as Ned emphasizes the extent of damage in their house, summarized by Al (43). At this point the two brothers overlap in two dramatic descriptions, Al with exaggerated generalization (43), Ned with emphatic prosody in (44).

> 39 Ned: oh my mum and dad cannot get to Pete's room
> 40   to see what it's like..= they ca*n't= get to George's
> 41 Al: = yeah =
> 42 Ned   =all the book-=
> 43 Al   =*natural *disasters= just do *not *stop *happening at *our
>   house.
> 44 Ned   ==*all the *bookcases *everything *fucking c-
> 45   our *house is **chaos.
> 46 Al   ==yeah.
> 47 Ned   it's *chaos..=the bookcases=
> 48 Olga: =the bookcases= came off = the wall?=
> 49 Al: [to O]   =Olga =
> 50 Ned: ==the bookcases all fell down= *books *everywhere *furniture=
> 51 Al: =you know =
> 52 Ned: *moved=

The dramatic example here turns out to be a specifying of the more general description. Albert's general characterization (43) is fleshed out by Ned who supports the generalization by describing the bookcases. But it is Albert who gets to the worst case of all, the shelving containing the antique crystal, and the brothers produce a duet narrative.

53 Al: you know that-
54   that *nice *glass *china *display case in our *dining room?
55 Ned: =in the *dining room=
56 Cyn: =o-o-oh=   =
57 Al: **trashed.
58 Cyn: =forget it.=
59 Ned: =*absolutely= trashed.
60 Al: whole thing a=bsolutely..yeah =
61 Ned: =*every *single bit= of *glass and
62   *pottery in th-
63 Olga: and *crystal?
64 Ned: *all the crystal..*trashed.
65 Al: crystal
66 Ned: *everything ..*trashed.
67 Cyn: =o-o-oh my go-o-o-d=
68 Al: =oh a er *antiques *genuine= *antiques
69 Ned: =and the *amount of *money= we have lost
70   is going to be **astronomical.
(UCDisclab:QUAKE)

The round thus began with what happened to items on shelves in each of the participant's campus rooms, moving from a vivid local example in the immediate environment, through another male's room to the most extreme case personally known, the parental home of Albert and Ned. At this point what triggers the dining room narrative is the two strong generalizations in (43, 45). To illustrate the generalization, Ned and Albert move emphatically through a coordinated but elliptical description, with considerable rhythmic emphasis. The line length is shorter, with stronger stress and more focus on predicated descriptors, compared to the beer bottle description where more action is mentioned and there are human participants. The final evaluation by Ned, in a longer, syntactically complex sentence, changes the rhythm to summarize the major outcome.

Rounds can also lead to conventionalized story-telling, since they can provide occasions to be given the floor and to produce a tale that can use prior models as scaffolding and the obligation of mutual appreciation as support.[11] In the following example, women at a Senior Center were discussing what they thought of changes in clothing fashions, and moved into the topic of making graduation dresses. The following is an excellent example of the frequent feature in all-female groups of women telling real-life narratives of their own embarrassing experiences to create amusement.

(7)   Making grade school graduation dresses
       Setting: Senior Center
       1   Ann: We had to *sew our own dress in elementary school.
       2   Bev: Yeah.

Ann told a story about how hard it was to finish in time, which ended with an evaluation.

       14 Ann: I remember I was so traumatized with that dress [laughs}

After general laughter, Bev started her own story on a similar theme.

       16 Bev: what did *I pick but an Indian *linen..

Bev's story quickly moves into a problem. Her laughter (31) suggests that she already had the intention of making a humorous report on her solution. Deb's laugh (33) collaborates in the key.

       29 Bev: and I uh if you did not leave enough yeah?
       30   for your seams you know and then
       31   uh, I had [laugh] all but one sleeve for puffed sleeves?
       32   and one was not gonna be as full as the other one so-o
       33 Deb: [laugh]
       34 Bev: my grandmother used to bring a lot of things from overse-
       35   you know, from uh, Europe, she used to travel a lot, my
       36   dad's mother? and she had some beautiful ribbon
       37   so I used it for the sash I remember it was an orchid.
       38   sash. and uh, that- that dress did up, but uh,
       39   what was I to do about the sleeves.
       40   so I walked crooked up the stage.
       41 All: [laugh]
       (UCDisclab: WCON1)

Here, Bev reports a situation which for a young girl would be a painful dilemma, the lack of fabric for making the dress sleeves symmetrical for a major public event. Her story about the sash (34–40) sustains the suspense; "*but what was I to do about the sleeves?*" and takes the listeners explicitly to her problem of a crooked dress. Then she states the punch line, the embarrassing solution of walking crookedly (40). This story is typical of women's humorous narratives about themselves (Ervin-Tripp and Lampert 1992). We can surmise that Bev knew at the start that she would present a problem narrative with a witty outcome. This is a prototypic narrative.

Adult round participants use prior models as scaffolding, with the possible aim of developing mutual appreciation as similar events. Kirschenblatt-Gimblett (1979) studies "story-dominated conversations" of Eastern European Jewish adults finds "in these story-dominated events, there is a preoccupation with narratives as things in themselves. For this reason, and because the narratives are preformulated and relatively self-contained (they can be understood without reference to any preceding conversation or narration), there is a tendency for story-dominated events to be organized like beads on a string" (p. 291).

In sum, rounds are a type of a speech context that can be heavily affected by notions of genre because the model given by others is followed. Thus there can be cycles of jokes, cycles of humorous personal narratives, cycles of stories of one's room in an earthquake. If rounds provide a mutually cooperative audience that allows floor to the speaker, there is the possibility of elaborating a performance in terms of the cultural norms. Rounds can thus involve continuity of genre, continuities of latent topic, continuities of key, emulation of form, and presupposition or ellipsis.

5.3. *Environmentally cued narratives*

More common than rounds in our conversational data are story triggers in the local environment. Here, unlike rounds, there are no models provided in the preceding conversation. There is considerable variability of structure.

(7)   Bird burials
       1   Ellen: don't look...there's a dead bird.
       (20 turns)
       21 Ellen: a-a-aw let's bury it.
       22 Dina: =let's= not [laugh]
       23 Bill: =I - I= don't think so! some cat will probly =get it =
       24 Ellen: =my dad= always
       25   did it for us
       26   =[laugh] =we'd put it in a shoebox and bury it.
       27 Dina: =[laugh]=   how sweet.
       28 Bill: a-aw
       29 Ellen: then we'd make crosses out of popsicle sticks.
       ......
       33 Dina: that's cute though...that's really nice.
       34 Ellen: we'd have a funeral for it and everything.
                   we'd say a prayer [laugh] and bury the thing.
       (UCDisclab: LCON2)

This is an example of the reminder report, which describes scripts rather than presenting a conflict with a resolution. There is a serial connective *then,* but the use of *would* marks this as a description of customary practice. There is, however, audience evaluation (27, 33) in this case, as if this were a narrative.

Children's conversations often include reference to what is in their immediate environment, since their activities tend to build on available resources for play. The following is an example of environment-cued fantasy of ten-year-olds in California. The imaginary characters and the disruption of order are characteristic of boys' stories as early as four (Nicolopoulou, Scales and Weintraub 1994).

> (8)   Microphone story
>   Two ten-year-old boys alone in a testing room eating lunch notice the microphones strung from the overhead light.
>   1   Sam: what's this for?
>   2   Jer: it's a microphone
>   3   [S & J start to sing into microphones]

Singing or other stage performances are frequent reactions to microphones at this age. At this point, Sam begins to build up a scene of disorder.

>   4   Sam: [laughing] I was screaming!
>   5   [laughing} (hey..I'll be acting like this)
>   6   hey Jeremy Jeremy Jeremy I'm gonna be laughing in this
>   7   and the light falls down [laugh]
>   8   what would you do if the light fell?

The past tense (4) marks irrealis and a possible story beginning. In (5–6) the tense is moved to the future and in (8) to the conditional, setting the stage for more fantasy. In (8) we see the imaginary disruption of order, which creates a problem to be solved by the fantasy narrative.

>   9   Jer: I'll be under the table
>   10 Sam: [laugh] no.. and you did it!
>   11 Jer: I'd be outta this class [laugh]
>   ⟨5⟩
>   12 Sam: it'll hit you on your head! [laugh]
>   13 Jer: you know what I'd do,
>   14   I'd be Superman and catch it.
>   15   be Superman and get squashed like a pancake.
>   16 Sam: I'll be Flash and get the fuck out.
>   (UCDisclab: GFIVE3)

In this sequence, Sam changes his position from challenger (10, 12) to capping with a character shift (16). Besides being fantastic responses to an environmental stimulus, these stories show how posing alternative outcomes can be part of collaboration in competitive bouts of story-telling.

5.4. *Narratives presenting problems*

As opposed to stories that resolve the complicating situations they set up during being told, some narratives invite audience participation in a possible problem-solving process by formulating problematic situations or protagonist behavior. Ochs, Smith, and Taylor (1989), who studied what they call "detective stories" during dinnertime talk, noticed that such problem-solving narratives can be characterized by interactive negotiation of the incomplete resolution.

The two most frequent contexts for temporal series in young adults' talk in the data are personal characterizations and problem situations. The problem situations are presented with potential endings, which participants co-construct. These differ somewhat from "troubles talk" (Jefferson 1988) when they refer not to chronic problems but one-time events.

A Taiwanese engineering student is conversing with two Asian-American women about the topic of race relations.

```
(9)   Asian women
      1   Hel:   you know...I was talking with a friend about
      2          that asian caucasian dating thing...
      3          and my complaint to {[p] to my friend}
      4          is that that is that asian guys just don't ask
      5          =y'know?=
      6   Min:   = yeah = they're not as (xxx) as (xx)
      7   Hel:   do you agree?
      8   Yuan:  totally agree
      9   Hel:   so then if that's true then how come when you guys
      10         get like mad at at *us
      11         if we go out with caucasian people
      12         then you guys don't ask..
      13         you guys don't get off your butts
      14         ⟨1⟩*answer me
      15  Yuan:  it's becau:se..
      16  Hel:   ⟨1⟩ you expect us to wait
      17  Yuan:  ==*ri:ght
      18  Hel:   =**yeah=
```

```
19 Yuan:  *ri::ght
20 Hel:   no, seriously
21 Yuan:  ⟨4⟩ hm I don't know I don't what to say
22 Hel:   ==yeah..i don't know either
```

This segment poses a problem of tension between Asian men and women, in which Helen presents a challenge to Yuan in the *you guys* form (12, 13) and pressures him (14) to answer the challenge, then herself providing the answer (16). In the conversation, Asian males are accused of causing the problem about which they are angry (10) both by their behavior (12, 13) and by their unrealistic expectations (16). The topic of male anger triggers a description from Min in which the theme is Asian male anger. The story is basically in the form of a long quotation.

```
23 Min:   ==did you guys see in the Daily Cal
24        about stuff..about the vandalism in Dwinelle
25        I actually like saw it..but um..there's this..
26        there's this like group of people who call themselves
27        the ⟨1⟩ Asian Male something or other they like
28        wrote like all over spray painted or marked =all over=
29 Yuan:  =o:h AMU?=
30 Min:   ==*yea AMU..they like wrote kill whitey and then like
31        in the girls' bathroom downstairs they're like like y'know
32        basically just slamming on asian woman
33        for dating caucasian men
34        like stay within your own kind..stay within your own group..
35        know what I mean? and it was just
36 Min:   scrawled *all over the stalls and the walls was writing
37 Yuan:  hm-mm
38 Hel:   I was like like when I saw that..I was just like...
39        god those people are *really angry [laugh] y'know?
```

Helen's evaluation (39) explicitly refocuses the topic again on anger, and triggers a story from Yuan which begins with the response marker *well* (40), suggesting he intends the listeners to find a continuity from the topic to his story.

```
40 Yuan:  well, I just met a caucasian guy yesterday
41        and we were just talking right?
42        and he he he speaks a little bit of Chinese
43        and he got a job uh got a job with a company like
44        uh doing tradings and stuff
45        and he was just telling me
46        yeah...you know...some Asian women...man
```

```
47        some Chinese women you just take them and
....[clarification of bam~bang]
48        bang them...you know
49        like ⟨2⟩ have sex with them
50        yeah bang them...and then yeah so y'know
51        I'm just going to work here a couple of years
52        and then go back to Thailand and get a wife
53        you know what am I supposed to response-
54        to response to that?
55  Hel:  you can bop him
56  Yuan: all I can say is you know
57  Min:  tell him you're pissed
58  Yuan: all I can say is being in this world
59        there's somebody who like to hit other people
60        and there's somebody who like to get hit...you know
61        so ⟨1⟩ what can you say?
62  Hel:  did you hit him?
63  Yuan: no
64  Hel:  why not?
65  Yuan: cause whoever the girl that wants to go out with
66        him, that's her problem...that's not my problem.
```
(UC Disclab: ASDAT)

This story picks up the racial anger theme, identifying the speaker with the anger of the graffiti writer implicitly by an example of what could produce that anger, white men's disrespect for Asian women. The story here has a structure of a prototypic narrative involving a conflict, but the conflict is unresolved. The narrator evidently did not show his anger to the Caucasian antagonist, and was left feeling dissatisfied. The businessman's statement (46–49) is presented without comment. There is a possible narrative transition marker *then* (50) but no overt reply is reported, and the action shifts to interior reflection. Yuan describes information about his own plans (51–52) implying a conflict with the stance of the businessman.[12] He leaves the story with a question about what he should have done (61). In the context of the graffiti topic, the two women have no hesitation in assuming Yuan's anger, and provide an answer to his question (55, 57). It is not until Helen (62) elicits a story completion that we find out the outcome as what did not happen, with an account of his reasoning only when prompted (64–66). The story has two unusual features: the failure to report the ending, which had to be prompted, and the solicitation by the teller of alternative outcomes. These mark the story as a problem situation.

5.5. *Narratives as performances*

Every narrative, insofar as it attempts to get some point(s) across, has an evaluative aspect. However, only some narratives receive a very animated and dramatic enactment so that a performance aspect is attributed to them (e.g., Bauman 1986; Hymes 1972). In such cases, the teller foregrounds the evaluative component of the story, with less emphasis placed on the events comprising the story. Cortazzi (1993), in contrasting performance narratives with interview narratives, asserts that performance becomes highlighted if the topic is appropriate to the audience, and if participants have reciprocal relationships and shared norms for evaluation. Schiffrin (1981) talks about one feature, that is, usage of historical present tense, that "makes the past more vivid by bringing past events into the moment of speaking..." (p. 58). Among some of the other common features that are employed as tools for highlighting the evaluated point of the story are constructed speech and animated intonation (Tannen 1989).

The following segment coming from two sisters sitting in a cafe demonstrates how constructed speech can be used to constitute a story. Sara is a topic change; she is involved in Mimi's job hunt. Bringing her up brings up also talk about her personality, first a descriptor from Mimi "standoffish" and then a carefully staged mocking mimicry, which Lina launched (9) before Mimi's comment about weirdness (10) suggesting it is an independent but perhaps corroborating expression. The mimicry is a "story", in the form of a dialogue. But it is only a fragment, with no event sequence.

(10)   Sisters in a cafe talking about a job search
    5   Lina: xxso you decided to call Sara?
    6   Mimi: yeah. it's weird cause she's kinda..I don't know
    7   don't you think that she's kinda standoff-
    8   she's kinda-
    9   Lina: she left this message
   10 Mimi: her and Jill are both kinda weird I think
   11 Lina: =she always goes she goes=
   12 Mimi: =they're =
   13 Lina: [slow whiny] "I'm calling for Mi-i-mi-i"
   14 Mimi: she's- she =calls me Mi-i-mi-i =
   15 Lina: =did you hear her message?=
   16 Mimi: yeah.
   17 Lina: she goes [slow whiny] "I'm calling for Mi-i-mi-i.
   18   um if you want you can work at the video store.
   19   um tell her to call me, bye Mi-i-mi-i" [laughs]
(UCDisclab: SISTRS)

Lina establishes the frame for her mimicry (9) while Mimi is still doing general description, the second line of which overlaps Mimi (11, 12). It is not until line 17 that Lina gets the floor for a full quotation mimicking Sara's voice, a production she appears to be planning by line 11. As a conversational tactic this example corroborates and illustrates the points made by Mimi, but the urgency of her production, and her overlaps while accelerating till she gets the floor suggest another feature, a goal of achieving a good performance, in this case of a witty mimicry. Also, as obvious from the content of the conversation, not much of what the story conveys is new information. The only conversational purpose of the story appears to be to display a shared assessment of a third person in a vivid way.

In the Turkish child database, totally "spontaneous" narratives by a child were not very common. Teachers, at times explicitly, disallowed children to tell stories outside of the time allotted for story-telling. When interviewed, a teacher reported that she really did not like it when Hasan, who told story (11) broke into his "quite fantastical and irrelevant" stories in the middle of "serious" group activities. But even without encouragement, children occasionally told some stories that were not precipitated by any remark, question, or topic in the preceding conversation. What seemed to trigger such narratives was probably the tellability attributed to the events by the storytellers. The content tends to be not banal, but out-of-the-ordinary events lending themselves to highly theatrical performances that attempt to build and uphold some suspense in the audience. Labov (1972) proposes that eventfulness is an intrinsic aspect of events and is expressed by evaluative devices: "evaluative devices say to us: this was terrifying, dangerous, weird, wild, crazy; or, amusing, hilarious, wonderful; more generally, that it was strange, uncommon, or unusual — that is, worth repeating. It was not ordinary, plain, humdrum, everyday or run-of-the-mill" (p. 371). Children also tended to repeat such narratives, and consolidated highly elaborate structures through repetition. As Goffman (1974) aptly writes "effective performance requires first hearings, not first tellings" (p. 508). The following narrative is from a 4-year-old boy replaying a particularly dramatic reported near-death experience of a (nonexistent) sibling.[13]

(11) Brain-washing
   During a gymnastic session at the preschool, a four-year old boy spontaneously launched into a dramatic story about his non-existent younger brother. When Hasan was asked to retell the story the second telling was very like the first.
   1 Res: tell *(it)* again.
   2 Hasan: my sibling opened medicine/medicine box — took *(it)*?

[self-correction]
3   was able to open *(it)*?
4   broke that lid?
5   ate them up
6   ate all all all *(of them)* up?
7   Res: a-ah! [=expressing surprise]
8   eee? [=so then?]
9   Hasan: ate them?
10   *(the ones)* which were mine?
11   *(he/she)* deserved so got sick
12 Res: then?
13 Hasan: then *(we)* took *(him)* to doctors
14 Res: what did *(they)* do at the doctor's?
15 Hasan: what's this? {re: taperecorder}
16 Res: this — *(we)* will listen *(to it)* later
17 Hasan: are *(you)* going to listen *(to it)*?
18 Res: uh-huhu
19   what did *(they)* do later at the doctor's?
20 Hasan: doctors ehh.. ee tube — *(they)* inserted a tube towards
21   *(his/her)* belly
22 Res: hmmh
23 Hasan: and after that e eh.. *(his/her)* stomach — e (they) cleansed
24   *(his/her)* brain.
25 Res: Uuuuh! [=expressing astonishment]
26 Hasan: yes!
27 Res: is *(he/she)* fine now?
28 Hasan: ee if *(they)* hadn't washed *(his/her)*brain,
29   he/she would have died {postposed pronoun}
30 Res: god forbid!
31   now *(he/she is)* fine, that means
32 Hasan: *(they)* washed *(his/her)* brain
33   after that *(he/she)* got well
34   and never took medicine without permission again.
(Aylin Küntay: Eryavuz preschool)

From the perspective of the 4-year-old boy, the events are so impressive that he seems to be carrying them around in a story-package that waits to be opened up in every appropriate occasion. The exigency of conveying the story gets reflected in the animated tone of voice he uses to tell the story. In turn, such enthusiasm may have led to the development of a full-fledged narrative structure. The temporal sequencing of the orienting events into a personally evaluated complicating action (1–11), the building up of suspense through an extended resolution (20–26), which also receives an evaluation by the presentation of a counterfactual event (28–29)[14] and the usage of a narrative-ending coda to return to the present time (34) depict all the essential elements of a Labovian story structure.

Not all the out-of-the-blue stories exhibited the Labovian elements in a very straightforward fashion. For example, first-person fight stories, while constituting a major portion of the boys' spontaneous tellings, never attained structural complication. There seem to be two main reasons for this: (1) young narrators do not necessarily take on the task of using the sequential unfolding events strategically to create suspense, and (2) the action structure of fight stories that reinforce a self-aggrandizing story is so predominant in the minds of the speakers that they do not go beyond elaborating on the manner of their participation in a fight.

5.6. *Tactical narratives*

Many conversational narratives are produced to support requests, claims, positions in an argument, or gossip about the character of others. A vivid example of the tactical use of narratives was Goodwin's (1990:243 ff.) instance of a story told in the midst of a dispute to humiliate the opponent. Support may be in the form of a description, or of a single vignette, as in example (10). Structurally, such narratives are often highly abbreviated, containing only enough information to support the position. Also, they may begin in the middle of a sequence. Example (13) contains a narrative but it does not conform to Labov's criterion of temporal iconicity.

Below is an example of a tactical narrative from the Turkish child database. In a context of a long conversation, Emre has been telling the adult researcher about some horror movies. The adult states (1) a generalizing conclusion that he does not get scared of anything if he can watch such violent movies, a statement Emre challenges by a story. Here the child provides a continuous narration demonstrating an instance of a personal history narrative brought in to support a reply that runs counter to the assumption behind the question. The result is an elaborate narrative with extensive presentation of emotional reaction.

(12) Scary films (Age: 4;11)
1 Ad: so you don't get scared of anything?
2 Emre: get scared–
3   for example I get scared of *sey* [how do you say]

4   in the cartoon very good–
5   at first there was a very ugly man
6   I didn't get scared of him
7   but then he got uglier in the film
8   I didn't watch it
9   and then I left the TV without turning it off
10   since I got so much frightened
11   my mother was in the kitchen
12   I immediately ran to the kitchen
(Aylin Küntay: Eryavuz Preschool)

The narrative is introduced clearly as an example (3) of the generalization (1) and is constructed as a contrast between a stimulus and non-response (5–6) in agreement with the adult's assumption, and a contrasting (*but then–*) stimulus and fear responses (7–9) in disagreement with her generalization. The next line (9) *and then* escalates to a more vivid example of fear. He provides explanations (10, 11) in the form both of motivational evaluations and place information before the climax and marks the ultimate challenge to the adult's generalization by illustrating his flight (12) as occurring *immediately*. The evaluation (10) can also be seen as a reply to (1) tying the example back to its prompt. Thus the narrative follows a direct reply, is marked as an example, and is punctuated with recurrent challenges to the stimulating question. It never loses its marking as a reply.

In the following example, the conversational topic had begun with questioning of Ann about her plans to become a feminist therapist, which she illustrates with a quotation narrative, which is the second-hand story of a friend. In the first narrative, Ann introduced a report of a conversation telling about repeated, customary harassment, told in generalized terms, without specifics.

Her point relating this story to her career goals never was completed, because Cathy interrupted with a specific narrative.

(13)   Temper
   8   Cath: =*wo-o-h =
   9   you wanna hear about *harassment from a *guy
   10   (like) *right after we *saw you,
   11   this guy grabbed my *butt, on my way to dinner, on the
               sidewalk//
   12 An: *o::h =my *go:::d   =
   13 Iris: =oh my *go:::d=
   14 Cath: ==**no:: it was kind of funny though.
   15   I- you- you know I

```
16          =knew him from the **party        = the night be*fore.
17 Tere:    =you **knew who he **was, right/=
18 Cath:    *but.. and he's nice looking
19          and he's a nice guy/
20          but it was just kind of {[fast] *weird
21          because I didn't recognize him at first}
22          I *had to turn around and like,..
23          *actually it took me about a *block to even make the
24          connection/
```

In this report, Cathy identified her story as an example of the general topic
introduced by Ann, supporting Ann's point. She uses a preface (9) to take the
floor, identifies the location of the event (10) and moves directly to the high
point. The audience reaction (12, 13) confirms the appropriateness of the story
and gives her warrant for holding the floor later to speculate about her own
reactions. The orientation, evaluation, and her resulting behavior all follow. The
audience even collaborates and confirms (17). This story presented a problem
appropriate to the topical context, and was followed by a round of harassment
stories.

```
64 Cath:    ==(well you know what *maybe)
65          it's kind of *cool sometimes
66          if you're in the right frame of mind.
67          I **really have to be in the right frame of mind,...
68          **drunk. {[laugh] (   )} ...
69          *no, I        *really- I      *do have to be in
70          =the right frame of mind.           *Simon was just =
71 Tere:    =guys do it to me all the *ti:me,.. I mean guys I *know=
72 Cath:    lucky I didn't *backhand him for that....
73          that's *all I have to *say about it..
74          it was there- I mean if it had been,..
75          if *that had been say like mid*week last week when I was
76          really up*set about stuff,..
77          *I would've turned around and- and...
78          **nailed the guy,.. I swear to god
79          I would've *kicked his nuts through the roof of his mouth,
80 Iris:    ==umhm,
81 Cath:    ==**anybody who fucks with me that way last week I
82          would've killed.
```

Cathy shifts the topic from harrassment to mood in contrasting situations,
a shift not followed by the other women (71). She then creates hypotheticals

about her willingness to retaliate when in a bad mood (77–79), building to an
extreme (82). Her anger about the unresolved event even leads to an ambivalent
reply to Teresa's teasing (93), which may have been based on a misinterpreta-
tion of Cathy's laugh (92, 95).[15]

```
91 Cath:   I have a *temper *anyway but
92         [laugh] I *really have a temper wh=en (a guy) =
93 Tere:                              ={[high] **do you=
94         **really?}
95 Cath:   [laugh] **Terry that was not even funny,..
96         *yeah it was but...*it wasn't. <3>
97         *well, yeah.
```

Next Cathy produces a story, but it is not built up temporally as a narrative;
rather, Cathy presents the high point (100) that provides proof of her claims to
a fiery character (99).

```
 99 Cath:  =*you= guys wanna see me in one of my bad moods,
100        *Iris saw me sh- throw my shoe through my window.
101 Iris:  [laugh] oh *yea::h I {[laugh] remember that.}
102 Cath:  *I don't remember what I was ma:ad about,
103        I *broke my window with my shoe.
104 Tere:  **go:d,
105 Iris:  **I remember what you were mad about....
106        you were *gonna uh- um..
107        you had been waiting all *day to ga- go out,..
108        your mom said she was gonna be back in the *morning,..
109        = and she didn't come back,=
110 Cath:  =**....h and left        = me without a *car.
111 Iris:  ==yeah....
112 Cath:  *that was when I was sharing a car with my *mo:m.
113        that was like my-,..
114        *that was a while ago....
115        that was like my *junior year in high school
116        or something
```
(UCDisclabCAFE1)

What turns out to be a story about a temper tantrum was not presented as
a narrative. Cathy, whose conversational focus is on her own personality and
capacities, says she remembers only her own burst of temper and its outcome,
not what caused it. It is left to her friend Iris to go back in time (105), and
reconstruct the context for the outburst. So we do not have, in any sense, the
iconicity of temporal series in the story and in the event, the build-up of conflict

to a high-point, and the resolution and coda that one sees in a full narrative. Rather, a speaker seizes a piece of a past sequence for her local conversational needs and gives a fragment of the event sequence.

6. Conclusions

When we see data from other societies, we recognize that there are conditions where long, well structured, personal experience narratives are heard frequently. Alves (1995), for example, found that even Portuguese village children speaking to other children can tell such stories spontaneously, because, he says, such tellings are encouraged and modeled. Americans ask "have you heard this before?" as if retelling to the same audience is undesirable, thus ruling out the repeated rehearsal that elaborates the descriptive, dramatic or humorous features of stories. Ochs, Smith and Taylor (1989) have recorded families in which long personal narratives are not modeled and parents do not report their personal experiences as narratives, instead treating children's reports of the past as problem situations.

Audience participation norms are culturally variable, as we have seen from Watson-Gegeo and Boggs (1977) and others. In our data there is some evidence of occasional backchannel encouragement. Among the questions to be considered in cultural information are these: Can a story be retold or must we ask if it is new? Under what conditions is retelling authorized, and how? Does the story-teller have to demand the floor by prefacing or do listeners recognize and orient to cues of upcoming narratives? Are there occasions and people that can be expected to produce elaborated stories? Many of these cultural factors have their effect through altering the very performance conditions which we have proposed affect the prototypical structure in narratives.

There are also *production conditions* that facilitate longer and more elaborated stories. Among them are:

(a)   The opportunity to rehearse and reshape a story. Stories that are retold already have a basis in form, and a reteller has the knowledge of how the first occasion was evaluated by the audience. Even a story that is someone else's gives the teller this advantage.

(b)   Stories are likely to be less elliptical where less shared knowledge can be presupposed, and orientation must be supplied. Stories across generations are like this.

(c)   On the other hand, shared experience can be motivating of shared interest, as we see in the stories shared by family members or veterans. Prompts, collaboration, and evaluations from an audience indicate attentiveness and willingness to hear a long story, leading the speaker to turn what could have started as a tactical move into a performance.

(d)   Elicited, prefaced or audience-prompted stories can be seen by tellers and audience to be held to an aesthetic standard involving the cultural norms for the genre — to be entertaining, exciting, and so on. Moreover, these occasions, unless they are daily routines, are likely to draw on the tellers' most shaped, retold, and dramatic experiences. If the speaker is free to choose a rehearsed and reshaped story, there is likely to be more plot build-up than in conversationally occasioned novel accounts.

(e)   Stories that are told in response to narrow questions, or to make particular conversational points, are more likely to select a time in the narrative to begin which does not entail a build-up or elaboration. The telling may include just the high point, or just constructed speech, or just a description. Stories that are told to illustrate a problem can lack resolutions, and alternative outcomes may be solicited from or volunteered by the participating group.

In sum, the presence and absence of the features of the prototypical story can be systematically related to the conversational circumstances.

Notes

1.   The second author's dissertation concerns both spontaneous and elicited narratives of children in two Turkish preschools.

2.   Throughout this paper, the terms "narrative" and "story" will be used interchangeably. However, the distinction between narrative and story is a valid one, which is central in some accounts. For example, Rimmon-Kenan (1983) has a three-way distinction between "story", "text", and "narration", where **story** refers to a series of of logically and chronologically related events, and **narration** is the manner of talking about these event sequences. The origin of the story/narrative bifurcation comes from the Russian formalists' split between *fabula* and *sjuzhet* (Propp 1968) and gets disseminated into other researchers' work (for example, Chatman's (1978) distinction between story and discourse). Such accounts strive to isolate a paradigmatic core from actual narrative versions, by moving away from the surface language phenomena towards a deeper structure. Since our main concern in this particular study is only the actual use of language in extended discourse, the distinction will not be honored in the writing.

3. For example, the rhetorical approach (for e.g., Abrahams 1968, 1976; Bauman 1986, 1992; Ben Amos 1976; Hymes 1971), which grew out of the folkloric tradition as a challenge to structuralist approaches, regards stories not as highly confined and named entitites in a given culture, but as parts of situated face-to-face communicative events and interactional sense-making situations.

4. In fact different prototypes appear when one compares elicited stories from people of different cultural backgrounds. For example, Minami and McCabe (1991), Michaels (1981), and Rodino *et al.* (1991) have compared elicited stories from different cultural sources, and have shown contrasts in children's story organization in terms of high points, the degree of focus on events or on people's characteristics, and audience encouragement of elaboration or brevity of presentation. So even if we are talking about the prototypic story, we need to identify what features and structural components are commonly highlighted or ellipted in a given culture.

5. Transcriptions are based on Gumperz and Berenz (1993); *is stress; = overlap=; == latched response; ... pauses; ⟨ ⟩ seconds of pause; { } feature boundaries; / falling terminal juncture.

6. This takes us to another issue, what is even tellable to outsiders, since some backgrounding is too difficult to make explicit, such as disability experiences or some war experiences which only can be shared with co-participants (Fussell 1975).

7. These data were obtained by assignments to students, so they are biased to ages 18–30 with a few exceptions involving families or senior centers.

8. Eryavuz Center and Ubaruz Center will be used as pseudonyms for the two preschools. Although social class is not one of the factors that is explored systematically in the study, an attempt was made to include children representative of families of different socio-educational backgrounds. Almost all of the children in Eryavuz Center came from higher-middle to upper-class families. Ubaruz Center catered to the children of the staff of a major university, and therefore included children of all backgrounds, mostly lower-middle class and middle-class.

9. Ages are given after quotations in the case of child speakers.

10. Looking only for marked sequences leads to the omission of stories like the earthquake event.

11. The kind of structural elaborations found by Nicolopoulou (1996) when children have audience support in preschool narratives-for-drama suggest that many other manipulations of audience relations to story-telling could alter structural complexity.

12. Linda Young (1994) has described an Asian communication pattern in which background information is presented first, often without further explanation, relying on inference.

13. A later interview with Hasan's father revealed that Hasan didn't have any brothers or sisters. However, the father reported that their neighbor's son, to whom Hasan may be referring as a sibling, had been hospitalized recently for swallowing some headache pills.

14. Such usage of postposed third-person pronouns is very rare in Turkish. In this context, it signifies some ambivalent attitude or emotion on the part of the narrator towards the protagonist — empathy mixed with disapproval and antagonism.

15. Laughter is common in women's self-critical and revealing speech (Ervin-Tripp and Lampert 1992).

References

Abrahams, Roger. 1968. "Introductory Remarks to a Rhetorical Theory of Folklore." *Journal of American folklore* 81.143–158.

Abrahams, Roger. 1976. "Personal Power and Social Restraint in the Definition of Folklore." In *Folklore Genres*, D. Ben-Amos (ed.), 16–30. Austin: University of Texas Press.

Alves, Julio. 1995. "The Story behind the Stories: Boys' narratives and the (re)production of gender discourses." In *Texts and Identities: Proceedings of the Third Kentucky Conference on Narrative*, Joachim Knuf (ed.). Lexington: University of Kentucky.

Bauman, Richard. 1986. *Story, Performance, and Event.* Cambridge: Cambridge University Press.

Bauman, Richard. 1992. "Contextualization, Tradition, and the Dialogue of Genres: Icelandic legends of the *kraftakáld.*" In *Rethinking Context: Language as an interactive phenomenon,* A. Duranti and C. Goodwin (eds.), 127–145. Cambridge: Cambridge University Press.

Bauman, Richard. 1993. Disclaimers of Performance. In *Responsibility and Evidence in Oral Discourse,* J.H. Hill and J.T. Irvine (eds.), 182–196. Cambridge: Cambridge University Press.

Ben Amos, Dan. 1976. *Folklore Genres.* Austion: University of Texas Press.

Chatman, Seymour. 1978. *Story and Discourse.* Ithaca, N.Y.: Cornell University Press.

Cortazzi, Martin. 1993. *Narrative Analysis.* London: The Falmer Press.

Ervin-Tripp, Susan M. and Aura Bocaz. 1989. *Quickly, before a Witch Gets me: Children's temporal conjunctions within speech acts.* Berkeley: Institute of Cognitive Studies, University of California (Berkeley Cognitive Science Report, 61).

Ervin-Tripp, Susan M. and Martin Lampert. 1992. "Gender Differences in the Construction of Humorous Talk." In *Locating Power: Proceedings of the Second Berkeley Women and Language Conference,* Kira Hall, Mary Buchholtz and Birch Moonwoman (eds), 108–117. Berkeley, Calif.: Berkeley Women and Language Group, Linguistics Department, University of California.

Ervin-Tripp, Susan M., Amy Strage, Martin Lampert and Nancy Bell. 1987. "Understanding requests." *Linguistics* 15.107–143.

Fussell, Paul. 1975. *The Great War and Modern Memory.* New York: Oxford University Press.

Goffman, Erving. 1974. *Frame Analysis.* London: Harper and Row.

Goodwin, Marjorie Harness. 1990. *He-said-she-said: Talk as social organization among black children.* Bloomington: Indiana University Press.

Gumperz, John J. and Norine Berenz. 1993. "Transcribing Conversational Exchanges." In *Talking Data: Transcription and coding methods for language research,* Jane Edwards and Martin Lampert (eds), 91–122. Hillsdale, N.J.: Lawrence Erlbaum.

Hymes, Dell. 1971. "The Contribution of Folklore to Sociolinguistic Research." *Journal of American folklore* 84.42–50.

Hymes, Dell. 1972. *Towards Communicative Competence*. Philadelphia: University of Pennsylvania Press.

Jefferson, Gail. 1978. "Sequential Aspects of Storytelling in Conversation." In *Studies in the Organization of Conversational Interaction*, J. Schenkein (ed.), 219–248. New York: Academic Press.

Jefferson, Gail. 1988. "On the Sequential Organization of Troubles Talk in Ordinary Conversations." *Social Problems* 35.418–441.

Kirschenblatt-Gimblett, Barbara. 1979. "The Concept and Varieties of Narrative Performance in East European Jewish Culture." In *Explorations in Verbal Performance*, R. Bauman and J. Sherzer (eds), 283–308. New York: Cambridge University Press.

Labov, William. 1972. *Language in the Inner City: Studies in the Black English vernacular*. Philadelphia: University of Pennsylvania Press.

Labov, William and Joshua Waletzky. 1967. "Narrative Analysis: Oral versions of personal experience." In *Essays on the verbal and visual arts*, J. Helm (ed.). Seattle: University of Washington Press.

Luebs, Margaret. 1992. "Earthquake Narratives." *Proceedings of the Eighteenth Annual Meeting of the Berkeley Linguistic Society*, 157–165. Linguistics Department, University of California, Berkeley.

Michaels, Sarah. 1981. "Sharing Time: Children's narrative styles and differential access to literacy." *Language in Society* 10.423–442.

McCabe, Alyssa. 1997. "Developmental and Cross-cultural Aspects of Children's Narration." In *Narrative Development — Six approaches*, M. Bamberg (ed.). Hillsdale, N.J.: Lawrence Erlbaum.

Minami, Masahiko and Allyssa McCabe. 1991. "*Haiku* as a Discourse Regulation Device: A stanza analysis of Japanese children's personal narratives." *Language in Society* 20.577–599.

Nicolopoulou, Ageliki. 1996. "Narrative Development in Social Context." In *Social Interaction, Social Context, and Language*, D.I. Slobin, J. Gerhardt, A. Kyratzis and J. Guo (eds). Mahwah, N.J.: Erlbaum.

Nicolopoulou, Ageliki, Barbara Scales and Jeff Weintraub. 1994. "Gender Differences and Symbolic Imagination in the Stories of Four-year-olds." In *The Need for Story: Cultural diversity in classroom and community*, Ann H. Dyson and Celia Genishi (eds), 102–123. Urbana: NCTE.

Ochs, Elinor and Lisa Capps. 1996. "Narrating the Self." In *Annual Review of Anthropology*, W. Durham, E. Valentine Daniels and B. Schieffelin (eds.). Palo Alto: Annual Reviews.

Ochs, Elinor, Ruth Smith and Carolyn Taylor. 1989. "Detective Stories at Dinnertime: Problem-solving through Co-narration." *Cultural Dynamics* 2.238–257. Newbury Park, Calif.: Sage.

Propp, Vladimir. 1968. *The Morphology of the Folktale*. Austin: University of Texas Press.

Rimmon-Kenan, Shlomith. 1983. *Narrative Fiction: Contemporary poetics*. London: Methuen.

Rodino, Ana Maria, Cynthia Gimbert, Carmella Perez and Alyssa McCabe. 1991. "Getting your Point across: Contrastive sequencing in low-income African-American and Latino children's narrative." Paper presented at the 16th Annual Conference on Language Development, October, Boston University, Boston, Massachusetts.

Ryave, Alan. 1978. "On the Achievement of a Series of Stories." In *Studies in the Organization of Conversational Interaction,* J. Shenkein (ed.), 113–132. New York: Academic Press.

Schiffrin, Deborah. 1981. "Tense Variation in Narrative." *Language* 57(1).45–62.

Tannen, Deborah. 1989. *Talking Voices.* Cambridge: Cambridge University Press.

Umiker-Sebeok, Jean. 1979. "Preschool Children's Intraconversational Narratives." *Journal of Child Language* 6.91–110.

Watson-Gegeo, Karen Ann and Stephen T. Boggs. 1977. "From Verbal Play to Talk Story: The role of routines in speech events among Hawaiian children." In *Child Discourse,* Claudia Mitchell-Kernan and Susan Ervin-Tripp (eds), 67–90. New York: Academic Press.

Young, Linda. 1994. *Crosstalk and Culture in Sino-American Communication.* Cambridge: Cambridge University Press.

Coherence in Multi-Party Conversation

Episodes and Contexts in Interaction

Per Linell and Natascha Korolija

Linköping University, Sweden

1. Introduction: Coherence-building in conversation

For participants in discourse, it is of fundamental importance that actions and utterances, at each moment, "make sense". We can think of sense-making as consisting in the actors' (and, at a second stage, analysts') building of coherent links between chunks of discourse (that which has to be made sense of) and some kind of context(s), i.e., things accessible to the conversationalist in prior co-text, in the concrete, surrounding situation, or in some kind of background knowledge.

But coherence with what is already given is counterbalanced by the need for renewal and progression in conversation. Each segment of discourse therefore represents some kind of resolution of the tension between the two opposing needs, that of staying on topic and that of renewing topics. Often, topics accrue by way of stepwise progression, but at other times participants create more abrupt shifts with clear boundaries. In the latter case, continuities are disrupted, and partial fractures structure the conversational flow into — what we will call — *episodes*. These are discursive events or action sequences, each delimited from prior and subsequent discourse, and internally bound together by something, e.g., a coherent topical trajectory and/or a common activity. Structurally, episodes belong to an intermediate level, above utterances and turns but below whole speech events and their major phases.[1] Exactly what we mean by episodes will emerge later in this paper.

What is it that makes episodes *internally coherent*? The most common answer to this question is undoubtedly: topical content. Episodes are usually "about" something, and this "aboutness" is what constitutes topicality. But topicality cannot be analyzed independently of sequential structure and activity types in discourse. Topics are characteristic of actors' *activities* of using discourse and contexts to build islands of coherence and intersubjectivity in and through the interactions, i.e., in the *acts* of referring, predicating, and connecting thoughts (idea units) with one another in a discourse with a common floor (an interaction with a single shared focus of attention). We would therefore not look at the discourse as a static text, but, instead, stress the participants' activities to create intersubjectivity by topical coherence. Schegloff (1990) argues that local sequential dependencies (between actions and utterances) are the most basic building-blocks in discourse, something which makes topical coherence possible (rather than the other way around). Similarly, Maynard (1980:263) maintains that "[t]opicality [...] is a matter not only of content, but is partly constituted in the procedures conversationalists utilize to display understanding and to achieve one turn's proper fit with prior turns."

One of our fundamental assumptions is therefore that topics, sequential structure and participation structure must be analyzed together (Maynard 1980; Erickson 1990; Ainsworth-Vaughn 1992; Goodwin 1995) The same thesis, though formulated within a different theoretical framework, shows up in Bublitz (1988), who regards topics as the combination of content ('topic subjects') and the 'topical actions', which introduce, sustain, change or close (what would in our terms be) topical episodes. This means that the perspective on topics is no longer exclusively content-based (a traditional text-linguistic perspective); it must *also* consider the organizations of sequences, the trains of interactional events and actions (Schegloff 1990), or, in our terms, episodes.

Topicality and coherence are for us 'discourse notions' (Keenan and Schieffelin 1976; Givón 1992; Chafe 1994:120), which are closely connected; they (partly) constitute each other (Brown and Yule 1983). Topicality pertains to matters of continued, sustained salience or importance (as opposed to things subjected only to peripheral or momentary attention; Givón 1995). Therefore, episodes, rather than single utterances, support topics. Cohesive devices, such as repetition of key words, semantic associations, use of pronouns, ellipsis, and other anaphoric devices, use of tense and aspect, etc., which tie utterances together, indicate that there is a topic space with a common focus (Grosz 1977), and they help create this space within an episode in discourse. But coherence is, for us, not a property of the conversational text itself, but something which emerges in the minds of the conversationalists (and analysts) (Gernsbacher and Givón 1995). At the same time, we insist on the importance of the conversation-al interaction as the locus for negotiating and constructing coherence (Goodwin 1995).

2. Local and global coherence

Our focus, in this paper, is on coherence between (and within) rather large chunks of discourse (i.e., episodes), rather than on coherence relations between adjacent sentences in texts. In this sense, we deal with coherence at a "global", or at least intermediate, level of structure. But this must not be taken to imply that coherence of these kinds is necessarily the results of global planning on the part of speakers. In interaction, and particularly in informal multi-party inter-action (for examples, see below), it is very difficult to predict and steer exactly what is going to happen. Rather, it seems plausible that a lot of manifest global coherence is actually the additive product of many local decisions on an utterance-to-utterance level. We could use here the parable of Simon's (1969) ant; Simon describes how the ant, on its way home (the global goal), finds its way across the beach sand, detouring, climbing over or under obstacles, backing up, interrupting its progress to talk with a fellow ant, but eventually reaching the goal. Now, creating a conversational episode takes of course more than an ant's cognition (and more than one individual), but the analogy is this; many local steps add up to what in retrospect may look like a coherent global strategy. Even (an attempt at) an episode initiation of a kind that is agenda-bound (and hence somehow pre-planned) is in fact a local contribution (and it does not always succeed in establishing an episode). However, it is also evident that speakers do indulge in some global, strategic or tactical planning when they talk. Hence, both local decisions and global planning contribute to coherence within and between episodes.[2]

Yet, while we assign a primary role to local decisions, it is equally important to recognize that certain activities typically exhibit a *lack* of local topical coherence beyond adjacency pairs. In some cases of episodes with global coherence but little local coherence beyond single question–answer pairs, the global coherence builds upon some macro-topical agenda, such as gathering personal data about a client in a professional–lay interaction. In such inter-mediate cases, the framing activity type, along with the macro-topical agenda, works to hold together the episode.

In other cases, the activity frame seems to fulfil this function alone. This is the case in many types of quizzes, certain psychological tests, etc., where each question-answer exchange "is about" something particular, but there is no coherence between these adjacency pairs, i.e., the various questions posed are semantically entirely unrelated.

(1) MEMORY MASTERS (Excerpt from a Swedish TV "Memory Masters" show. Q = question-master (program host), C = contestant)[3]

Q:1   va kallar man en anläggning för hästavel?
C:2   stuteri.
Q:3   rätt. vem vann världscupen i utförsåkning 1975?
C:4   Stenmark.
Q:5   fel. hur lång tid tog de att bygga slottet i Versailles?
C:6   sa du Versailles?
Q:7   ja.
C:8   hur exakt måste man vara?
Q:9   de får du inte fråga.
C:10   tretti år.
Q:11   fel, förtisju år. va e en cineast?
C:12   en filmkännare.
Q:13   rätt. vad var Caruso bra på?
        ((fortsätter))

Q:1.   what do you call an establishment for horse breeding?
C:2.   stud-farm.
Q:3.   correct. who won the world cup in down-hill skiing in 1975?
C:4.   Stenmark.
Q:5.   wrong. how long did it take to build the castle of Versailles?
C:6.   did you say Versailles?
Q:7.   yes.
C:8.   how exact does one have to be?
Q:9.   you mustn't ask that.
C:10.   thirty years.
Q:11.   wrong, forty-seven years. what is a cineaste?
C:12.   a connoisseur of films.
Q:13.   correct. what was Caruso good at?
        ((continues))

With the exception of embedded repair sequences (cf. turns 6–9; note the restriction even on such sequences imposed by moves such as Q:9), there is no topical connection between successive questions, and their related answers, in this kind of activity. Yet, at one level, it is perceived as coherent and meaningful; both parties understand that they are engaged in an activity in which unrelated quiz questions are being asked, the point being that of testing B's ability to retrieve memory information very rapidly and thus to answer questions correctly on the spot. Something similar applies to many psychological tests.

Hence, the activity-type context makes up for the absence of any co-textual coherence between question–answer pairs.

We conclude therefore that though topic organization is common, it is not a universal property of discourse at the episode level. Topicality is not the only phenomenon that can make episodes coherent. In general, we can say that the ways of organizing topicality, coherence and episode structure in discourse are activity-specific. Quizzes and psychological tests are special activity-types.

3. Episodes and the dynamics of topic progression in conversation

In the course of a dialogue, interlocutors both interact with each other and develop topics in and through their discourse. Talk-in-interaction is produced on a moment-to-moment, utterance-to-utterance, basis; discourse is built by "incrementation" (e.g., Schegloff 1996). Bits and pieces of discourse are selected and strung together in a process of local production, one 'idea unit' makes another one possible and relevant, and once this new unit materializes, opportunities for further continuations, i.e., more idea units, are created etc. One single contribution does not build a topic; a series of contributions, bound together by response links, will be needed to establish topic. In this way a topic becomes a joint accomplishment and a product of the dialogue dynamics of responses and initiatives (Linell 1990).[4] A topic is both the project and product of coherence-building (cf. also Goffman 1983).

The response-initiative principle means basically the following. At each point in time interlocutors are expected to say something which ties up with, is relevant with respect to, what has been said before, or is otherwise *given* in the present micro-situation, i.e., the current, local contexts. At the same time something *new* should be introduced. Bergmann (1990) termed these responsive vs. initiatory aspects 'topic maintenance' and 'topic progression', respectively. If participants succeed in developing topics in this stepwise manner, the resulting discourse may look like a seamless web in which topics shade into each other ('topic shading', Schegloff and Sacks 1973; 'topic drift', Hobbs 1990). However, as we already noted, interlocutors do not go on developing aspects of the "same" topic or closely related topics for ever; sometimes, they need to change topics.[5] If these topic shifts are more or less abrupt, we get some sort of boundaries, i.e., (at least partial) discontinuities or fractures within the discursive flow, dividing the resulting "text" into episodes.

Episodes must be regarded as suitable units of analysis for (especially) multi-party conversations, because episodes are, in general, natural units of social interaction,[6] they are held together by a common floor and focus of attention, they are usually topically continuous, and they represent a level where the interdependencies between discourse and its contexts are most clearly brought out.

Although topics and episodes tend to be mutually constitutive, there is no simple or necessary correlation between episode and topic. First, as we have already pointed out, although *most* episodes are topically coherent, this is not true of all episodes (e.g., quizzes).

Secondly, topics do not remain constant and immobile within episodes. Topic maintenance is in itself a dynamic process (e.g., Foppa 1990), and there are always some topical *trajectories within episodes*. Sometimes these movements inside topic spaces are so radical that the end of the episode appears to be "about" something completely different from the topic of the beginning, without there being any recognizable internal boundary (a seamless, "stepwise topical transition", Sacks 1992; topic 'shift', Bublitz 1988). Such episodes may be called bitopical or *polytopical*, as opposed to those episodes which are relatively monotopical (though continuously developing, these appear to be "about" one topic). However, we shall not be concerned, in this paper, with patterns of episode-internal coherence. Rather, we shall focus on what happens at episode boundaries.

Finally, and most importantly, boundaries between episodes are seldom completely abrupt, nor are most new episodes initiated totally "out of the blue". Contexts at hand are deployed as resources when conversationalists initiate new episodes. It is primarily this third point we shall develop in the following, where we will propose to use such contextual resources for classifying episodes.

4. Contextual resources in conversation

It appears that when a speaker, in collaboration with interlocutors, tries to initiate talk about something new (or an interaction of another kind than just before), he or she does this most often by using some resource in the contexts potentially accessible to the interlocutors. Correspondingly, when a new episode has been initiated, we (as actors or analysts) can usually retrospectively find a contextual source. We may say that speakers implicitly assume that these contextual resources can be taken and treated as given. Speakers can use them, as they guide their interlocutors into doing or talking about something new. A new topic (or activity) must be anchored or *grounded*, i.e., contextualized and understood in relation to something (Clark and Schaefer 1989; Wilkes-Gibbs 1995). Our analysis is based on a theory of such *contextual resources* used in the initiation of new episodes.

Nothing is a context of a piece of discourse in and by itself, as it were "objectively". Instead, we have *contextual resources*, potential contexts that can be made into actual, relevant contexts through the activities of the interlocutors in dialogue. For this reason, the following is a list not of contexts per se, but of phenomena that can serve as contextual resources.

There are *immediate* contextual resources of basically two kinds:

(Ia) the *prior* (up to the simultaneously occurring) *discourse* in the encounter, i.e., what is often called *co-text*. Actually, this should be generalized to cover the whole sequence of relevant actions prior to the utterance (or action) in focus; in some cases, this sequence may contain primarily, or even exclusively, non-verbal actions.

(Ib) the surrounding concrete (spatially and temporally specific) *talk-and-interaction situation*, i.e., the immediate perceptually available environment (*"here-and-now"*) with its physical spaces, persons (and their physical positions, e.g., seating arrangements), objects, artifacts (including media as carriers of linguistic, and other, signals), and extra-discursive events.

We must also deal with *mediate* (abstract) contextual resources of a number of partially overlapping kinds. These contextual dimensions are not directly and publicly manifest in the perceptually available situation and behaviors. Some are, however, more directly linked to the unfolding specific topics of the discourse:

(IIa) what actors already assume, believe, know or understand about the things talked about in the discourse in question; this is often termed '*models*' of the discourse-in-context.[7] Such models are seen as something which gets continuously updated through discourse. Closely connected with such models are the actors' (undoubtedly partially different) models of their *current and upcoming communicative projects*; these are of course also successively updated through discourse.

Another two types are also rather closely related to the situation at hand:

(IIb) *specific knowledge about persons involved*; this (subjective or inter-subjective) background knowledge is based upon actors' partly shared experiences and knowledge about each other's biographies;

(IIc) the *abstract situation definition*, or the '*frame*' defining the encounter as an instance of a certain activity type (Levinson 1979) or situated activity system (Goffman 1961) or communicative genre, e.g., a court trial, a family dinner-table conversation, a speech therapy session etc.

Related to (IIc) is the *specific organizational* context (and the actors'
knowledge thereof) consisting of working conditions, documents, regulations,
hierarchies among (professional) role incumbents, educational backgrounds
surrounding the actors, etc. which are relevant especially for those who act in
their professional roles.

At the most abstract end, we find the most general kinds of background
knowledge:

(IId)   *general background knowledge*, i.e., fundamental or general assump-
        tions about the world which may be said to belong to the culture's
        'collective memory' and therefore are usually taken as given by
        actors. One should also mention here actors' knowledge of language,
        communicative routines, and action types.

This cursory account of contextual resources needs a couple of comments
straight away.[8] One is that contexts are semiotic phenomena; they are meaningful only in relation to discourse. Discourses and relevant ("realized") contexts
are co-constituted. This means that if we think of extra-discursive entities, such
as bodies, objects, artifacts etc (cf. Ib), as contextual resources, these must be
cognitively apprehended and actively deployed in order to function as contexts.
In one sense, this moves features of the co-text and the concrete environment
(Ia,b) closer to the abstract contextual resources (II), the latter sometimes being
called 'cognitive environments'.

Another point is that it is immediately evident that contexts and contextual
resources vary and overlap considerably;[9] they may be situational or cultural,
local or global, common to interlocutors or not etc. Contexts and contextual
resources are seldom completely shared by actors in a given situation. For
example, the same activity can be framed or perspectivized (IIc) differently by
different actors. Likewise, parties may possess different kinds of background
knowledge, entertain conflicting interests, and direct their attentions differently
during a conversation. Even if we imagine cases of highly cooperative encounters involving mutually well-acquainted parties, there cannot be one single
context for each discourse. Rather, there is a complex matrix of contexts,
assembled from an array of contextual resources.

Yet, if we wish to look at the specific function of contextual phenomena to
be used as resources for anchoring new episodes in conversation, it may be
reasonable to assume that only one or two dimensions are focused upon in each
such moment. It may also be useful to group the relevant types of contextual
resources in terms of prior discourse (Ia), concrete surrounding situation
(interactional setting) (Ib), and (various kinds of) abstract background knowledge
(II). Incidentally, this is a triplet which often recurs in discussions of givenness.[10]

5. Topical Episode Analysis

Topics are notoriously difficult to analyze in substantial terms, i.e., exclusively in terms of what the discourse is "about". Most analysts therefore work with topic boundaries (and transitions), which are easier to identify (Brown and Yule 1983; Adelswärd 1988). Using episode boundaries as a resource for unitization is in fact a common method of doing topic analysis. Our model is based on transitions across episode boundaries. Boundaries, or fractures, involve greater leaps or more abrupt shifts (of topic or activity) than between contributions within coherent stretches. Yet, across these discontinuities, there are usually some coherence mechanisms bridging adjacent segments, thus impeding new episodes from appearing entirely "out of the blue".

Criteria that can be used for assigning an episode boundary, and the beginning of a new (RC) episode, include:

a. a new episode is, at least to some extent, about new referents in new constellations and situations; hence episode-internal cohesive devices (e.g., certain pronouns) are usually not used over boundaries;[11]

b. conversationalists often form a new participation structure in the new episode (note also that a conversation can develop into several parallel episodes with separate floors; Edelsky 1981; Parker 1984) (see also sect. 8 below);

c. the prior episode has faded out,[12] and the new episode often starts at a different prosodic level (in terms of intonation, loudness, speech rate etc.);

d. the new episode is initiated by means of a reference to an item from a new contextual domain (cf. the contextual resources above).

In Korolija and Linell (1996), we describe a coding system (Topical Episode Analysis; TEA) for episodes in conversation, especially multi-party conversation. In this paper, we shall not go through the merits and drawbacks of this coding system, let alone of coding systems for conversation in general. We shall, however, account for the eight categories posited in TEA, and use some examples to demonstrate how participants deploy various contextual resources for episode initiation.

In applying TEA, the analyst should work with the tape-recorded spoken interaction, as well as the transcript of this, in order to find episode boundaries and to assign categories to the episodes so identified. This is of course a heuristic, a more or less 'text-based' method, for identifying structures (and, indirectly, processes) in manifest discourse. Coherence in discourse is, for us and many other analysts,[13] something which is brought about in the minds of the human subjects (actors, participants, analysts) in and through their dialogue with each other and with various contexts. That is why even partially 'incoherent' texts can often be heard as coherent in significant ways. We will return to this point later.

TEA looks at what happens when new episodes are initiated. It should be noted that this does not amount to an analysis of the topical content of entire episodes. Givenness and topicality are not the same (Givón 1995:78 *et passim*). In our case, we must distinguish between, on the one hand, resources that are accessible ("given") and used at points where new episodes are initiated, and, on the other hand, topics as subjects of continued, sustained salience or importance. It is a contingent matter if topics to be sustained throughout major parts of episodes are signaled effectively, and exploited as coherence-building resources, already in the episode initiations. We will not deal specifically with episode-internal coherence here.

In dialogue, an episode must involve the contributions of more than one speaker, just as it takes more than one to establish a topic. One may therefore want to require a certain minimal size, for something to qualify as an episode. We have, for the purposes of TEA, chosen to define an episode as consisting of at least *three turns, at least two of which must be substantial turns by different speakers.*[14]

6.   Categories of episodes in conversation

Our eight TEA categories are the following:

RC: Re-contextualization of an element from the prior episode:
Some aspect or element in the immediately prior episode (typically occurring towards the end of that episode) is taken as a starting point for a new episode, in which the element is placed within a new context space.[15] There are two main types of RC:

a.   re-contextualization via an association to a fact, a concept or a referent mentioned (but peripheral) in the prior episode (*topically tangential or peripheral link*)

b.   re-contextualization via a meta-comment on the form or meaning of some expression in the prior episode, etc. (*meta-link*).

The first type (RC:a) is exemplified in example 2. It is taken from a family gathering at Midsummer's eve. Present are Eva, 36, who suffers from a global aphasia, her husband Ulf, 40, the researcher Bengt, 45, and Eva's parents Arnold and Nora, both about 65, who are the hosts. The ongoing episode was triggered by a question from Arnold, "Why don't birds fall out of their nests?", something which he apparently just had read on the backside of a milk carton. Ulf, who has been the main speaker in this episode, has given Arnold the explanation or answer. In U:1 he tells Arnold that he himself has read the same text. The topically tangential re-contextualization, however, does not concern birds but bats, which are claimed to be sleeping while hanging upside down. In U:16, Ulf makes a peripheral association to bats and begins to tell the others about a particular incident when Eva was attacked by bats; a new (RC) episode unfolds.

(2)   (TEMA K: H204:234)

	((från en pågående episod))
U:1	ja har *också* läst paketet du
	((samtliga skrattar tyst))
E:2	mm
B:3	de va därför du visste de
N:4	ja visst annars visste du inte
A:5	((skrattar till))
U:6	näe ja har nog själv haft (.) mina funderingar på de
A:7	((skrattar))
B:8	ja har nog aldrig sett nån fågel hänga upp å ner å sova. har du?
U:9	näe de har ja inte gjort (.) men en *mus* (.) har ja sett
N:10	fladdermus, ja
U:11	ja:
B:12	=ja fladdermöss, ja
N:13	mm
	(2s)
U:14	de finns här också gott om
B:15	mm
	RC**************************************
U:16	kommer du ihåg den där gången vi skulle åka å överraska (.) Ilse? å henn– när dom bodde ute i stuga där nere i stugan?
E:17	ja:
U:18	å fladdermössen flög på den vita tröjan?
E:19	ja
U:20	de va otäckt
E:21	=mm
U:22	då va du rädd
E:23	mm

U:24   =mm. ⟩⟩dom slog bara ner⟨⟨ °houup° de va så vitt
A:25   ja ä de vitt så gör di dä
        ((episoden fortsätter))

        ((from an ongoing episode))
U:1   you see I have *also* read the parcel
        ((all laugh quietly))
E:2   mm
B:3   that's why you knew it
N:4   yes of course otherwise you wouldn't know
A:5   ((gives a laugh))
U:6   no I guess I have had (.) my reflections on it
A:7   ((laughs))
B:8   I don't think I have ever seen a bird sleep while hanging
        upside down. (.) have you?
U:9   no I haven't (.) but a *mouse* (.) I have
N:10   bat, yes ((note: Swedish for 'bat', fladdermus, is literally
        'fluttering mouse'))
U:11   ye:s
B:12   =yes bats, of course
N:13   mm
        (2s)
U:14   there are lots of those around here
B:15   mm
        RC**
U:16   do you remember that time when we were supposed to go
        and surprise (.) Ilse? an' her– when they stayed in the cot-
        tage down there in the cottage?
E:17   ye:s
U:18   and the bats flew against the white sweater?
E:19   yes
U:20   that was horrid
E:21   =mm
U:22   you were scared then
E:23   mm
U:24   =mm ⟩⟩ they just swooped down⟨⟨ °houup° there was such
        white
A:25   yes if there's white they'll do that
        ((the episode continues))

The meta-linguistic type (RC:b) is exemplified in example 3, which stems from a long-running Swedish radio show, where four more or less permanent participants gather to discuss recent trends in fashion and society. G has been the current main speaker, and in G:1 he is about to conclude why the letter 's' seems to have become fashionable, permeating a lot of recent Swedish film titles. The item or fragment which is re-contextualized here is not a specific referent or a theme but the way in which G pronounces the letter 's'; in H:6 H makes a meta-comment on this. Thus, G's articulation of 's' in the preceding episode gives rise to a new episode. This example illustrates that co-text is constituted not only of content but also of form, the way content is *expressed* (Korolija 1997).

(3)   (Tema K: NKR 6:1131)

((från en pågående episod))

G:1   ja tycker allså de e fullkomlit u– uppenbart att [es] står för
        Sverige för *trygghet* för för att vara *barn* igen
A:2   för *succé*!
G:3   för succé
S:4   mm
G:5   [es] e en bokstav som som helt enkelt e e—
        RC***

H:6   men du hur gör du när du *väser* sådär, du väser lite
S:7   ja tänkte just de, de finns väsljud
H:8   ja:
S:9   =som e hotfulla å de e ju [es]
H:10   ja: men du *väser* ju lite när du säger [es]
A:11   sir väs mhm orm
H:12   e e de för att du vill sätta folk i.. allså få folk i disciplin?
G:13   ⟩ja kan ja kan eftersom ja har gått så länge hos en tal-
        pedagog säga [es] [esh] [es] som ja vill⟨ vid de här laget
        ((episoden fortsätter))

((from an ongoing episode))

G:1   what I mean is that it is completely ob– obvious that [es]
        stands for *Sweden* for *security* for for being a *child* again
A:2   for *success*!
G:3   for success
S:4   mm
G:5   [es] is a letter which which quite simply is is—
        RC***

H:6   but how do you do when you *hiss* like that, you hiss a bit
S:7   I thought that's right, there are hissing sounds
H:8   ye:s
S:9   which are threatening and [es] is one of them
H:10   ye:s but you *hiss* out a bit when you say [es]
A:11   sir hiss mhm snake
H:12   is is it because you want to put people in.. that is get people
       disciplined?
       ((the episode continues))
G:13   )I can I can because I have attended speech therapy for so
       long say [*es*] [esh] [es] any way I please⟨ by now
       ((the episode continues))

AN: Analogous episode to prior episode
Somebody, often another speaker than the main speaker of the prior episode,
initiates a story, an argument, a telling of an experience, or the like, this new
unit being somehow analogous (or parallel) to the (or a) topic in the prior,
adjacent episode. The new AN episode is concerned with a different train of
events or set of circumstances, and is therefore usually about a different set of
referents, than the previous one (cf. 'second stories', another speaker 'telling his
side; Pomerantz 1980). One case would be a new joke told after a first one in a
round of joke tellings. Often the adjacent episodes can be described as having
the same 'point' (cf. Ryave 1978; Sacks 1992, II:249ff.) or as instantiating the
same type of 'speech event'; they are then used to index some kind of super-
topic, often implicit, over and above the series of episodes.

    The AN episode in example 4 is taken from the same encounter as example
2. The episode, initiated in U:12, constitutes the beginning of a story round of
analogous episodes on the topic of 'what you can do with things found at a
dump'. Arnold has just told the other participants about a boat that his youngest
son (who is absent on this occasion) found in a container, repaired and made
seaworthy with the help of another family member. The point in this episode —
and also in the following ones (not cited here) — is that things are often thrown
away with no good reason. Analogous episodes in a row tend to have a cul-
minating narrative point, that is, the story developed in the actual episode tends
to upgrade the assessment or outdo the point in the immediately prior episodes,
even if the narrative theme appears to be the same.

(4)   (TEMA K:H202: 515)

((från en pågående episod))
A:1   å di satte (0.5s) ja de va väl ett hål i botten eller var de va
       nånstans så här stort (2s) så han tog'en på bilen
B:2   mm.
A:3   = å den har han gjort i ordning nu
N:4   han e jättefin han e som en ny båt nu
E:5   (hä, e)
A:6   mm.
N:7   såna grejor utanpå me satt dit ny– nytt allting
E:8   mm
A:9   ja
U:10   ja
N:11   han va så kunnig me allt sine grejer
       AN**
U:12   ja läste om en kille som va faktist ((harklar sig)) miljonär (.)
       han hade inget arbete, han åkte omkring å plockade runt i
       containerna
B:13   mm
U:14   han hade en lastbil så plockade han runt de sen hade han
       auktion på de där
B:15   mm
A:16   här har du mera plugg ((serverar potatis))
U:17   de va en ren *vinst* de han fick in faktist
B:18   javisst, de e klart
N:19   mm.
U:20   å han var förvånad då va va folk slänger
       ((episoden fortsätter))

((from an ongoing episode))
A:1   and they put (0.5s) well I guess there was a hole in the
       bottom or wherever it was this big (2s) so he took it on top
       of his car
B:2   mm.
A:3   =and now he has got it in order
N:4   it is first-rate it's like a new boat now
E:5   (he, e)
A:6   mm.
N:7   even those exterior gadgets put ne– new everything
E:8   mm

A:9   yes
U:10   yes
N:11   he was so clever with all his things
       AN***
U:12   I read about a guy who actually was a ((clears his throat))
       millionaire (.). he had no job, he drove around an' poked
       about in the containers
B:13   mm
U:14   he had a lorry an' so he picked out things, then he sold them
       by auction
B:15   mm
A:16   here's more spuds for you ((serves potatoes))
U:17   he actually got a net *profit* out of that
B:18   yes that's obvious
N:19   mm.
U:20   an' he was surprised to find what people throw away
       ((the episode continues))

RI: Reinitiation (renewal) of or return to a prior, non-adjacent topic in the same discourse
The speaker goes back abruptly to a prior topic that was activated in a non-adjacent part of the preceding discourse. Reinitiations are sometimes cued by return markers like 'but anyway', 'now', 'to return to what we talked about before'.

The re-initiated episode in example 5, again from the same Midsummer celebrations, must be understood in relation to the episodes leading up to it. In the ongoing (dyadic) episode, Ulf is testing his aphasic wife Eva's memory and/or skill at articulating important family dates, civic identification numbers, something which becomes a focused activity in the ongoing interaction. Bengt objects to Ulf's "cross examination" in an intermediate episode (not reproduced here); turns 65–73 constitute the concluding utterances in this episode. In A:74, Arnold, however, re-initiates the issue of number and birth dates, framing the topic in a playful mode. Arnold, who was a rather passive participant in the preceding two episodes here becomes an (active) main addressee; the others, sharing the speakership, come to guess what the final figures in his birth registration number are.

(5)   (TEMA K: H204:470)

```
       ((från en pågående episod))
U:1    är de den tionde?
E:2    =ja
U:3    mm tjugonde mars ((A skrattar tyst))
       va har du för slutsiffrer i ditt födelsenummer?
E:4    eh– dittonhunratjutvå
U:5    näe
E:6    =näe
U:7    nittonhundra
       (4s)
E:8    eh. (k) artonhundra?
U:9    näe nittonhundra
E:10   näe a:h?
       (3s)
U:11   nittonhundra.. va visar ja nu för siffra?
       ((54 turer utelämnade))
N:65   hon visste't direkt då?
B:66   ja just de
U:67   ja hon sa de på en gång. ja Ulf Erik sa hon klart
B:68   =ja
U:69   hja när dom fråga va ja hette
B:70   =mm. (1s)
U:71   mm.
E:72   mm.
U:73   mm. (1s) mm.
       RI*****************************************
A:74   mina slutsiffrer ä rätt bra
U:75   dina?
A:76   ja:
U:77   har du nåra slutsiffrer du? ((skratt))
A:78   ja: ((U skrattar)) (2s) ja:
U:79   mm.
A:80   de årtalet glömmer ja aldrig
       ((N och A skrattar)) °ja de är svårt å komma ihåg°
       ((man fortsätter att gissa sig fram till Arnolds slutsiffror;
       episoden fortsätter))

       ((from an ongoing episode))
U:1    is it the tenth?
```

E:2   *yes*

U:3   mm March the twentieth ((A laughs silently)) what are the
           final figures in your birth registration number?

E:4   eh– dineteenhunredtwentytwo

U:5   no

E:6   =no

U:7   nineteenhundred (4s)

E:8   eh. (k) eighteenhundred?

U:9   <u>no</u> nineteenhundred

E:10   <u>no</u> a:h? (3s)

U:11   nineteenhundred.. which figure am I showing now?
           ((54 turns excluded))

N:65   she knew it directly then?

B:66   yes that's right

U:67   yes she said it immediately. yes Ulf Erik she said clearly

B:68   =yes

U:69   well when they asked her my name

B:70   =mm. (1s)

U:71   mm.

E:72   mm.

U:73   mm. (1s) mm.
           RI**

A:74   my final figures are quite good

U:75   yours?

A:76   ye:s

U:77   so you mean you have some final figures? ((laughs))

A:78   ye:s ((U laughs)) (2s) ye:s

U:79   mm.

A:80   I'll never forget that date ((N and A laugh)) °yes it's difficult
           to remember°
           ((they continue to make guesses about Arnold's final figures;
           the episode continues))

A new episode is often triggered by some 'local matter' (Bergmann 1990),
something in the surrounding speech situation, i.e., the immediate and perceptually accessible environment with its physical spaces, persons, objects, artifacts,
extra-discursive events etc. Such matters are, by definition, given in the concrete
situation, but have not been topicalized in the immediately prior discourse space.
When they do become thematized, we get cases of what Bergmann (1990) terms
local sensitivity. We distinguish here between two major cases, *SE* and *SO*.

SE: Reference to an event taking place in the situation

The new episode is triggered by some event, usually one occurring immediately before the utterance topicalizing it. The event involved attracts the attention of one, or, more typically, several (or all) actors, which makes it easy for anyone of them to comment on the event without much ado.

Episodes initiated out of sensitivity to events (SE) are typical of interactions with small children or interactions where the participants move around freely in the surrounding milieu. The excerpt below is taken from a multi-party conversation which is characterized by frequent fractures due to the child present, Anita, about four years old. Anita is together with her mother Vivan and her aunt Ulla, both around 30, visiting Anita's grandparents Tora (53, who has aphasic symptoms) and Nils, 60, one spring afternoon. Vivan and Tora are in turns V:1 to V:3 involved in a dyadic exchange, when Tora in T:5 sees that Anita has got hold of a pair of plastic nippers which Tora herself uses when she needs to pick up things from the floor. What Tora objects to, and what also becomes the focus in the episode beginning in T:5, is that Anita uses the nippers not only as a toy but to pinch the other family members.

(6)   (TEMA K: H61:1423)

	((från en pågående episod))
V:1	kan ja göra de nu?
T:2	ja: då (2s)
V:3	fast ni ska äta här sen, mena ja
N:4	°usch ja då°
	SE***
T:5	näej *JOO* ja– titta som ne– *NEJ NEJ* ((till Anita))
V:6	<u>NEJ</u> du de *där* kläms! ((till Anita))
N:7	°hmm°
T:8	((börjar nynna))
V:9	de ä ingen leksak de där
A:10	ja ha:r de–
V:11	ne:j de *ä* de inte!
A:12	(xx ja har xx)
V:13	de ä en sån där mormor har fått *låna* (0.5s) °eller om hon
	har fått den. ja vet inte°
T:14	amen d de–
N:15	du har lånat den, va?
T:16	va?
N:17	har du fått den där klipp– klipparn?
T:18	ja va e. ha haft

N:19   °har du fått den°?
T:20   de vet ja inte om– d– om–
        ((episoden fortsätter))

        ((from an ongoing episode))
V:1   may I do that now?
T:2   ye:s of course (2s)
V:3   even if you're supposed to eat here, I meant
N:4   °ugh yes°
        SE***
T:5   no: YES well– look as no– NO NO ((to Anita))
V:6   NO now listen *that* hurts! ((to Anita))
N:7   °hmm°
T:8   ((begins to hum))
V:9   that's no toy you see
A:10   I ha:ve that–
V:11   no: it *is not*!
A:12   (xx I have xx)
V:13   that's one of those gradma has *borrowed* (0.5s) °or if she
        was given them. I don't know°
T:14   but th– that–
N:15   you have borrowed it, right?
T:16   what?
N:17   have you been given that pair of nippers?
T:18   I was e. ha had
N:19   °were you given them°?
T:20   I don't know if– it– if–
        ((the episode continues))

SO: Reference to an object present in the situation
Here the presence of an object (person, arrangement etc.), which has been there
during (the whole or parts of) the discourse, is used as a resource for talk. In
comparison with SE, this case usually demands more of referential specification
to guarantee a successful introduction.

Sensitivity to object (SO), in the example (7) we have chosen, refers to the
anatomy of one of the participants. Five businessmen, aged 40–55, have
gathered for dinner. They know each other quite well; for seven years they have
had these monthly happenings at which they play tennis, talk about share-
holdings and have fun. They are still seated at the dining room table, when J, in
J:8, suddenly notices C's arms and his remarkably conspicuous blood veins.

Initially, the episode about the veins (between J and C) goes on in parallel with the dyadic continuation (between G and B) of the preceding episode (there is a bifurcated floor), until the new topic eventually becomes the focus of the whole gathering.

(7)   (Gruppsam: Conrad:497)

       ((från en pågående episod))

G:1   ⟩nä men de där me⟨ dåliga (0.8s) dåliga blåbär ⟩ja hörde att du⟨ (1.7s) sa nåt om de ((porslin slamrar)) (1.5s) dålit me blåbär

B:2   ⟩ja ja⟨ de var de uppe i Dalsland i

J:3   ((harklar sig))

G:4   m:

B:5   =vart fall °va°

G:6   de har de varit här me (0.7s) *otrolit* dålit (0.9s) men sen blev de

V:7   °mm°

       SO***

J:8   de va ena *jädra* ådror du har på armarna du (0.7s) de har ja aldrig sett förut

G:9   sen blev de lite *senare* Bosse (1s) efter eh (.)

C:10   ((skrattar till))

G:11   =regnen (1.1s) (i slutet på juli augusti) °så°

C:12   nä de (0.8s) är inte så svårt att hitta dom vet du

B:13   kom ju då (xx)

G:14   senare så blev de plötslit en eh en

J:15   nä:

G:16   =del bär (0.6s) när man trodde att de va f– kört

C:17   de e illa om man *skär* sej °⟩i å för sej⟨° (0.7s) ⟩men de e inte så f– så stor fart ⟨ på

B:18   °ja ja°

J:19   ⟩va kommer de sej⟨ att dom ligger så ytlit då? (2.7s) ((bestick skrapar))

C:20   ja: de ingick i de de (0.6s) ((harklar sig)) extra extra start-paket som ja hade när ja föddes

J:21   ((skrattar))

       ((samtliga fokuserar nu C; episoden fortsätter))

G:1   ((from an ongoing episode))

G:1   ⟩no but this about⟨ bad (0.8s) bad blueberries ⟩I heard that
    you⟨ (1.7s) said something about that ((the crockery clatters))
    (1.5s) we're short <u>of blueberries</u>

B:2   ⟩yes yes⟨ that was up in Dals<u>land in</u>

J:3   ((<u>clears his throat</u>))

G:4   <u>m</u>:

B:5   =in any case °right°

G:6   it's been about the same here (0.7s) *unbelievably* bad (0.9s)
    but then it got

V:7   °mm°

    SO**

J:8   I'll be *damned* if I ever saw such veins as those you have on
    your arms (0.7s) <u>I have never noticed that before</u>

G:9   <u>then we got some *later*, Bosse</u> (1s) after eh (.)

C:10   ((gives a laugh))

G:11   =the rain (1.1s) (by the end of July August) °so°

C:12   <u>no it's (0.8s) not so</u> hard to locate them you know

B:13   <u>it came then (xx)</u>

G:14   later <u>there</u> suddenly turned out to be some eh some

J:15   <u>no</u>:

G:16   some berries (0.6s) when one thought it was d– over and
    done with

C:17   it's bad if you *cut* yourself °⟩for that matter⟨° (0.7s) ⟩but it's
    not so d– <u>full speed</u>⟨ on

B:18   °<u>yeah yeah</u>°

J:19   ⟩how come⟨ that they lie so superficially then? (2.7s)
    ((cutlery scrapes))

C:20   we:ll it was included in the the (0.6s) ((clears his throat))
    extra extra start package that I had when I was born

J:21   ((laughs))

    ((all participants now focus on C; the episode continues))

*AG: Reference to (some aspect of) the abstract activity type: taking up a predefin-
ed, agenda-bound topic or subactivity*

AG covers all those cases in which somebody, drawing upon knowledge of the
purpose of the encounter or activity type, and the tasks involved, takes up some
point on the agenda assumed to be known in advance. Here belong all the cases
in institutional, task-oriented discourse, where participants know before-hand
what will or can be brought up and where such topics can therefore be nomi-

nated or elicited without further ado.

The next example is drawn from a criminal court trial on a case of shoplifting. The prosecuting attorney (P) is just closing his interview with the defendant (D) whereupon the judge J, in J:4, directly introduces a new topic (and trial phase), namely D's personal record.

(8)   (TEMA K: A14:16)

((från en pågående episod:))

P:1   men de anser du att du har inte gjort de för du hade inte avsikt å (D: nä) å gå igenom kassan utan att betala för varorna

D:2   aldri.. de hade ja inte.

P:3   ja tack.

AG***

J:4   ja, här finns ett personbevis beträffande dej, Lisa, som visar att du e skriven i Askby, du e gift, förekommer inte i kriminalregistret, å du e hemmafru å din man e upptagen till ungefär hundra tusen kronor, din mans inkomst– –

D:5   ja, de e väl något mer

J:6   å bostadsbidrag. å tre barn har du hemma.

((from an ongoing episode))

P:1   but then you claim that you haven't done it 'cause you had no intention to (D: no) pass the cash-point without paying for the goods

D:2   never. I didn't.

P:3   OK. thanks

AG**

J:4   well, here is a personal identity document concerning you, Lisa, that shows that you are registered in Askby, you're married, doesn't appear in the criminal records an' you're a housewife an' your husband is registered for about a hundred thousand kronor, your husband's income– –

D:5   well, it's a bit more

J:6   an' a housing allowance. an' you have three children at home

Certain activity types in private situations also involve subactivities which are partly routinized and usually performed by a certain role incumbent, e.g., the host giving a welcoming toast, a dinner guest giving a speech of thanks, etc. These cases belong to AG too. Also, we can classify encounter openings (greetings, how are you's etc.) and closings (leavetaking, farewells) here.

As an example of an agenda-bound episode in an informal setting we have chosen a toasting event. G, who is the host in the businessmen's dinner (cf. example 7), takes the opportunity to welcome his friends in G:4. AG episodes in non-professional interactions rarely disturb the interaction, that is, they are more or less expected to break into the ongoing conversational activities.

(9)   (Gruppsam: Conrad:1300)

    ((från en pågående episod))
B:1   de: kommer han ju kunna göra bra affärer på om han lyckas
        me de
G:2   ((harklar sig)) hm: (0.8s) °otrolit°
B:3   °visst°
        AG**
G:4   *nu* skulle man kunna säga skål och (0.5s) °välkomna° (0.7s)
B:5   tack
L:6   skål
G:7   hoppas de smakar bra
V:8   mm (1s)
J:9   skål
        ((episoden fortsätter))

    ((from an ongoing episode))
B:1   on tha:t he will be able to make some good deals if he is
        successful with it
G:2   ((clears his throat)) hm: (0.8s) °incredible°
B:3   °sure°
        AG**
G:4   *now* one could say cheers and (0.5s) °welcome°
        (0.7s)
B:5   thank you
L:6   cheers
G:7   I hope it'll taste good
V:8   mm (1s)
J:9   cheers
        ((the episode continues))

BA: Invoking other topics which are situationally near at hand (belonging to situationally activated background assumptions)
The next general category is in several ways difficult. It involves a number of

topic initiations that share the property of being somehow near at hand in the situation given. When such topics are invoked, the initiations usually do not appear to be entirely out of the blue (as opposed to UA below). What is taken as given in BA (making this category somewhat akin to AG) is inherent in the *social* situation as such, but the situation is considered as a token rather than as a type; BA exploits background knowledge about the specific persons, place and time, i.e., assumptions about the 'deictic centre' of the situation (the persons etc. indexed by 'I', 'you', 'here', 'now'). There are several mutually related sub-categories of BA, including (a) commenting on the social situation in general (e.g., the fact that people are there together), (b) exploring each other's relevant biographies, (c) invoking items from a common biography, and (d) invoking topics about absent members' activities.

That certain topics are near at hand, or inherent in the social situation, and 'not out of the blue' (other than perhaps for an analyst) is illustrated by example 10, which belongs to the same multi-party conversation as example 6. We meet the participants when Vivan, in V:1, summarizes what had to be done when her automatic fire alarm abruptly started to ring time after time. This episode has just petered out, when Ulla, in U:5, begins to tell the other ones about Isabelle, her teen-age stepdaughter, i.e., an absent family member; that is, Ulla invokes an item from their common biography (BA: c). Isabelle has not been mentioned earlier in the co-text.

    (10)   (TEMA K:H61:1247)

	((från en pågående episod))
V:1	=vi fick ta ut batteriet på brandvarnarn– för de va världens liv i den där
T:2	jaha – –
N:3	°aha°
	(4s)
T:4	hm 'hm... ((nynnar)) (6s)
	BA**************************************
U:5	Isabelle kom hem ti mej ida å ville ha frukost sådär vid halv elva nå'n gång.. när ja lå å sov (xx)
T:6	ja ((suckar))
N:7	°Isabelle°?
V:8	så sent
U:9	° ja sen ville 'on sova hos mej då (xx xx)°
V:10	va då (sova hos dej)
T:11	((gäspande)) räcker de då? (2s) kom ka on komma– e v– finns– fin– fick de vara dä?

U:12   klockan halv elva, ja låg å sov, va e de *nu*, tänkte ja
        ((skratt))
        ((episoden fortsätter))

        ((from an ongoing episode))
V:1   we had to take the battery out of the automatic fire alarm–
        because it made a hell of a sound
T:2   I see – –
N:3   °aha°
        (4s)
T:4   hm hm... ((humming)) (6s)
        BA**
U:5   Isabelle came to my place today an' asked for breakfast at
        about half past ten, around then.. when I was asleep (xx)
T:6   yes ((sighs))
N:7   °Isabelle°?
V:8   that late
U:9   °yes then she wanted to get some sleep at my place (xx xx)°
V:10   what do you mean (sleep at your place)
T:11   ((yawns)) is that enough then? (2s) came ca she come eh v–
        is– is– could it be that?
U:12   at half past ten, I was asleep, what *now*, I thought
        ((laughter))
        ((the episode continues))

UA: Contextually unanchored episodes
This is the case when somebody brings up a topic 'out of the blue', without any
grounding in prior discourse (RC, AN, RI), local matters (SO, SE) or such
abstract background knowledge which is situationally relevant and intersubjectively available (AG, BA). Instead, there seems to be some non-transparent
association or mental leap behind it. It therefore appears to be completely new,
and, in some cases at least, unmotivated even from the point of view of the
speaker's interlocutors. Note that the speaker himself presumably sees some
connection with, or is triggered by, something in the contexts, but the defining
characteristic is that the speaker and/or the others do not take anything like this
for granted, but must take pains to establish the new topic from scratch.
Therefore, prototypical UA episodes are either marked by the speaker as locally
unmotivated (e.g., by the use of a 'discontinuity marker', either a general one,
such as "by the way", "incidentally", "that reminds me of", (which may occur
also with RC, AN, BA) or a marker more limited to UA such as "before I

forget", "if I may change the subject", etc.), or are marked by the addressee (or other interlocutors) as not (initially) understood as situationally relevant (through questions ("why do you bring that up?") and other means).[16]

The unanchored episode below, beginning in E:7, is taken from a ladies' dinner. Five female academics, aged 28–56, gather a couple of times a year to dine, besides seeing each other daily at work. On this occasion, E, the hostess, all of a sudden comes to think of some photographs from a memorable event, and she wants to show the photos to the other ones who were co-present at the time (E:7). The group has earlier, up to A:6, discussed plants and various aspects of gardening, and E's initiative in E:7 abruptly demands a re-orientation of focus. Note that E:7 is prefaced with "hey" (Sw. oh), a marker which indicates that something has suddenly come to her mind. The others' weak uptake (C:8, B:9) may be heard as uncertainty of what it is all about, and E goes on to elaborate on her new topic (E:10):

(11) (Gruppsam: Eva:1879)

          ((från en pågående episod))
B:1   va de den vi hade me oss? ((om en blomma))
C:2   ja
V:3   ja
C:4   =den va så *läcker* tycker ja
E:5   ja ⟩de va den⟨
A:6   den drack *jätte*mycke ⟩mesamma den kom till lan– hit till stan⟨
          UA**************************************
E:7   oh ⟩ja måste komma ihåg⟨ ja ha– har foton (0.6s)
C:8   hm
B:9   °hm°
E:10   = på den där *gossen* Bettan å Asta ska få—
C:11   =han me den bil–
B:12   =ne::j den lille söte
E:13   hja honom me bilen jag undrade va de *va* ⟩för nåt konstit ja sa⟨ (1.6s) ((skratt)) dom måste ha gjort fel (va)? rullen å *så* va? (0.8s)
          ((E fortsätter att berätta om framkallningen av fotografierna))

          ((from an ongoing episode))
B:1   was that the one we brought with us? ((about a plant))
C:2   yes
V:3   yes

C:4   =I thought it was so *exquisite*

E:5   yes ⟩it was⟨

A:6   it drank *extremely* much ⟩right away when it came to the count– here to the town⟨
        UA**************************************

E:7   hey ⟩I <u>must</u> remember⟨ I ha– have photos (0.6s)

C:8   <u>hm</u>

B:9   °<u>hm</u>°

E:10   =<u>of</u> that lad Bettan and Asta will get—

C:11   =the one with the car–

B:12   =no: <u>that</u> little cute one

E:13   <u>well</u> the one with the car I wondered what it *was* ⟩sort of strange things I said⟨ (1.6s) ((laughs)) they must have been mistaken (right)? the roll of film and *so on* right? (0.8s)
        ((E continues to tell about the development of the roll of film))

Note that even in UA, some participants (or at least speakers) may possess the resources to (tacitly) frame or contextualize contributions, i.e., to make them understandable in situ and thus construe them as coherently used in context, but analysts may lack such knowledge (which is often parties' biographical knowledge). The rule of thumb for the coder is, however, to try to take *the interlocutor's* (rather than the speaker's) *perspective* and look at his/her uptake. (In addition, we of course attend to the speaker's discontinuity markers, cf. above.)

The different categories that can be used as contextual resources in the initiation of new episodes, constitute a consistent system. Indeed, they can be roughly ordered in a hierarchy as follows:

- RC, AN and RI are discursively (co-textually) anchored; in RI the topic may be said to be given in the co-text, although not in the immediately prior stretch of discourse, whereas in RC and AN, some aspects (elements, precursors, seeds) of the new topics are somehow identifiable in the prior episode.
- SO and SE are cases where the topic is situationally evoked (motivated) but not co-textually anchored.[17]
- AG and BA involve references to referents or topical aspects which are anchored in, known to be part of, some kind of (supposedly) shared background knowledge, either the (abstract) situation definition (frame of the communicative activity) (AG) or the participants' own personal biographies (BA).
- UA comprises cases where the topic is treated as not given in any of the above-mentioned senses, i.e., it is intersubjectively unanchored.

AG, BA and UA are all, in one way or another, initiated 'out of the blue',[18] neither co-textually bound nor (deictically) anchored in the concrete situation, i.e., we deal with talk about absent referents or abstract aspects, introduced without premonition (grounding) in the prior co-text. However, these are matters of degree; least 'out of the blue' are agenda- or activity-defined topics (AG), whereas UA represents the other pole. There are also cases in between (BA). These considerations may motivate collapsing the categories into fewer super-ordinate categories. Such a collapsed system may include:

- T (= (locally) co-*t*extually anchored initiations) = (RC, AN)
- R (= *r*einitiation of same topic) = (RI)
- S (= *s*ituationally evoked initiations) = (SO, SE)
- O (= *o*ther abrupt, more *o*ut-of-the-blue, initiations) = (AG, BA, UA)

An analysis of episodes may involve several subtasks, focussing on episode initiation types, participation frameworks etc. This is, however, not the place for going through applications possible and results achieved with TEA.[19] Rather, we have used the categories and examples to demonstrate the general mechanisms and resources that speakers seem to deploy, when they create episodes in multi-party conversation. Such an analysis shows that contextual resources are of crucial importance. As Goodwin (1995:131) puts it, "context" is "the phenomenal environment that provides for the ongoing intelligibility of talk, action and situation". It is when participants are about to initiate new episodes (and thereby new topics) that they actualize contexts the most.[20] This applies in particular to the kinds of contexts underlying the taxonomy proposed, i.e., prior co-text, concrete situation, and (certain kinds of) background knowledge. (When contexts are used inside episodes, it appears to be mostly a question of *local* co-text and the (discourse-in-context) models of current topics (§ 4: IIa).)

7. Topical episodes as islands of temporarily shared understanding

In the flow of discourse and thought, people focus on limited chunks of information at each moment (Chafe 1979, 1994). At the same time, consciousness is in constant motion. Chafe (1994) opens his book on these issues by a quote from William James: "As we take, in fact, a general view of the wonderful stream of our consciousness, what strikes us first is this different pace of its parts. Like a bird's life, it seems to be made of an alternation of flights and perchings" (James 1890, 1:243; Chafe, *op. cit.*: 3). This observation holds true at the local level of sentence-sized utterances, but also at the level of episodes in conversation.

In joint discourse, actors focus attention and interpretive efforts on a few aspects of the world. If humans (and animals) did not organize the stream of fragments, glimpses, impressions and associations in some coherent manner, by means of linkages, memory traces, perceptual schemes etc., we would probably not survive in a bewildering environment. In perception and cognition, we construct the world as apprehended by actively organizing it, selecting some features and disregarding others, segmenting the flow of impressions and events. "If we were not able to do such framing, we would be lost in a murk of chaotic experience and probably would not have survived as a species in any case", says Bruner (1990:56). Thus, in our flow of consciousness, streams get *cognitively organized locally*, and so experience comes to us consciously apprehended and cognitively constituted (Schutz 1973). Focusing our attention to only a limited number of aspects, we bring about order in a comprehensible, situated and temporary, micro-world; we build 'islands of understanding'.

When we look at talk-in-interaction, we can study the processes of *collaboratively and (partially) intersubjectively constructed cognition*, what Schutz (1973) called the 'synchronization of two streams of consciousness'. Similarly, Gernsbacher and Givón (1995:viii) describes "coherence" as "emerg[ing] [...] in the two collaborating minds." We can think of the building of topical episodes and the construction of a coherent text and an associated topical space as starting from a fragment and then building around and beyond this an *island of temporarily shared understanding*.

Discourse involves building and using fragments of understanding and contexts. Our realities are only partially shared and fragmentarily known. As interlocutors in dialogue, we are "struggling to establish temporary dyadic states of intersubjectivity in a contextually understood and only partially shared world" (Rommetveit 1988:18). Hence, most situations are characterized by interlocutors' having partly discrepant understandings of the discourse, its various components (contributions) and relevant contexts. But topics in jointly attended discourse constitute interactants' attempts at achieving intersubjectivity in understanding some particular things that they find themselves talking about.

We have used the metaphor 'island' in this section. Actually, this may underscore the insulation between episodes too much. Our analyses suggest that there are connections and bridges built between episodes, and in particular between episodes and contexts. Perhaps some other spatial metaphor is more appropriate. What language users do as they move into new episodes is like walking from one room to another, between spaces which are partially enclosed and partially connected.

8. Fragmentation in multi-party conversation

Constitutive of the activities involved in conversation is the tension between coherence and fragmentation. In the preceding section, we discussed fragmentation vs. focusing of attention and shared understanding from a cognitive and intersubjective point of view. However, conversation also involves interaction and participation frameworks. In at least multi-party conversations, one can point to the fragmentation of interaction resulting from actors' temporary forming of parallel activities and different floors (Parker 1984; Erickson 1982). In multi-party conversations, there are many sources of fragmentation in interaction and in the resulting intersubjective cognitive processes. In particular, there are reasons to believe that episode structure develops differently under such circumstances, as compared to dyadic interaction or monological soliloquy.

There are episodes both in dyadic talk and in multi-party conversation. However, we may assume that boundaried events like episodes (as opposed to stepwise topic progression) are more clearly borne out in multi-party conversation, which, in comparison with dyads, involves more divergent possibilities of topic and action progression. For example, multi-party constellations increase the differentiation among actors in access to topics and knowledge (Drew 1991), and facilitate interventions by actors who have been temporarily disattentive, or simply off the floor. There may be several parties actively contributing to developing topics, rather than, as in many interviews, two people creating question–answer sequences with one party in control of topics and the other party responding to his or her questions. Among factors contributing to the multiplication of abrupt topic shifts in conversation, we might expect the following:

- familiarity among participants in unrestrained, spontaneous interaction;
- no pre-defined tasks or agenda (but still some demand for talk, i.e., an "open state of talk"; Goffman 1983);
- no ban on local sensitivity (the more informal the situation is, the more probable are references to things in the concrete environment);
- people's movements in physical space (which tend to disrupt discourse, relative to e.g., the interaction in a group of people seated at a table);
- limited conversational skills of some participants (e.g., children, aphasics, foreign language speakers).

Returning to our TEA categories, results suggest a typology of conversational activities with regard to coherence, as defined by the different prevalences of episode initiation types. We could, for example, think of three types, characterized by over-representation of (i) deictic references to the concrete situation (SE, SO), (ii) co-textual coherence (few episode boundaries, many RC and AN), and (iii) global control (often an implicit or explicit agenda) (AG), respectively. The two last-mentioned types fit normative demands for "staying on topic". While (iii) is typical of many genres of institutional discourse, (ii) is what skilful conversationalists are often normatively expected to accomplish ("the art of conversation"). The many concrete-situational dependencies of (i), on the other hand, is typical of talk supporting manual work, and situations characterized by an "open state of talk". In addition, this pattern seems to appear in many conversations with small children, and perhaps conversations with people with communicative disabilities (Linell and Korolija 1995). It is reasonable to suppose that the mental efforts needed to retrieve referential sources and to sustain focused attention are lower in this kind of talk exchanges.

9. Concluding remarks: Coherence inside, between and across episodes

We have argued that episodes constitute the most appropriate level to start from, if we want to do topic progression analysis, at least in informal multi-party conversations. Yet, there are other kinds of topical structure than episodes. Some researchers have proposed a multi-level hierarchical structure (e.g., Gee 1991, cf. also Chafe 1979). While Gee's system, designed for narrative analysis, seems to be too hierarchical to be of general validity, we must recognize some other levels of topical structure. Although this matter must be properly researched, we suggest the following:

–   *intra-episodic movements*: e.g., topic drift and topical redirections (small topical leaps to new aspects, which may be regarded as boundaries between sub-episodes, akin to Gee's 'stanzas' and Reichman's (1978) 'context spaces');
–   *supra-episodic structures*: series of topical episodes making up a macro-topic or super-topic (Chafe 1994: 137);
–   *trans-episodic themes*; narrative or topical themes[21] (discourse threads) can become leitmotifs repeated or developed in and through several episodes or stories (cf. story sessions, story rounds); such a theme can also function locally as a resource for episode initiation (link over to new RC or AN episodes; recontextualized aspect vs. basis of analogy, respectively).

There are, in other words, several strands of coherence in discourse and conversation (Givón 1995).

Topic progression and coherence have been extensively dealt with in the literature. However, few researchers have, like us, been concerned with coherence at a middle-range level, rather than at a local level of single utterances, turns or speech acts. In addition, we have treated coherence in multi-party conversation, especially topically fairly unconstrained ones, rather than coherence in well-edited written texts or discourse in institutional contexts or with pre-determined topics. There are reasons to believe that local and global coherence takes different forms in informal multi-party conversations, than in well-edited texts; we are concerned with what Givón (1995:363) calls "flexible, opportunistic, negotiated aspects of coherence". Naturally, there are many analyses of topics and episodes in multi-party conversation before (Tannen 1984; Bublitz 1988; Watts 1989; Erickson 1990, to mention just a few), but there are very few attempts at developing explicit models of episode structure. Finally, we have argued for a theory of contextual resources as an integrated part of the theory of topic progression and coherence between episodes. We, in fact, assign a crucial role to contexts and contextual resources; they provide the links of coherence, when the textual flow of discourse is fractured as a result of conversationalists' moves to introduce new topics and activities into their ongoing interaction.

Our analysis also deals with topic progression in conjunction with participation framework, thereby highlighting the point that topics can only be initiated, sustained and closed through the organization of sequences of discursive actions (Schegloff 1990). Inside episodes, turns are used to support progression in a more or less stepwise manner from something given to what is, at each moment, new. Such developments ("topic glides") can therefore not be classified as distinct topic shifts, nor, a fortiori, as transitions between episodes. It is the more or less abrupt or disjunctive shifts, those which, by definition, form episode boundaries, that we have described in this paper. Such shifts have often been called 'noncoherent' (Crow 1983) or 'total' (Reichman 1978). Our analysis shows that fractures in talk-in-interaction do not imply total incoherence. On the contrary, speakers and their interlocutors take measures, deploy contextual resources and cue their 'topical shifts' in various ways, in order to secure some kind of coherence across boundaries. This of course still leaves some vexing questions open: What is "real" incoherence like in discourse and interaction? Or do our minds always build coherence, even when we are faced with what *seems* textually totally incoherent?

Notes

1. Dumesnil and Dorval (1989) distinguish between six levels of analysis for discourse: speech occasion, speech event, talk activity, episode, sequence, speech act. 'Episodes' appear at a 'meso-level' between phases of speech events and local sequences. Our units of Topical Episode Analysis (see Korolija and Linell 1996, and below) are in general slightly bigger than Dumesnil and Dorval's 'episodes', which, like Reichman's (1978) 'context spaces', correspond to what we would regard as 'subepisodes'.

2. Many researchers have explored notions of local vs. global coherence, e.g., McLaughlin (1984: 36ff.), Craig and Tracy (1983), Hobbs and Agar (1985), Givón (1995:362, 385).

3. Examples are given first in their (spoken) Swedish originals and then in rough English translations. The Swedish data are available at Department of Communication Studies, Linköping University. For access to data from the data corpus Gruppsam, we thank Kerstin Nordenstam, University of Göteborg.

    Transcription conventions: *italics* denote emphatic stress; <u>underlinings</u> simultaneous talk or other activities; (1s) a timed pause in seconds; (.) a micro-pause; (xxx) undecipherable speech; = means that the following utterance is latched on to the previous one without any intervening silence whatsoever; – – means that current speaker is interrupted (or suddenly stops speaking). ° ° denotes speech in a low volume; * * indicates that the words enclosed are spoken with laughter in the voice; ⟩ ⟨ indicates that the words enclosed are spoken at a faster speech rate. A line like: AG*************** marks an episode boundary as assigned by the analyst (here a boundary preceding an episode of type AG, see below).

4. Cf. in this context the notion of 'communicative dynamism' of Prague school text linguistics (Firbas 1971).

5. We work with a notion of 'topic' defined at a 'middle-range' level of discourse structure (Givón 1983), rather than at a sentence/utterance level (cf. Ochs Keenan and Schieffelin 1976). Accordingly, we will also discuss given-new distinctions at the level of episodes. In the literature, hierarchies of 'givenness', 'familiarity', or 'accessibility' have concerned smaller units than episodes, i.e., utterances or sentences, and have been used to explain regularities in the use of different sorts of referring expressions (Prince 1981; Clark and Marshall 1982; Hawkins 1978; Givón 1983; Ariel 1988; Gundel *et al.* 1993). For example, Ariel (op. cit.) notes various regularities between the grammatical forms of referring expressions and the assumed accessibility of the corresponding referents in the hearer's mind. If a referent is presented as entirely new, it is usually introduced through a full indefinite noun (phrase); full nominal expressions (definite descriptions) and proper names are therefore 'low accessibility markers'. Conversely, demonstrative expressions (*this X, that Y* etc) mark 'mid accessibility', and pronouns and gaps are used for 'high accessibility'. A referent is treated as given or new, familiar or unfamiliar, easily accessible or less accessible etc., depending on its cognitive status, on its assumed accessibility in the listener's consciousness, on whether it has been mentioned in the local co-text, whether it is perceptually accessible in the situation, whether it belongs to background knowledge which is contextually activated, or whether it is assumed to be brand new for the recipient. Chafe (1994) discusses most of these theories and shows that several dimensions are involved. He also argues that the given/accessible/new hierarchy be construed in terms of degrees of activation cost.

6. An analysis of the stream of social behavior in terms of 'episodes' was proposed already by Watson and Potter (1962) (and applied by them to conversation). An influential work is Harré

and Secord (1972), whose notion was later used by, among others, Hare and Blumberg (1988). Other researchers use the term 'episode' in slightly different ways. van Dijk and Kintsch (1983) seem to be influenced by the theory of episodic memory. Chafe (1979) proposes units such as episode/paragraph and larger memories/stories (where 'memory' and 'episode' are cognitive units, and 'story' and 'paragraph' the corresponding "verbalized" units of expression.). For van Dijk (1982) too, episodes are semantic, rather than interactional, units.

Crow (1983) uses the term 'conversational episode' in his analysis of topic progression in couples' conversation. The concept also appears in the hierarchy proposed by Dumesnil and Dorval (1989) (cf. fn. 1).

7. Such a 'model' is usually described as a structured set of implied, presupposed and/or communicated propositions about the 'discourse-world'. The term 'model' has a clearly cognitivist ring (cf. Johnson-Laird 1983), but similar concepts have been proposed by scholars of divergent persuasions. Accordingly, there are many terminological (and conceptual) proposals here; context spaces (Reichman 1978), focus spaces (Grosz 1977), situation models (van Dijk and Kintsch 1983), mental models (Johnson-Laird, op. cit.), discourse models (Kamp 1984), discourse-world model (Beaugrande and Dressler 1981:194), to mention just a few.

8. A more comprehensive account of contexts and contextual resources can be found in Linell (1995). See also, in particular, Goodwin and Duranti (1992).

9. We have chosen to use 'context(s)' as the more general term, preferring to use 'situation' (and the adjective 'situational') about the surrounding social and physical setting with its concrete (Ib) and abstract (IIc) features. Others may reverse the terminological conventions.

10. Such triplets have a well-established tradition in the literature (e.g., Ochs Keenan and Schieffelin 1976; Clark and Marshall 1982). Clark and Marshall (1982) talk about 'prior conversation', 'joint perceptual experiences', and 'joint membership' (i.e., mutual and shared background knowledge). Cf. also Givón's (1989) partly similar notions of textual, deictic and generic contexts, and Givón's (1995:350) 'episodic model of the current text', 'model of the current speech-situation', and 'model of permanent generic-lexical knowledge'.

11. See e.g., Givón (1995). Cf. also Reichman's (1978) notion of 'context space'. These units, however, are smaller than our episodes, i.e., we are more conservative in assigning boundaries between units.

12. Episode initiations, at least the abrupt ones, are more basic and salient than episode closings (cf. Ellis *et al.* 1983). Fractures in discourse are thus achieved by the introduction of something new. Episodes are ended, or closed, in either of three basic ways; by explicit closing of a topic (quite frequent in institutional encounters), by fading out (as indicated by pauses, lowered tempo, the use of (sequences of) confirmatory and other topicless utterances), or by (being interrupted by) the initiation of a new episode. For an attempt to classify topic transitions on the basis of (prior) topic closure types, see Ainsworth-Vaughn (1992).

13. E.g., Givón (1995:342, *et passim*); Gernsbacher and Givón (1995).

14. A 'substantial' turn is, by definition, expanded beyond being a minimal response. This means that an episode cannot consist of an isolated turn, nor of only one substantial (but non-monological) turn followed only by a minimal response (or several such responses). (Such short sequences may well represent **attempts** at initiating episodes.) However, if a speaker, in a dyadic or polyadic situation, manages to hold the floor for a long monological turn, this must be regarded as an episode. Under normal conditions, the speaker is then almost certain

to receive some minimal responses or back-channel items from the others, which will make the event jointly constructed also overtly, not only 'virtually' (i.e., simply by being other-oriented).

15. On the concept of (local, discourse-internal) recontextualization, see Linell (1995).

16. UA is also something of a residue category, to be used when there is no strong evidence in favour of any other coding. However, the incidence of UA has been very low in our studies carried out so far.

17. Referents in the new episodes can therefore often be introduced by anaphoric and deictic means in RC+AN+RI and SE+SO, respectively.

18. In a still wider (and therefore uninteresting) sense, all initiations (in which, by definition, you do not stay entirely on the prior topic) may exhibit features of 'out of the blue' introduction.

19. For some discussion and results, see Linell and Korolija (1995) and Korolija and Linell (Forthcoming).

20. The same applies, however, to all the more or less isolated utterances that never develop into episodes. For an example, see A:16 in example 4.

21. Cf. the musical term 'theme'.

References

Adelswärd, V. 1988. *Styles of Success: On impression management as collaborative action in job interviews.* Linköping: Institute of Tema Research (Linköping Studies in Arts and Science, 23).

Ainsworth-Vaughn, N. 1992. "Topic Transitions in Physician–Patient Interviews: Power, gender, and discourse change." *Language in Society* 21.409–426.

Ariel, M. 1988. "Referring and Accessibility." *Journal of Linguistics* 24.65–87.

Atkinson, M. and Heritage, J. (eds). 1984. *Structures of Social Action: Studies in conversation analysis.* Cambridge: Cambridge University Press.

Beaugrande, R. de and W.U. Dressler. 1981. *Introduction to Text Linguistics.* London: Longman.

Bergmann, J. 1990. "On the Local Sensitivity of Conversation." In Marková and Foppa 1990.201–226.

Brown, G. and G. Yule. 1983. *Discourse Analysis.* Cambridge: Cambridge University Press.

Bruner, J. 1990. *Acts of Meaning.* Cambridge, Mass.: Harvard University Press.

Bublitz, W. 1988. *Supportive Fellow-Speakers and Cooperative Conversations.* Amsterdam: John Benjamins.

Button, G. and N. Casey. 1984. "Generating Topic: The use of topic initial elicitors." In Atkinson and Heritage 1984.167–190.

Chafe, W. 1979. "The Flow of Thought and the Flow of Language." In *Discourse and Syntax,* T. Givón (ed.), 159–181. New York: Academic Press (Syntax and Semantics, 12).

Chafe, W. 1994. *Discourse, Consciousness, and Time*. Chicago: The University of Chicago Press.

Clark, H.H. and C.R. Marshall. 1982. "Definite Reference and Mutual Knowledge." In *Elements of Discourse Understanding*, A. Joshi, B. Webber and I. Sag (eds), 10–63. Cambridge: Cambridge University Press.

Clark, H.H. and E.F. Schaefer. 1989. "Contributing to Discourse." *Cognitive Science* 13.259–294.

Craig, R.T. and K. Tracy (eds). 1983. *Conversational Coherence: Form, structure and strategy*. Beverly Hills: Sage.

Crow, B.K. 1983. "Topic Shifts in Couples' Conversation." In Craig and Tracy 1983.116–135.

Dorval, B. (ed.). 1990. *Conversational Organization and its Development*. Norwood, N.J.: Ablex.

Dorval, B. and C. Eckerman. 1984. "Developmental Trends in the Quality of Conversation Achieved by Small Groups of Acquainted Peers." *Monographs of the Society for Research in Child Development*, no. 206.

Drew, P. 1991. "Asymmetries of Knowledge in Conversational Interactions." In *Asymmetries in Dialogue*, I. Marková and K. Foppa (eds), 21–48. Hemel Hempstead: Harvester Wheatsheaf.

Dumesnil, J. and B. Dorval. 1989. "The Development of Talk–Activity Frames that Foster Perspective-focused Talk among Peers." *Discourse Processes* 12.193–225.

Edelsky, C. 1981. "Who's Got the Floor?" *Language in Society* 10.383–421.

Ellis, D.G., M. Hamilton and L. Aho. 1983. "Some Issues in Conversation Coherence." *Human Communication Research* 9.267–282.

Erickson, F. 1990. "The Social Construction of Discourse Coherence in a Family Dinner Table Conversation." In Dorval 1990.207–238.

Firbas, J. 1971. "On the Concept of Communicative Dynamism in the Theory of Functional Sentence Perspective." *Sbornik Praci Filosoficke Fakulty Brnenske University* A 19.135–144.

Foppa, K. 1990. "Topic Progression and Intention." In Marková and Foppa 1990.178–200.

Gee, J.P. 1991. "A Linguistic Approach to Narrative." *Journal of Narrative and Life History* 1.15–39.

Gernsbacher, M.A. and T. Givón (eds). 1995. *Coherence in Spontaneous Text*. Amsterdam: John Benjamins.

Givón, T. 1983. "Introduction." In *Topic Continuity in Discourse: A quantitative cross-language study*, T. Givón (ed.), 1–42. Amsterdam: John Benjamins.

Givón, T. 1989. *Mind, Code and Context*. Hillsdale, N.J.: Lawrence Erlbaum.

Givón, T. 1995. *Functionalism and Grammar*. Amsterdam: John Benjamins.

Goffman, E. 1961. *Encounters: Two studies in the sociology of interaction*. Indianapolis: Bobbs-Merrill.

Goffman, E. 1983. "Felicity's Condition." *American Journal of Sociology* 89.1–53.

Goodwin, C. 1995. "The Negotiation of Coherence within Conversation." In Gernsbacher and Givón 1995.117–137.

Goodwin, C. and A. Duranti. 1992. "Rethinking Context: An introduction." In *Rethinking Context*, A. Duranti and C. Goodwin (eds), 1–42. Cambridge: Cambridge University Press.

Grosz, B. 1977. *The Representation and Use of Focus in Dialogue Understanding*. Technical Note 151, Stanford Research Institute.

Gundel, J.K., N. Hedberg and R. Zacharski. 1993. "Cognitive Status and the Form of Referring Expressions in Discourse." *Language* 69.274–307.

Hare, P.A. and H.H. Blumberg. 1988. *Dramaturgical Analysis of Social Interaction*. New York: Praeger.

Harré, R. and P.F. Secord. 1972. *The Explanation of Social Behaviour*. Oxford: Basil Blackwell.

Hawkins, J. 1978. *Definiteness and Indefiniteness: A study in reference and grammaticality prediction*. London: Croom Helm.

Hobbs, J. 1990. "Topic drift." In Dorval 1990.3–22.

Hobbs, J. and M. Agar. 1985. "The Coherence of Incoherent Discourse." *Journal of Language and Social Psychology* 4.213–232.

James, W. (1890). *The Principles of Psychology*. 2 vols. New York: Henry Holt.

Johnson-Laird, P. 1983. *Mental Models*. Cambridge: Cambridge University Press.

Kamp, H. 1984. "A Theory of Truth and Semantic Representation." In *Formal Methods in the Study of Language*, J. Groenendijk, J. Janssen and M. Stokhof (eds), 1-41. Dordrecht: Foris.

Korolija, N. 1997. "Re-cycling Co-text: The impact of prior conversation on the emergence of episodes." Ms. Linköping: Department of Communication Studies.

Korolija, N. and P. Linell. 1996. "Episodes: Coding and analyzing coherence in multi-party conversation." *Linguistics* 34:799–831.

Labov, W. and D. Fanshel. 1977. *Therapeutic Discourse*. New York: Academic Press.

Levinson, S. 1979. "Activity Types and Language." *Linguistics* 17.365–399. Reprinted in: *Talk at Work*, P. Drew and J. Heritage (eds), 66–100. Cambridge: Cambridge University Press.

Linell, P. 1990. "The Power of Dialogue Dynamics." In Marková and Foppa 1990.147–177.

Linell, P. 1995. "The Dynamics of Contexts in Discourse." In *Form and Function of Language*, S. Millar and J. Mey (eds), 41–67. Odense: Odense University Press (RASK Supplement, Vol. 2).

Linell, P. and N. Korolija. 1995. "On the Division of Communicative Labour within Episodes in Aphasic Discourse." *International Journal of Psycholinguistics* 11.143–165.

Linell, P. and N. Korolija. Forthcoming. "Topical Episode Analysis (TEA): A manual." Ms. Linköping: Dept of Communication Studies.

Marková, I. and K. Foppa (eds). 1990. *The Dynamics of Dialogue*. New York: Harvester Wheatsheaf.

Maynard, D. 1980. "Placement of Topic Changes in Conversation." *Semiotica* 30.263–290.

Maynard, D. and D. Zimmerman. 1984. "Topical Talk, Ritual and Social Organization of Relationships." *Social Psychology Quarterly* 47.301–316.

McLaughlin, M. 1984. *Conversation: How talk is organized.* London: Sage.

Ochs Keenan, E. and B. Schieffelin. 1976. "Topic as a Discourse Notion: A study of topic in the conversations of children and adults." In *Subject and Topic*, C. Li (ed.), 335–384. New York: Academic Press.

Parker, R. 1984. "Conversational Grouping and Fragmentation: A preliminary investigation." *Semiotica* 50.43–68.

Pomerantz, A. 1980. "Telling My Side: 'Limited access' as a 'fishing' device." *Sociological Inquiry* 50.186–198.

Prince, E. 1981. "Toward a Taxonomy of Given–New Information." In *Radical Pragmatics*, P. Cole (ed.), 223–255. New York: Academic Press.

Reichman, R. 1978. "Conversational Coherency." *Cognitive Science* 3.283–327.

Reichman, R. 1990. "Communication and Mutual Engagement." In Dorval 1990.23–48.

Rommetveit, R. 1988. "On Literacy and the Myth of Literal Meaning." In *The Written World*, R. Säljö (ed.), 13–40. Berlin: Springer.

Ryave, A.L. 1978. "On the Achievement of a Series of Stories." In *Studies in the Organization of Conversational Interaction*, J. Schenkein (ed.), 113–132. New York: Academic Press.

Sacks, H. 1992. *Lectures on Conversation*. Vols. 1–2, G. Jefferson (ed.). Cambridge: Basil Blackwell.

Schegloff, E.A. 1990. "On the Organization of Sequences as a Source of 'Coherence' in Talk-in-Interaction." In Dorval 1990.51–77.

Schegloff, E.A. 1996. "Turn Organization: One intersection of grammar and interaction." In *Grammar and Interaction*, E. Ochs, E.A. Schegloff and S. Thompson (eds). Cambridge: Cambridge University Press.

Schegloff, E.A. and H. Sacks. 1973. "Opening up Closings." *Semiotica* 8.289–327.

Schutz, A. 1973. *Collected Papers*. Vol. 1, *The Problem of Social Reality*. The Hague: Martinus Nijhoff.

Simon, H. 1969. *The Sciences of the Artificial*. Cambridge, Mass.: MIT Press.

Tannen, D. 1984. *Conversational Style*. Norwood, N.J.: Ablex.

van Dijk, T. 1982. "Episodes as Units of Discourse Analysis." In *Analyzing Discourse: Text and talk*, D. Tannen (ed.), 177–195. (Georgetown University Round Table on Languages and Linguistics 1981). Washington: Georgetown University Press.

van Dijk, T. and W. Kintsch. 1983. *Strategies of Discourse Comprehension*. New York: Academic Press.

Watson, J. and R.J. Potter. 1962. "An Analytic Unit for the Study of Interaction." *Human Relations* 15.245–264.

Watts, R. 1991. *Power in Family Discourse*. Berlin: Mouton de Gruyter.

Wilkes-Gibbs, D. 1995. "Coherence in Collaboration: Some examples from conversation." In Gernsbacher and Givón 1995.239–267.

Choosing the Right Quantifier

Usage in the Context of Communication

Linda M. Moxey and Anthony J. Sanford
University of Glasgow

1. Introduction

Formal approaches to quantifier meaning have stressed issues of the scope of quantification and the way in which natural language quantifiers fit with mathematical theories such as Generalised Quantifier Theory (Barwise and Cooper 1981). From a formal perspective, quantification concerns the mapping of elements or sets onto other sets. Many kinds of mappings are possible, and from this perspective, there are many possible kinds of quantifiers. Thus, for some formal semanticists at least, natural language quantifiers are a subset of theoretically possible quantifiers, and part of the interest lies in determining what are the restrictions on natural language quantifiers with respect to the possibilities generated by a particular theoretical framework (Barwise and Cooper 1983; Westersthål 1989). We have argued in several other places (e.g., Moxey and Sanford 1993a; Sanford, Moxey and Paterson 1994) that psychological approaches have stressed the role of quantifiers in reasoning, where the quantifiers in question have been restricted to those expressible within first-order predicate calculus, and hence capable of generating interesting results within the context of the syllogism. The other approach has treated the vast bulk of quantifiers (including *many*, *few*, *a lot*, and so on) as though their meanings could be expressed in terms of the proportions or numbers which they denote. This is also true of the treatment of other quantity expressions such as frequency adverbs, and probability terms. The seriousness of the issue is nicely illustrated by recent proposals to devise a restricted language for expressing uncertainty based entirely on the scaling of natural language expressions to quantities (Mosteller and Youtz 1990;

see Clark 1990, for a rebuttal based in part on more linguistic considerations).

The approach which we take here is more plainly functional. We believe that neither the formal logico-linguistic approach, nor the scaling approach can explain why and when we choose the quantifiers we do. While paying attention to these other approaches, we have been engaged in research aimed at tracking down which quantifiers are chosen when in communication. In this paper, some aspects of this research are reported.

We shall complete this introduction by briefly describing the outcome of a study in which subjects have to communicate which of several pictures they have in mind, using quantifiers, so that another person can choose the correct picture. The astonishing finding was the range and number of ways people did this. In section 2 we provide a summary of laboratory-style studies reported in several other places, in which we attempted to uncover various aspects of the effect various quantifiers have on the mental representations of listeners and readers. Section 3 reports some very preliminary observations made on the basis of a corpus of naturally occurring quantifiers, which gives some different support for the idea that quantifiers do not simply denote amounts. In section 4, we give a fuller description of some work on choosing the appropriate quantifier in communication vignettes, where we attempt to test some of our predictions. We end with a discussion of some issues for future investigation.

In order to get a picture of how quantifiers may be used in communication, Moxey (1986) carried out an experiment in which subjects were required to describe each of six sketches in such a way that another person would be able to correctly identify the sketches. Each sketch comprised 100 pin-figures, representing surgeons at a local hospital. The number of male and female surgeons varied in the figures as follows: 90:10, 75:25, 60:40, 40:60, 25:75, 10:90. The male and female surgeons were differentiated stereotypically in the sketches. Subjects were told not to count the figures, nor to use numbers in their communications, but just to use language expressions. Subjects wrote the sentences on each picture. These were coded for choice of quantifier. Later, the experimenter presented the sentences thus produced by each subject to another subject, called the subject's partner. The partner was given the six sketches, and invited to match each description to a sketch, to try to guess which ones the descriptions referred to. This study produced two kinds of data: choice of expression, and efficacy of the choice in terms of the partner's accuracy. Production and interpretation data was obtained from 185 subjects; production data alone was obtained from 223 subjects.

These six sketches, with 223 subjects, led to the production of no less than 182 different descriptions. Of course, some expressions are rare and some are minor variants on others: A summary is given in table 1, in which only combinations which occur more than 5 times are listed. The range of proportions with which they are associated is indicated along with the absolute frequency of occurrence.

Table 1. *Quantifiers occurring 5 or more times in Moxey's 1986 data*

quantifier	preceding words	range denoted	frequency
all	almost	75–90	12
	nearly	75–90	13
	practically	75–90	10
	virtually	90	6
	others		5
any	hardly	10–25	19
few	none	10–25	25
	a	10–25	30
	only a	10–40	29
	only a very	10	6
	quite a	25–75	16
	very	10–25	82
	others		9
handful	others		10
lot(s)	no modifier	40–90	25
	a	25–90	37
	quite a	25–60	11
	others		1
many	no modifier	25–90	29
	others		14
mainly	no modifier	60–90	18
majority	no modifier	60–90	12
	a	60–90	13
	a large	75–90	6
	a slight	60	6
	the	40–90	38
	the vast	75–90	20
	others		28
minority	others		14
most(ly)	no modifier	25–90	70
	others		1
number	no modifier	10–90	12
	a large	60–90	8
	the	10–90	27
	others		87
proportion	other		34
some	no modifier	25–75	18

First there is a richness of modifiers, especially in the case of *all* and *few*. Second, the ranges associated with the expressions are frequently large (e.g., *many* covers 25–90%; Note that this does not include constructions such as *many...are not*). Moxey examined the relationship between the sizes of the ranges associated with expressions and the likelihood that they would lead to a communication error (an incorrect selection on the part of the subjects' partners). This was done where the number of occurrences of an example was 5 or more, and of 659 usable cases, 558 were matches, and 101 were mismatches, i.e. roughly 15% were mismatches. There was a reliable correlation between the size of the range associated with an expression and the likelihood of an communication error occurring. Thus the vagueness of the quantities denoted by expressions influences communicative efficacy, as one might expect.

A further point is that a large number of expressions were used for the same range. From the point of view of the communication task, therefore, these expressions must have been intended to communicate similar amounts. We may then ask why so many expressions are used if they amount to the same thing.

In summary, this preliminary work showed that subjects will recruit many and various ways of communicating a quantity, that the mapping of expressions onto amounts is a many to one mapping, and that the mapping of amounts onto expressions is also a many to one mapping. In an effort to get more closely to grips with these issues, Moxey and her colleagues carried out a number of laboratory studies.

2. Laboratory studies of quantifier function

The major thrust of our research to date has used essentially laboratory tasks rather than the analysis of dialog to investigate the basic properties of quantifiers (see Moxey and Sanford 1993a; Sanford, Moxey and Paterson 1994 for reviews). This research consists of a rebuttal of the idea that quantifier meaning can be represented in terms of the quantities which they denote, and a set of studies showing that they have other major communicative functions.

2.1. *Quantity*

If *A few students failed the exam*, we can ask how many students that is, or what proportion it is. Variants on this question have predominated in experimental psychology approaches to quantifiers. Such an approach makes sense when it is realized that standard questionnaires often use quantifiers and frequency adverbs to save the respondent from having to use numbers. There is considerable variability in the numbers which people assign when invited to do so, and a number of studies demonstrated that some of this variability derives from the context in which the quantifier is used (see Pepper 1981, for a thorough review to that date). A nice anecdote by Parducci (1968) makes the point with respect to frequency adverbs: A student thinking about contraceptive failure would regard 5% of the time as *often*, while missing 5% of lectures might be considered to be *hardly ever*. In general, the higher the baserate expectation, the higher the numbers assigned to the quantifiers, especially to those quantifiers which tend to denote larger amounts (see also Wallsten, Fillenbaum and Cox 1986).

In our own work (Moxey and Sanford 1993b), we asked subjects to indicate what percentage a quantified statement denoted for 10 quantifiers in three contexts, where baserate was manipulated in the contexts. The higher the baserate expectation, the higher the numbers assigned. Our study was unique in that a given subject contributed only **one** reading, so that contrast effects did not influence the results. This is very important, since faced with the choice, everyone would agree that *very few* of something meant less than *few* of something. Such contrast effects in judgements are very well documented in psychology (e.g., Poulton 1973). However, when one group of subjects made a judgement about *few*, and another made a judgement about *very few*, there were no real differences in the numbers they were taken as denoting. From a communicative point of view, we claim that if a person chooses to use *few*, this cannot be taken as denoting a number or proportion any different from *very few*. Many psychological results on scaling quantifiers and related expressions, such as probability terms or frequency adverbs, are obtained with repeated judgements and so cannot be used to make inferences about normal communication.

Like other words whose meanings interact with context (such as *good*), quantifiers pose problems for a simple dictionary definition, and because they are only very fuzzily related to amounts when a proper independent groups procedure is used, Moxey and Sanford (1993a) looked to other determinants of quantifier choice in communicative settings. Natural language quantifiers can convey far more than is conveyed by mere numerical denotation, as the following example illustrates:

Student: 60% of our class have advanced maths qualifications.
Visitor: Is that a lot?

It may be argued that whether something is *a lot* or not depends upon what is expected. When a listener doesn't know what to expect, use of a quantifier may help by setting up a reference point. To substitute *a lot* for 60% in our example is equivalent to saying something like *in my opinion, given what is relevant in the situation, the number in the class with advanced qualifications is high* (Sanford, Moxey and Paterson 1994). To the extent that it is believable that the student is an expert on baserate in this situation, the quantifier is more informative than the number, since it contains an internal reference to baserate expectation.

We are not claiming that *very few* denotes the same quantity as *few*. Clearly, subjects asked to order them from smallest to largest would all place *very few* first on the list and *few* second. Indeed in comparative contexts, it is clear that *very few* is intended to mean a smaller amount than *few*:

Student: Few of the class passed the exam, I hear.

Tutor: Very few.

What we are saying is that even a fine numerical scale of 1–100 does not enable subjects to differentiate between these expressions numerically when not explicitly asked to compare them. However the quantity information denoted by these terms is represented, it cannot be usefully represented on a numerical scale such as the 1–100 percentage scale.

The remainder of this section addresses ways in which quantifiers differ beyond the numbers they denote.

2.2. *Perspectives: Monotonicity and focus*

One of the obvious distinctions amongst quantifiers is that some are negative. This property can be tested for by the licensing of negative polarity items in simple declarative sentences (Ladusaw 1979; Zwarts, In press). For instance, the negative polarity item *anymore* can only be used in negative contexts except for special effects:

(1)   Few people believe that anymore.
         *A few people believe that anymore.

Negative/positive polarity is a major way of dividing up quantifiers in a formal context, within theories such as Generalised Quantifier Theory (Barwise and Cooper 1981). A related division is based on monotonicity. If what is true of one subset of the universe of discourse is also true of another, then the proposition is monotone with respect to those sets. In the case of monotone decreasing expressions, what is true of a superset is true of it's proper subset:

(2)   *IF* Few of the students went to the party *THEN* few of the
         students went to the party early.

To the extent that this is acceptable, few X is monotone decreasing.

In contrast, if what is true of a proper subset is also true of the superset, then the expression is monotone increasing:

(3)   **IF** many of the students went to the party early, **THEN** many of the students went to the party.

Note that the quantifiers in these two example cannot be intersubstituted.

These patterns of allowable inference are fundamental to the formal treatment of negativity.[1] At a level more of interest to those concerned with language as a means of communicating, Moxey and Sanford (1987; Sanford, Moxey and Paterson, In press) have shown that there is what appears to be an important functional difference between monotone increasing and monotone decreasing (negative) quantifiers. Each of these types of quantifier leads to a different focus pattern.

To illustrate, consider the case of the paradigm statement *Some As are Bs,* the sets necessary for interpretation include *those As which are Bs* (at least one), *possible As which are not Bs,* and *possible Bs which are not As* (also all As, all Bs), as shown in figure 1.

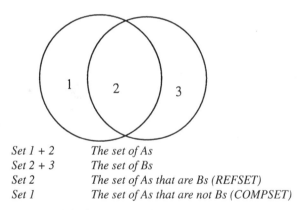

Set 1 + 2	The set of As
Set 2 + 3	The set of Bs
Set 2	The set of As that are Bs (REFSET)
Set 1	The set of As that are not Bs (COMPSET)

Figure 1.   *Given a statement of the form Quant of the As are Bs, the logically possible sets may be represented by this Euler Circle diagram.*

Taking ease of pronominal reference as an index of which of these sets is in focus (e.g., Sanford and Garrod 1981), it is obvious that (4) is acceptable and (5) is not:

(4)   Some of the football fans went to the match. They cheered as their team scored.

(5)   Some of the football fans went to the match. They stayed at home instead.

The NLQ *some* would appear to put focus on *those As which are Bs* (what Moxey and Sanford termed the **Ref**(erence) **set**). In contrast, the NLQ *few* can put focus on *those As which are not Bs* (those who did not attend), what we termed **Comp**(lement) **set reference**:

(6)   Few of the fans went to the match. They cheered as their team scored.

(7)   Few of the fans went to the match. They stayed at home instead.

Systematic exploration shows that compset reference is licensed by those quantifiers which are monotone decreasing. In order to assess whether compset focussing occurs outside of invented examples, Moxey and Sanford (1987) presented subjects with quantified statements, followed by the plural pronoun *they*, for instance:

(8)   Few of the football fans were at the match. They...

The subjects' task was to continue the *they* sentence in a way which made sense. The results showed clearly that some quantifiers seemed to license the use of compset reference, while others did not. The following have been shown to be compset licensing: *not all, not quite all, not very many, not many, few, very few, hardly any,* and *less than X,* where X is a number or a percentage. The following are not compset licensing: *nearly all, many, some, a few,* also *more than X,* and *X* where X is a number or a percentage. The expressions *only a few* and *only X,* where X is some number or percentage, seem to license compset but only very weakly in that compset continuations only appear under some circumstances.

The most accessible subset of the logical possibilities set up by a quantified statement is a function of quantifier, with monotone decreasing expressions licensing complement set reference, and monotone increasing or nonmonotone quantifiers requiring refset reference. These results can be thought of as illustrating where the attention of the listener lies. Further studies using self-paced reading time methods (Sanford, Moxey and Paterson, In press) and eyetracking (Sanford, Moxey and Paterson 1994) demonstrate that these focus effects play a role in comprehension as well as production, and that mismatches between quantifier-induced focus and subsequent anaphora leads to slower reading.

Further analysis of the continuations produced by subjects showed that quantifiers which induce compset reference patterns also cause subjects to think about reasons for the predicate being false. For instance, *Few of the fans went to the match* causes subjects to write about why fans did not go to the match. We therefore view these focus effects as a major means of manipulating the pattern of thought of the listener, and in section 4 we attempt to illustrate this.

2.3. *Levels of interpretation*

Moxey (1986; Moxey and Sanford 1993b) investigated the idea that quantifiers could signal inferences about the beliefs of a speaker prior to the speaker discovering the facts about something which formed the basis of the quantified statement. When *not many* is used, for instance, it might signal that the speakers prior beliefs were to the effect that she expected more to be the case. This is in fact the same argument as that made by Clark (1976) and Wason (1965) to the effect that negation serves to deny presuppositions.

The notion of presupposition is not sufficiently psychological for our purposes, however. A pragmatic presupposition depends upon **someone** making the supposition, and from the psychological perspective, the question naturally arises as to **who** might be making that supposition (i.e., who had a certain expectation that was not matched by the facts). There are several possibilities, including: (i) The speaker expected more to be the case, and (ii) the speaker believed the listener would have expected more to be the case (levels 2 and 3 in figure 2). Moxey and Sanford (1993b) examined the possibility that prior expectations of the speaker, and beliefs of the speaker regarding the prior expectations of the listener might be conveyed by comment-generating quantifiers. We used three settings which created three different baserate frequency expectations as confirmed by a pretest: number of local doctors who are female (low expectation), number of people persuaded by a political speech (medium), and number of people who enjoyed a party (high). Subjects were presented with a quantified statement, containing one of ten quantifiers, about one of the above numbers. We asked one group of subjects what percentage the quantifier was intended to denote (level 1). A second group was asked to say what proportion they thought the speaker had expected before the speaker discovered the facts (level 2). A third group had to say what proportion the speaker thought the listener might have expected before the listener heard the quantified statement (level 3). Subjects only made one judgement.

If there were no effects of quantifier on the second and third questions, then the responses might be expected to be in line with the independently measured[1] baserates, since the speaker was described as a local news reporter, who is likely to have had the same expectations as the subjects. However, variability in prior expectations as a function of quantifier should tell us something about the functions of the quantifier. For instance, if *a few* does not trigger a denial that more was expected, and *not many* does trigger such a denial, then with level 2 and/or 3 questions, the percentages reported for *not many* should be higher than for *a few*. The values obtained in the experiment suggested that the following quantifiers were associated with the listener believing that the speaker had

Figure 2.   Three levels of interpretation illustrated with one quantified utterance (after Moxey and Sanford 1993a).

expected more than turned out to be the case: *very few, few, not many*, and *only a few*. These quantifiers produced relatively high proportions in response to the question. This is consistent with the idea that these quantifiers presuppose a higher level than is being asserted, and signal denials of the presupposition. Here, though, presupposition is the listener's perception of an expectation on the part of the speaker. In contrast, use of *a few* produced low answers to the expectation questions.

Similar results held for the percentage which the listener inferred that the speaker thought the listener to have expected in advance. However, there was an important difference in the group: *few* **did not seem to signal that more had been expected**. Perhaps *few* sounds more formal and aloof in usage than *not many* because by using it the listener does not engage or accommodate the prior beliefs of the listener. We shall examine this distinction below. In addition to the results with negative quantifiers, the expression *quite a few* appeared to signal that less had been expected than turned out to be the case, this holding for both levels 2 and 3.

So, quantifiers can convey information about the speaker's prior beliefs as well as about the current situation. This may be summarized as:

— **More expected than was the case (level 2 and 3)**: not many, only a few
— **More expected than was the case (level 2 only)**: few, very few
— **Less expected than was the case (level 2 and 3)**: quite a few

Of course, whether all of this potential information forms a standard part of interpretation, or whether it is optional, depending upon the particular circumstances of a communication, remains to be established.

2.4. *Conclusion*

These laboratory studies show that quantifiers cannot be characterized simply in terms of the quantities they denote, but that they also have rhetorical functions, conveying quite subtle information about prior expectations, and leading the listener to pay attention to particular subsets of the logical possibilities, and search for knowledge about particular aspects of general knowledge which is relevant to a quantified proposition. When quantifiers lead to questions about reasons-why or why not the quantified statement is the case, we term them **comment generating**.

Barton and Sanford (1990) showed that comment-generating quantifiers influence causal attribution patterns in simple attribution paradigms. Much work in attribution is concerned with the explanation of some single event, such as *John kicks a dog*, in the light of subsidiary evidence, such as *Other people kick that dog*. The consistency of the behavior (whether John has kicked the dog in the past), its distinctiveness (whether John ever kicks any other dog), and consensus pattern (whether other people kick this dog) combine to determine the pattern of attribution (e.g., Kelley 1967; Hilton and Slugoski 1987). These elements depend upon assumptions about quantification. Thus to say *Few other people kick the dog* indicates that the majority of people do not kick the dog (a comment generator), while to say *a few people kick the dog* is to say that there is a small number of people who do kick the dog (not a comment generator). Barton and Sanford (1990) showed how attribution patterns vary with this variable. For instance, in (10) subjects think there is something special about John, while in (11) they think that there is something special about the dog:

(10)   John kicks the dog at the corner.
        Few other people kick the dog at the corner.

(11)   John kicks the dog at the corner.
        A few other people kick the dog at the corner.

For further details, see Barton and Sanford (1990). These studies also showed that frequency adverbs behave in the same way. Thus *rarely* may be equated with *few* in that both are comment generators, while *occasionally* may be equated with *a few*, and are not (see also Moxey, Sanford and Barton 1990).[2]

On the basis of these distinctions it should be possible to go some way towards predicting which quantifiers will be used when in normal communication situations. In section D we describe a recent attempt to develop the means to test questions of quantifier choice within a controlled paradigm.

3.   A substitution task using naturally occurring sentences

In order to obtain a fuller picture of quantifier usage, and to evaluate the importance or otherwise of the factors described above, we have recently undertaken an analysis of a large corpus of email material obtainable over the internet. Since focus is central to our analysis, it is important to discover how focus manifests itself in truly natural language constructions, for instance. The occurrence of compset focus using simple plural reference, as in example (8) above, for instance, is rare. Indeed, we have already established that in free continuation in laboratory tasks, it is rare (Moxey, Sanford and Barton 1990).

One of our goals, therefore, is to use the corpus data to try to track down precisely how focus and expectation differences might manifest themselves through other constructions. This work is ongoing, and for the present purpose, we report one of our first investigations which tests the idea that numerical substitution does not yield a good paraphrase of many quantified statements.

3.1. *Corpus*

The corpus is a large database of email and internet newsgroup material collected by J Hoeksema of the University of Groningen. The materials have been edited for repeat messages, and consist of a wide range of topics and styles of interaction.

3.2. *Experiment*

All cases of four quantifiers were extracted from the corpus as single sentences, yielding the following total numbers of cases: *not many* (78), *few* (1777, this number refers to *few* as a single expression and not in combination with *only, a, quite a,* etc.), *only a few* (244), and *a few* (4294). We randomly sampled 30 sentences of each of these expressions. The sentences were read by 25 subjects, undergraduates of the University of Glasgow. For each sentence, the subjects had to judge whether or not the quantifying expression (which was written in bold) could be replaced by any of the following phrases: **A small/large amount/number/quantity**. So, if *a few* means *a small number,* for instance, then substitution should be possible. Subjects were also asked to comment on the sentence if a paraphrase was judged not possible.

The results are shown in table 2. The most easily paraphrased expression is *a few*, which we would predict to be the best. In fact, the unacceptable items are trivial although quite large in number. We explain why below. We carried out a simple post-hoc classification of the comments made by the subjects:

(i)   *Negative.* The subjects mentioned that the paraphrase was no good because the quantifier was "more negative".

(ii)   *Emphasis.* The subjects mentioned that attention seemed to be directed to the wrong thing if the paraphrase was used.

(iii)   *Only required.* The subjects said that the paraphrase would be acceptable if *only* were incorporated into it.

(iv)   *Replace.* In this category, not only did the subjects say that the paraphrase would not work, they went on to suggest that the use of another quantifier would be better. Suggestions were restricted to *few, very few, not many* and *hardly any*.

Table 2. *(a) Proportion of acceptances of the given paraphrase, and (b) reasons given for not accepting the paraphrase*

	(a)			
	Not many	Few	Only a few	A few
Proportion acceptable	42%	49%	56%	63%

	(b)			
Category of comment	% comments in that category			
	Not many	Few	Only a few	A few
Negative	26%	14%	0.2%	0%
Emphasis	19%	12%	9%	1%
Only required	26%	5%	10%	1%
Replace	13%	12%	6.8%	0.3%
Other	16%	57%	74%	97.7%

(v) *Other.* This includes "no comment" and a few cases where subjects simply said the paraphrase would not sound right for reasons other than i–iv.

The data of some subjects falls into more than one of these categories, so the table is merely indicative of the problems of substitution. However, it is clear that *few* and *not many* are problems because of emphasis and negativity, which is entirely consistent with our laboratory results on the importance of focus. Those cases where *only a few* or *a few* were found to be unacceptable did not have to do with negativity; they occurred because of the presence of some measure statements in the sentences sampled. For instance, many subjects judged statements which included *a few miles* as not sounding right paraphrased as *a small number of miles*. This type of judgement, making up the main "other" category comments, has nothing to do with emphasis or negativity.

4.   Vignette studies of quantifier selection

It may be possible to evaluate the choice of which quantifier to use as a function of situation and intention through artificial, controlled, vignettes. In this section we describe choice in three vignettes designed to manipulate focus requirements and a requirement for speaker engagement.

4.1. *When refset patterns should be best*

Refset focus assumes the existence of some elements in the refset, while compset focus assumes the existence of some elements in the compset, and not necessarily any in the refset. This property is vital in communication, and should be a very obvious factor in the control of quantifier choice. Consider for instance the following vignette:

> Imagine a situation in which Mrs Jones is ill with a dangerous condition, and urgent surgical intervention has been suggested. However, the procedure was notoriously complex, and most patients do not survive for long after treatment. It is the duty of the surgeon to tell this to the patient.

What the patient wants to hear is that there is hope: This translates into a nonempty refset. On the other hand, it would be a lie for the doctor to tell the patient that the chances of survival are quite high when they are not. These two influences should join to cause selection of a low denoting quantifier, but one which puts primary focus on the refset.

Method

Procedure. The vignette shown above was printed on a page of paper, along with the following sentence:

> The doctor tells her "Q patients survive for long afterwards."

where Q was one of the following five quantifiers: *not many, few, hardly any, a few, only a few.*

Subjects were asked to rank-order the quantified statements (1 = best fit) in terms of their applicability to the situation in hand.

Subjects. These were 24 undergraduates from the University of Glasgow. None were aware of the hypotheses under test.

Results and discussion

The rank-orders obtained are shown in table 3. Application of a Friedman nonparametric analysis of variance by ranks was carried out, and yielded a significant effect of quantifier (X_r^2 = 64.18, df = 4, p < 0.001.). The rank assigned each quantifier was compared with the ranks assigned the other quantifiers by means of a sign test. The differences are shown in table 4.

Table 3. *Ranking results from the operation prognosis vignette*

Only a few	1.98
Few	3.96
A few	1.06
Not many	3.42
Hardly any	4.50

Table 4. *Sign test results showing the differences between rankings of quantifiers for the operation prognosis vignette. Where there is a significant difference at the 0.05 level or better, the letters identifying the preferred quantifier are inserted. Where there is no reliable difference, the letters n.s. are inserted.*

	only a few	few	a few	hardly any	not many
only a few (OAF)	x	OAF	AF	OAF	OAF
few (F)		x	AF	n.s.	n.s.
a few (AF)			x	AF	AF
hardly any (HA)				x	n.s.
not many (NM)					x

   A few is preferred over all other quantifiers, as expected. Next in rank is *only a few*, which is preferred to all other quantifiers except *a few*. None of the other differences are reliable.

   These findings are consistent with the idea that what has to be emphasized to the patient is the possibility of survival, through a refset focusing expression, *a few. Only a few* admits the possibility of survival, in that it is not monotone decreasing and only weakly allows reference to the compset. But the compset focussers are completely unacceptable, because they emphasize the high probability of death, and do not rule out the possibility that death may always occur. Since it is clear that people DO survive, we think that it is the compset focus which is the problem rather than allowing the null-set.

4.2. Compset focus and the requirement to disengage the listener

There are many situations in which it is desirable for the speaker to avoid any sign of recognizing that the listener suspects that some undesirable state of affairs may be the case. For instance, if a salesman is trying to sell something, and the customer asks about any problems with the product, then the salesman must not only use a quantifier indicating a low likelihood of a problem, he must also put focus on the high likelihood of a nonproblem (i.e., on the compset). This should lead to a preference for using *not many, few* or *hardly any* over *a few*. But there may be another factor constraining the salesman's choice of words, operating at level three in the Moxey and Sanford (1993b) classification: it may be undesirable for him to show that he recognizes that the customer may expect that there may be a problem with the product, even if the customer asks directly about potential problems. There is a big difference between answering a question about potential problems because it has been asked, and answering a question in such a way that it shows a recognition that the listener may already suspect that there **is** a problem. This can be seen as part of a salesperson's image: there is no question that the product is good, and there is no reason for anyone to suppose anything else. Focus is on being good, not on being bad.

Method
A vignette was constructed to meet two requirements:

1. The desired focus should be on the compset.
2. There should be no focus on the refset through recognition of a refset supporting presupposition.

Material. The "salesman vignette" was designed to meet these criteria. Subjects read the following material, presented on a single sheet of paper:

Imagine a situation in which a car salesman has been discussing with a client possible cars to be purchased. The client has asked about a number of cars, but keeps coming back to the same one. He asks about the reliability of the model, which is not known to him. The salesman replies,

"Well, put it this way, few of these cars need more than a basic service within the first three years."

A total of 5 sentences like this are presented to the subject, where the quantifiers used are *few, only a few, a few, not many, hardly any*. A further instruction said: not all of these statements are equally acceptable. Please rank-order the statements in terms of their acceptability for the salesman's answer to be appropriate to the interaction.

Subjects. There were 25 subjects, volunteers who were undergraduates from the University of Glasgow. They had no knowledge of the hypotheses under test.

Procedure. The 25 subjects were asked to rank-order the 5 statements in terms of their acceptability.

Results

The ranking results are shown in table 5. The ranks given to the quantifiers differ from one another by a Friedman nonparametric analysis of variance by ranks ($X_r^2 = 53.9$, df = 4, $p < 0.001$). Each quantifier was compared with every other quantifier by means of sign tests, the results of which are shown in Table 6.

Table 5. *Mean rankings for the salesman vignette (1 = good); 5 = poor)*

Few	1.88
Hardly any	1.96
Not many	3.00
Only a few	3.48
A few	4.68

Table 6. *Sign test results showing the differences between rankings of quantifiers for the car salesman vignette. Where there is a significant difference at the 0.05 level or better, the letters identifying the preferred quantifier are inserted. Where there is no reliable difference, the letters n.s. are inserted.*

	only a few	few	a few	hardly any	not many
only a few (OAF)	x	F	n.s.	HA	NM
few (F)		x	F	n.s.	F
a few (AF)			x	HA	NM
hardly any (HA)				x	HA
not many (NM)					x

Our major expectation was that refset focussers would be judged as inappropriate for the present vignette. Indeed, *a few* scores as the poorest choice of all, and is reliably less preferred than all other quantifiers. The expression *only a few*, which is essentially a weak compset focusser with a strong preference towards the refset, is also not a preferred expression, even though it explicitly points out that the small number is indeed small (Barton and Sanford 1990). However, it is preferred over *a few*. The poorest of the compset focussers in terms of preference is *not many*, which although preferable to *a few* was not reliably better than *only a few*. This is in complete contrast to the first vignette. The most interesting results, however, are those showing a difference between *few* and *not many*. In accordance with hypothesis, *few* is preferred over *not many*, (and is even as preferable as *hardly any*, even though the latter signifies a smaller number than *few* in a direct comparison).[3] Compset focus per se cannot explain this difference between *not many* and *few*; indeed, in production tasks, *not many* produces as many or more compset references than *few* (Moxey and Sanford 1987; Sanford, Moxey and Paterson, submitted). Rather, we believe that the difference is explained by a need not to engage the possibility that the customer might have expected any cars to have a poor record of reliability.

4.3. *Requirement to engage the listener*

If *not many* allows the listener's expectations into the arena of the discourse, and *few* does not, we would expect *not many* to be preferred when it is desirable to address the listeners expectations.

Method

Materials. The following vignette was designed to put a high weight on the need to take into account the expectations (in this case the hopes) of the listener.

> Imagine a situation in which John is keen on the local football club, but could not attend the most recent match. It is important to him that lots of fans went. He asked his friend how many fans did in fact go. In fact, none of the fans went at all. In order to hedge, John's friend does not say this immediately, but rather makes a statement like the ones below, in which after the hedged statement, he tells the absolute truth.

> Only a few of the fans went to match. ... In fact, none did.

The same statement was repeated with the quantifiers *a few, few, not many*, and *hardly any*.

We argue that here the preference should be for *not many*, with the other compset-focussers less preferred, but more preferred than the refset focussers. *Procedure.* Subjects were presented with the vignette and the five sentences with the instruction that not all of the possibilities for reply given below are equally acceptable, and to rank-order the alternatives.

Subjects. The 27 subjects were undergraduates from the University of Glasgow. They were volunteers and were unaware of the hypotheses under test.

Results

The rank orders, analysed by means of a Friedman nonparametric one-way analysis of variance, showed that there was an overall effect of quantifier ($X_r^2 = 54.56$, df = 4; $p < 0.001$). Separate sign tests were used to investigate the differences between pairs of quantifiers. The pairs which differ from one another are shown in table 8. There is an obvious preference for compset focussing expressions in that *few*, *not many*, and *hardly any* are all preferred over *a few*. Although *only a few* is preferred to *a few*, *few*, *not many*, and *hardly any* are all preferred to *only a few*. *Only a few* is a weak compset focusser, so this result is as expected and conforms to the findings with the salesman vignette.

Table 7. *Mean values of ratings of goodness of choice, and rank order values, for the football vignette (0 = good fit; 10 = poor fit)*

	ranking
Few	3.0
Hardly any	1.5
Not many	2.3
Only a few	3.8
A few	4.3

Table 8. *Sign test results showing differences between rankings of the quantifiers for the Football vignette. Where there is a significant difference at the 0.05 level or better, the letters n.s. are inserted. Where there is a difference at the 0.05 level or better, the letters identify the quantifier that was reliably most preferred.*

	only a few	few	a few	hardly any	not many
only a few (OAF)	x	F	n.s.	HA	NM
few (F)		x	F	HA	NM
a few (AF)			x	HA	NM
hardly any (HA)				x	HA
not many (NM)					x

Not many is prefered over *few*, which is consistent with our hypothesis, and reverses the preferences for these expressions in the salesman vignette.

6.   General discussion

Our main objective has been to describe some of our work on how a suitable quantifier might be selected during communication. The results do not come from spontaneous dialog, but we believe that we have isolated some of the variables which should predict usage in dialog. The vignette tasks are designed to test this possibility, while enabling us to keep control over the communicative setting, in principle at least.

As we have stressed elsewhere, our claim is that the vast variety of quantifiers in use cannot be explained in terms of denoting differentiable amounts. While this may be no surprise to some, the approach in terms of numerical denotation has dominated the psychological literature, and formal approaches have lacked contact with functional questions. We hope to have filled a gap here.

The evidence for looking beyond numbers comes in part from laboratory studies showing that the numbers which subjects assign to different quantifiers may overlap to such an extent that such an account would not be able to differentiate quantifiers, so that expressions would overlap in meaning. Furthermore, in a substitution task, negative quantifiers especially did not readily paraphrase into a small/large amount/ number/quantity, showing that other functions were being caried out by the quantifiers.

The primary reason for the failure of the substitution test is that quantifiers convey certain emphases or "negativity". In the review of our laboratory studies, we showed that negative quantifiers allow and encourage a different pattern of focus from the positive quantifiers. Quantifiers also appear to vary in terms of what they convey about the expectations of the producer, including what they convey about the producer's beliefs of the listener's prior expectations. The failure of the substitutions is consistent with this.

In order to test the applicability of these ideas to choice in a communicative setting, we have attempted to fabricate situations in which we have controlled the desirability of compset or refset focus, and the desirability or otherwise of the producer indicating any belief concerning the listener's prior expectations. There is still much work to do in refining this methodology to incorporate adequate control, but the results discussed above do appear to be promising.

The *few/not many* distinction, should it replicate in other tests, may provide a clue about a distinction between formal and informal expressions. People sometimes comment that *few* is a formal expression, even pompous. Perhaps the basis for this is that by not conveying speaker beliefs about listener expectations, it is sometimes plain to the listener that their beliefs are not being taken into account. The literature on attitude survey techniques has identified another possible candidate for just this kind of analysis: the pair *not allow/forbid*. (Hippler and Schwartz 1986). When respondents to questionnaires are not totally sure of what they believe about an issue, such as abortion on demand, they are more likely to endorse statement (a) than (b):

a.   Abortion on demand should not be allowed.
b.   Abortion on demand should be forbidden.

Perhaps this is because not allowed is a denial of allow at levels 2 and 3, while forbidden does not engage at level 3. It is thus more formal, and more pompous. Whether it will ultimately be possible to link the formality of expressions to levels of engagement of expectation remains to be seen: If it is, it will certainly not be through the analysis of quantifiers alone, but through a broader analysis.

To summarize, choice of quantifier seems to be determined at least by:

(1)   need to assert a large or a small amount, but this can be done only crudely with respect to communication;

(2)   the need to include an internal reference as to the significance of the amount (this may cause us to use a natural language expression rather than a number even when we know the number exactly);

(3)   the set on which emphasis is to be put (compset; refset);

(4)   whether or not a comment is being made about the amount (i.e., reason-why, reason-why-not, consequence of the number);

(5)   whether or not the speaker's beliefs about the expectations or hopes of the listener are to be admitted as relevant background to the utterance (which we wish to equate with formality).

There are of course many other aspects of quantifiers yet to be considered. In particular use of mass terms (*a lot*) when number might be used (see Moxey and Sanford 1993a for some suggestions), and the use of even more complex forms of negation such as litotes (*not a few, not infrequently*); litotes are good candidates for treatment within a focus framework. The functions of these are currently being investigated.

7.   The broader perspective

In real-life there are many ways of conveying quantitative information, and it is a future research goal to get a grip on these issues. For instance, if many Xs are Ys, then we could say the following:

a.   Many Xs are Ys *(quantifier on set)*.

b.   If you get an X you'll probably find it is a Y *(probabilistic statement)*.

c.   If you get an X I'm fairly sure it will turn out to be a Y *(degree of belief)*.

d.   Xs are usually/often Ys *(quantifier of frequency)*.

e.   if you get a bunch of Xs you should get some Ys *(set description of a sampling strategy)*.

This list is by no means systematic and by no means exhausts the options. Quite obviously which particular type of expression is used to describe a situation is going to be determined by the general requirements of the interaction in which it occurs, and even on the basis of existing knowledge we could begin to formulate a choice regime. Why is it worthwhile doing so with respect to conveying quantity? Apart from the general point that these types of expression are ubiquitous, it would seem that the kind of approach we are taking here is compatible with the application of argumentation theory to providing explanations for decisions under uncertainty made in expert systems (e.g., Fox, Krause and Elvang-Gørenson 1993). Argumentation is the process of constructing arguments about propositions, and the assignment of degrees or statements of confidence to those propositions depending on the nature and strength of the supporting arguments. The general inadequacy of numerical treatments alone is quite consistent with our line of work on quantifier choice. This link has not only convinced us of the usefulness of the approach which we have taken up to now, and of the potential value of understanding choice of expression within the specific microcosm of quantification and related terms, it has brought us face to face with the need to understand the interchangeabilty of modes of expression such as those exemplified by examples (a) through (e) above.

Acknowledgements

The authors would like to thank the British Academy and the British Council for their support of this work. Thanks are also due to Marie McGinley who collected some of the vignette data.

Notes

1. The focus of this paper is not these formal issues. However, for a treatment of formal classes of negativity (monotone decreasing, anti-additive, antimultiplicative, and antimorphic within a boolean framework, see Zwarts 1994). For our purposes, the monotone decreasing property may be considered the weakest form of negativity.

2. This is not too surprising since rarely (and seldom) are essentially monotone decreasing and show patterns of focus which resemble the compset pattern in amount quantifiers. It is also the case that *only occasionally* and *only a few* seem to be equivalent.

3. This can be demonstrated by the acceptability of the statement "Few people were at the meeting. In fact hardly any people were". To the extent that this is acceptable, *hardly any* must be asserting a value nearer to zero than *few*.

References

Barton, S.B. and A.J. Sanford. 1990. "The Control of Attributional Patterns by the Focusing Properties of Quantifying Expressions." *Journal of Semantics* 7.81–92.

Barwise, J. and R. Cooper. 1981. "Generalized Quantifiers and Natural Language." *Linguistics and Philosophy* 4.159–219.

Clark, H.H. 1976. *Semantics and Comprehension*. The Hague: Mouton.

Clark, H.H. 1990. Comment on Mosteller, F. and Youtz, C., "Quantifying Probabilistic Expressions." *Statistical Science* 5.2–34.

Fox, J., P. Krause and M. Elvang-Gørensson. 1993. "Argumentation as a General Framework for Uncertain Reasoning." In *Proceedings of the Ninth Conference on Uncertainty in Artificial Intelligence*, Washington, D.C., July 9–11.

Hilton, D.J. and B.R. Slugoski. 1986. "Knowledge-based Causal Attribution: The abnormal conditions focus model." *Psychological Review* 93.75–88.

Hippler, H-J. and N. Schwartz. 1986. "Not Forbidding Isn't Allowing: The cognitive basis of the forbid–allow asymmetry." *Public Opinion Quarterly* 50.87–96.

Kelley, H.H. 1967. "Attribution in Social Psychology." *Nebraska Symposium on Motivation* 15.192–238.

Klima, E.S. 1964. "Negation in English." In *The Structure of Language*, J.A. Fodor and J.J. Katz (eds). Englewood Cliffs, N.J.: Prentice-Hall.

Ladusaw, W.A. 1979. "On the Notion of Affective in the Analysis of Negative Polarity Items." Paper presented to the 1979 meeting of the Linguistics Society of America, Los Angeles.

Mosteller, F. and C. Youtz. 1990. "Quantifying Probabilistic Expressions." *Statistical Science* 5.2–34.

Moxey, L.M. 1986. "A Psychological Investigation of the Use and Interpretation of English Quantifiers." Unpublished Ph.D. thesis, University of Glasgow.

Moxey, L.M. and A.J. Sanford. 1987. "Quantifiers and Focus." *Journal of Semantics* 5.189–206.

Moxey, L.M., A.J. Sanford and S.B. Barton. 1990. "Control of Attentional Focus by Quantifiers." In *Lines of Thinking*. Vol. 1, K.J. Gilhooly, M.T.G. Keane, R.H. Logie and G. Erdos (eds). Chichester: Wiley.

Moxey, L.M. and A.J. Sanford. 1993a. "Prior Expectation and the Interpretation of Natural Language Quantifiers." *European Journal of Cognitive Psychology* 5.73–91.

Moxey, L.M. and A.J. Sanford. 1993b. *Communicating Quantities: A psychological Perspective*. Hove, UK: Lawrence Erlbaum.

Parducci, A. 1968. "Often is Often." *American Psychologist* 23.828.

Pepper, S. 1981. "Problems in the Quantification of Frequency Expressions." In *New Directions for Methodology of Social and Behavioural Science*, D. Fiske (ed.), 25–41. San Fransisco, Calif.: Jossey-Bass.

Pepper, S. and L.S. Prytulak. 1974. "Sometimes Frequently means Seldom: Context effects in the interpretations of quantitative expressions." *Journal of Research in Personality* 8.95–101.

Poulton, E.C. 1973. "Unwanted Range Effects from Using Within-subject Experimental Designs." *Psychological Bulletin* 80.113–121.

Routh, D.A. 1994. "On the Representation of Quantifiers." *Journal of Semantics.*

Sanford, A.J., L.M. Moxey, and K.B. Paterson. 1994. "Psychological Studies of Quantifiers." *Journal of Semantics* 10.153–170.

Sanford, A.J., L.M. Moxey, and K.B. Paterson. In press. "Attentional Focusing with Quantifiers in Production and Comprehension." *Memory and Cognition.*

Wallsten, T.S., S. Fillenbaum and J.A. Cox. 1986. "Base Rate Effects on the Interpretations of Probability and Frequency Expressions." *Journal of Memory and Language* 25.571–587.

Wason, P.C. 1965. "The Contexts of Plausible Denial." *Journal of Verbal Learning and Verbal Behavior* 4.7–11.

Westerståhl, D. 1989. "Quantifiers in Formal and Natural Languages." In *Handbook of Philosophical Logic, 4,* D. Gabbay and F. Guenthner (eds), 1–131. Dordrecht: Reidel.

Zwarts, F. 1994. "Polarity Items." In *The Encyclopedia of Language and Linguistics,* R.E. Asher and J.M.Y. Simpson (eds). Oxford: Pergamon Press.

Conflict Talk

Understanding and Resolving Arguments

Nancy L. Stein
University of Chicago

Ronan S. Bernas
Eastern Illinois University

David J. Calicchia
University of Chicago

1. Background

The goals of the present study were to investigate the ways in which two people resolve differences of opinion during an argument, to describe the conflict talk associated with different argument outcomes and to explore the content of argument memories when the outcome of an argument varies. In examining these issues, two dimensions, in particular, were thought to constrain the types of conflict talk and resolution strategies that are used during an argument: the gender of the arguers and the instructions they received before negotiation. As we unfold our conflict story, the importance of gender and instructional variables will become clarified.

1.1. *Understanding an argument and choosing sides*

When two people disagree about an issue and choose to support opposing sides, both have concluded that, for the moment, their stances cannot co-exist simultaneously with one another (Stein and Miller 1990; 1993a, b). For example, in arguing about whether or not to loan a friend money, one person claims that the money should be loaned while the other person claims that the money should not be loaned. No possibility exists for both of these outcomes to be realized simultaneously.

When two arguers recognize a conflict between them, both initially believe that their stance is more legitimate and more viable than that of their opponent. They also believe that their stance should be maintained and that more positive benefits will result from holding their stance than their opponent's stance. Otherwise, neither would engage in discussion about the issue.

Arguers almost always begin a negotiation by trying to convince the other about the greater legitimacy of their position. In the give and take of conflict talk, even children of preschool age attempt to provide reasons for supporting their side of the issue (Dunn 1989; Eisenberg and Garvey 1981; Goodwin 1990; Stein and Liwag, In press; Tesla and Dunn 1992) and reasons for opposing that of their opponent. The reasons given in support of a position are critical because they are connected to the goals that underlie a particular stance. Stein and Miller (1990, 1993a, b), in particular, contend that arguments are goal driven and that reasons function to illuminate the *consequences* of adhering to one goal versus another. Thus, the quality of reasoning given in support of or in opposition to a position is critical: the reasons determine the outcome of a conflict and whether personally significant goals will be allowed to be maintained. Thus, explanations in support of a favored position are inherent to the definition of an argument, even for very young children. The goal of explanation-based talk is to persuade and focus on the consequences of maintaining one position versus another.

According to Stein and her colleagues (Stein and Miller 1993b; Stein, Bernas, Calicchia and Wright 1995), arguers initially support one side of an issue over the other because they have more knowledge about the positive benefits of their position than that of their opponent. They also have more knowledge about problems with their opponent's position than they do with their own position. Thus, the content and structure of argument knowledge across the two positions is asymmetrical.

1.2. *Individual differences in prior knowledge about an argument*

Despite asymmetries in understanding the two opposing positions, however, arguers also vary in the amount and type of knowledge they have acquired about each other's stance (Grotevant and Cooper 1985; Koehler 1991; Stein and Miller 1993 a, b; Stein, *et al.* 1995). Some arguers may have access to only one of type of knowledge about an issue: reasons for supporting their side of an issue. Other arguers have acquired detailed knowledge about their opponent's position (Koehler 1991; Reyna, Woodruff and Brainerd 1992; Stein *et al.* 1995) and often understand some of the positive benefits of their opponent's stance. These more knowledgeable arguers may even be aware of the problems with their own position, even though they still believe in the less problematic nature of their own position.

These individual differences in initial argument knowledge (Grotevant and Cooper 1985), like those in other areas of expertise (Chi, Slotta and de Leeuw 1993; Ericsson and Smith 1991), may be critical in determining the ways in which a conflict is understood and resolved. If arguers attempt to focus on constructive resolutions to differences of opinion, where they consciously try to create common ground and avoid harm to their opponent, they may need to understand the strength of both positions so that an integration of the two can be formulated.

Being willing to re-evaluate each position and to consider the adoption of new goals is thought to be crucial to ending an argument in a constructive fashion. From past studies on conflict resolution and problem solving in family contexts (Smetana 1989; Vuchinich 1987; Vuchinich, Angellini and Gatherum 1995) and in large business organizations (Fisher and Brown 1988; Ross and Stillinger 1991), researchers have demonstrated that ending negotiations in a standoff, where each party maintains and intensifies their original stance, is not an effective solution over the long run. Standoffs lead to worsening conditions, overt acts of aggression and attempts at future retribution (Cummings and Davies 1994; Fisher and Brown 1988; Forgatch 1989; Gottman 1994; Stein and Miller 1993a; Vuchinich 1987; Vuchinich *et al.* 1995).

To create common goals, either a compromise or win–loss solution must be adopted. If a choice has to be made, a compromise is generally preferred because some goal revision is necessary for both partners (Stein *et al.* 1995) and the use of verbal or physical coercion is less frequent than in win–loss outcomes (Forgatch 1989; Gottman 1994; Vuchinich *et al.* 1995). The question is: How easily can arguers arrive at compromise solutions? If they are able to negotiate compromise, does their knowledge about each other's positions differ from those who opt for a win–loss or standoff solution? Does the conflict talk of compromisers differ from those who choose win–loss or standoff resolutions? Do explicit instructions to compromise increase the probability of creating common ground among arguers?

To investigate these issues, we carried out a study with high school students who were asked to resolve an argument that occurred between two friends in their high school class. Our goal was to examine the dynamic properties of understanding, talking about and resolving an argument. Participating students were presented with a summary of events leading up to their friends' argument and they were asked to choose whose side of the conflict they supported. Each participant was then paired with a fellow student participant who favored the opposite position. Then, the two participants were asked to resolve their differences of opinion through negotiation. Half of the participating pairs were asked to resolve their differences by compromising and half were asked to resolve their differences in a way they thought would result in the best solution.

1.3. *Review of past research on conflict*

Researchers who have investigated both adolescent (Hofer and Pikowsky 1993; Smetana 1989; Smetana, Yau, Restrepo and Hansen 1991; Vuchinich 1987, 1990; Vuchinich and Angelleli 1995) and young children's conflict (Ross and Conant 1993; Tesla and Dunn 1992) have shown that compromise is not a frequent outcome of dispute resolution. Vuchinich (1987, 1990) and Smetana (1989) have shown that in family conflicts that involve adolescents, most end in stand-offs, where differences are not resolved. Further, Vuchinich (1987; Vuchinich *et al.* 1995), Smetana (1989) and Tesla and Dunn (1992) indicate that as children get older, they do not necessarily compromise more or become more sensitive to another person's position. Rather, children often learn to become better arguers in order to maintain their own position.

Studies on adults (Ross and Lepper 1980; Vallone, Ross and Lepper 1985) also illustrate that a more entrenched commitment to one's original position and further exacerbation of the conflict is a frequent outcome of negotiation. As Sherif and Sherif (1953, 1978) noted, discussions of disagreements do not necessarily lead to better problem solutions, even among adults. The tendency to dominate, to adhere to one's own position and to devalue the validity of another's position, can be seen in arguments between adolescents, two spouses in a marriage (Beck 1988; Christensen and Heavy 1990, 1993; Christensen and Margolin 1988; Gottman 1994), two business associates (Fisher and Brown 1988; Ross and Stillinger 1991; Ury 1991) and two opposing scientists (Koehler 1991).

On the other hand, conflictual interchanges are thought to be one of the best vehicles for learning, conceptual change and switching argumentative stances. Developmental researchers who support this position (Dunn 1989, 1992; Murray 1972; Piaget 1932; Resnick 1991; Valsiner and Cairns 1992) contend that conflictual situations force a reconsideration of current beliefs about each position because of the explicit contrasts and comparisons that can be made between the two positions. The question is: What variables lead to effective conflict outcomes and what variables lead to destructive outcomes?

The present study was designed to examine in more detail talk during the negotiation process and the role that prior beliefs, knowledge, desires and commitments play in the negotiation process. With the exception of Vuchinich (1987), the different types of outcomes that result from negotiation have not been explicitly defined or discussed, nor has the temporal process of negotiation been explicitly described. Although researchers have discussed what constitutes a poor solution to conflict (e.g., stand-offs, hostile negotiations and threats of physical violence), the concept of a good solution is still elusive and in need of study (see Valsiner and Cairns 1992, for corroboration of this point). Are compromise solutions the "best" outcomes of conflict? If so, how is a compromise to be defined? What types of prior knowledge and feelings are necessary for compromise to occur? And, do the negotiations of compromisers differ from those of winners and losers?

Describing negotiation talk is also important in gaining a more accurate understanding of the gender differences associated with resolving a conflict. On the one hand, several researchers (Gilligan 1982; Ross and Holmberg 1990; Tannen 1990; West and Zimmerman 1977) have claimed that women more frequently lose an argument with men and they more frequently suggest a compromise solution. On the other hand, researchers who have studied conflicts among married couples (Christensen and Heavy 1990; Gottman and Krokoff 1989; Gottman and Levenson 1991; Weiss 1990) have demonstrated that wives more frequently initiate and win spousal arguments, show more tenacious behaviors, remember problems in more detail (Christensen and Heavy 1990) and focus more on a solution.

The present study was design to resolve some of the discrepancies and limitations of previous studies. Negotiations between adolescents were video and audio taped. The gender of arguers was varied so that an equal number of all male and all female dyads were compared to the same number of male–female dyads. Prior knowledge of each arguer was assessed before negotiation began and perceptions and reactions to the argument were assessed during the negotiation.

2. Method

2.1. Subjects

A total of 178 high school students participated in the study. Fifty-two percent ($n = 93$) were female and 48% ($n = 85$) were male. All students attended the same high school located in a southwest suburb of Chicago. Students from all four grade levels participated in the study. Forty-two percent ($n = 75$) were in ninth grade, 36% ($n = 65$) in 10th grade, 12% ($n = 21$) in 11th grade and 10% ($n = 17$) in 12th grade. Seventy-seven percent ($n = 137$) were African-American, 17% ($n = 31$) were Caucasian and 6% ($n = 10$) were from other ethnic backgrounds. Although participation in the study was voluntary, the students were paid for their involvement.

2.2. *Materials*

Two real life conflict scenarios were constructed by interviewing an initial group of 128 adolescents about memories for recent conflicts they had experienced and resolved. These adolescents lived in the same suburban school district and had the same demographic characteristics as the actual subjects who participated in the present study. Adolescents in the survey study were requested to report and narrate about two conflicts that occurred recently in their daily interactions with friends. The two most frequent types of conflicts mentioned were chosen as central themes around which we constructed real-life conflict scenarios for the present study.

The first conflict scenario (Borrowing Money Scenario) focused on an adolescent who borrowed money from a friend and who was tardy in repaying the loan. Because of the tardiness, the lender insisted that he or she would never lend money again to the borrower. The borrower objected to the lender's pronouncement and stated that he or she should be allowed to borrow money again from the lender. The text of the conflict scenario also included a description of the specific conditions that caused the borrower to be tardy in paying back the money and the negative consequences suffered by the lender as a result of the borrower's tardiness.

The second conflict scenario (Friendship Scenario) concerned an adolescent who had moved to a new high school and was spending time with new friends to better accommodate to the new school. The result, however, was that the adolescent ignored a long-standing friendship with a person who still attended the adolescent's former high school. A conflict arose when the adolescent's old friend asked the adolescent to join him (her) at a dance at the old high school. The adolescent turned down the old friend because a dance was also being held at the new school and the adolescent already had plans to attend this dance. The old friend felt that the adolescent was neglecting him (her), stated that the adolescent should be allocating more time to the old friendship and threatened to cut off the relationship permanently. The adolescent disagreed, contended that the old friend had to understand the current circumstances and argued that the friendship should be maintained. Appendix A contains the complete narrative accounts of both conflict scenarios.

2.3. *Design*

All 178 students in the study proper completed three tasks in the following order: (1) a screening interview; (2) a pre-negotiation interview; (3) a 10-minute negotiation session and (4) a debriefing interview. Dyads were created wherein partners held opposing positions and were equally committed to their opposed positions. Twenty-seven dyads were all male, 31 were all female and 31 were male-female, totaling 89 dyads. Forty-four of the dyads were randomly assigned to a Compromise condition, in which students were instructed explicitly to resolve their differences of opinion by effecting a compromise. The remaining 45 dyads were assigned to a Control condition, in which students were instructed to resolve their differences of opinion in a manner that each thought was best.

Half of the dyads discussed the Friendship Scenario, while the other half discussed the Borrowing Money Scenario. In both conflict scenarios, a male and a female protagonist were portrayed as disagreeing on the issue. Either the male or the female acted as the accuser, while the other one denied the accusation. The gender of the accuser was counterbalanced so that half of all scenario presentations portrayed a male as the accuser and half portrayed a female as the accuser.

2.4. *Procedure*

All the students completed the following three tasks:

2.4.1. *Screening interview*
Students read the two conflict scenarios. Students were asked to imagine that the two characters in the conflict scenario were their friends and that their friends had asked the student which side of the conflict he or she would support. For each conflict scenario, students indicated which protagonist's position they would support and the degree of commitment they felt to the protagonist's position. Degree of commitment was measured on a 5-point scale using the following values: (1) not committed, but I am even less committed to the other position; (2) a little committed; (3) somewhat committed; (4) very committed; and (5) completely committed. Students were then asked to generate as many reasons as they could for supporting and opposing *both* positions in each conflict scenario. Thus, the students generated reasons for and against their favored position *as well as* reasons for and against the opposing position.

Screening interview data were collected from 389 students. A total of 89 dyads resulted from pairing procedures that took into consideration position preference, degree of commitment to the favored position and gender. Thus, only 178 of the 389 students were asked to participate in the succeeding tasks.

2.4.2. *Pre-negotiation interview*
Approximately one week elapsed between the screening interview and the actual negotiation session. During the pre-negotiation interview, members of the 89 dyads were requested to reread one of the two conflict scenarios. They were

asked to re-evaluate the scenario so that they could discuss it with one of their fellow students. During the rereading phase, they were again asked to indicate which side of the issue they supported. If the students' response was different from the position they supported during the screening interview, they were reminded of the previous stance and were asked to support this original position at the beginning of the negotiation session.

Before students entered the negotiation, they were asked how they wanted to resolve their disagreement. They had to choose from three options: (1) they wanted to win and have their opponent agree to support their position; (2) they wanted to compromise and generate a position they both could support; or (3) they wanted their opponent to win and they would support their opponent's position (i.e., to lose). All pre-negotiation interview responses were audio taped.

2.4.3. *Negotiation session*

The two students in each dyad were brought together in a conference room, reminded that they held opposing positions on the conflict and were asked to resolve their differences of opinion. Students assigned to the Compromise condition were asked to resolve their differences by reaching a compromise. They were told that:

> *A compromise is a process by which you find a position that both of you can support. A compromise can include support for some of each of your concerns, or it can be an entirely new position, as long as you both feel you can support the position.*

In the Control condition, the two students were asked to settle their disagreement in the way they thought would be best.

Students in both conditions were given approximately seven minutes to resolve their disagreement. An extra three minutes was granted to students who expressed the need for more time. Only the two students involved in the negotiation were in the room during the resolution process. With the students' prior consent and permission, however, all negotiation sessions were video and audio taped. Near the end of the negotiation sessions, students in each dyad stated, on film, how each thought their differences of opinion had been resolved. Students had no obligation to agree with one another in how they characterized their resolution. They simply stated, in the natural flow of ending their negotiation, how the negotiation ended and provided explanations as to why they arrived at such an outcome.

3. Results

3.1. *Beginning the negotiation: The status of initial knowledge*

Our first analysis focused on: (1) the number of reasons generated in *support* of the favored and the opposed position; (2) the number of reasons generated *against* the favored and the opposed position; and (3) the specific *content* of supporting and problem-oriented reasons.

A supporting reason was defined as: (1) a reason that *explicitly* validated a claim (e.g., "I'm for him because..."") or (2) a social or moral imperative that implied support and validity for a claim (e.g., "He *had* to make new friends because he *needed* to learn his way around the new school"). A problem-oriented reason was defined as: (1) a reason that provided explicit *validity* for opposing a position (e.g., "I don't support him because... ") or (2) a social or moral imperative containing a negation that implied a valid reason for opposing a position (e.g. "He was *not* responsible in repaying the loan"; "He did *not* consider the consequences to her").

Reasons for and against the two positions were first parsed into clausal units, using the verb as the primary determinant of each clause. Clauses were then grouped so that each cluster represented one reason. Criteria of causal consistency, coherence and understandability (Stein *et al.* 1995; Trabasso, van den Broek and Suh 1989) were used to determine the number of clauses included in each reason. Reasons were then classified as supporting or problem-oriented according to our previous definitions. Inter-rater reliability for classifying reasons as supporting or opposing a position was 94% across three judges.

3.1.1. *The number of supporting and opposing reason for both positions*
A three-way ANOVA was carried out on the number of reasons generated. Experimental Condition (compromise vs. control) was the between-subjects factor while Position (favored vs. opposed) and Knowledge Type (supporting vs. problem-oriented reasons) were within-subjects factors. Experimental Condition was not significant and did not interact with any other factor. Position, $F(1,176) = 10.92$, $p < 0.01$ and Knowledge Type, $F(1,176) = 16.30$, $p < 0.0001$, were significant as was their interaction, $F(1,176) = 146.36$, $p < 0.0001$. Figure 1 depicts the interaction.

Post-hoc pairwise contrasts revealed that students generated more supporting reasons for their favored position ($M = 3.58$, $S.D. = 2.43$) than for the opposed position ($M = 1.38$, $S.D. = 1.90$), $F(1,176) = 130.90$, $p. < 0.0001$. They generated fewer problem-oriented reasons for their favored position ($M = 1.43$, $S.D. = 1.72$),

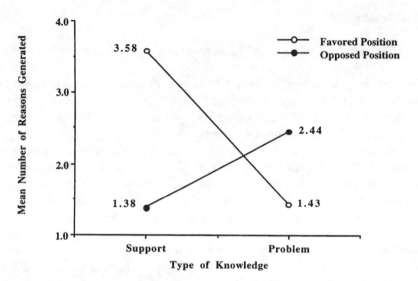

Figure 1.   *Number of supporting and problem-oriented reasons generated for the favored and opposed positions.*

however, than for the opposed position ($M = 2.44$, *S.D.* $= 2.21$), $F(1,176) = 32.12$, $p < 0.0001$. Thus, the hypotheses advanced by Stein and her colleagues (Stein *et al.* 1995; Stein and Miller 1993a, b) concerning the asymmetrical nature of initial argument knowledge were upheld. Upon entering the negotiation, arguers generated more supporting evidence for their own position than for their opponent's position and they generated fewer problem-oriented reasons for their own position than for their opponent's position.

3.1.2. *The content of supporting and opposing reasons*

A taxonomy was constructed to describe the nature of supporting and opposing reasons. Four categories of information accounted for almost all reasons: (1) claims or repudiations, (2) current or past operating conditions, (3) internal states of the characters involved in the conflict and (4) future conditions.

Claims and Repudiations were statements that expressed explicit agreement or disagreement with a position. Examples of Claims were: "I sided with Roberta…"; "I supported Michael's position…" Examples of repudiations were: "I disagreed with Roberta…"; "I did not support Roberta's position…"

Current and Past Operating Conditions included three distinct subcategories: Personal Beliefs, Constraining Circumstances and Action-Outcomes. *Personal Beliefs* were defined as expressions of opinion in terms of how the world operates, from the subject's point of view. Examples were: "One needs friends to survive in high school"; "New friends can be just as bad as old friends"; "Everyone forgets once in a while." *Constraining Circumstances* were identified as existing states of the world that subjects identified as influencing or constraining the characters' actions in the conflict scenario. Examples were: "Roberta is at a new school"; "They have been friends for a very long time." *Actions/ Outcomes* referred to actions and outcomes in the scenario that either facilitated or harmed one of the positions of the characters. Examples of Actions and Outcomes were: "Steve did call her several times"; "Her father gave her the money to repay the loan"; "Roberta already made plans to go to a different dance."

Despite the different content of these three sub-categories (e.g., beliefs, current and past operating conditions and action-outcomes), each functioned to lend support to a claim by providing the necessary conditions, constraints, circumstances or actions upon which further support for the claim could be made. Thus, the three categories were clustered together for the present analysis as *Current and Past Operating Conditions* because of their similar role in building support for an argument.

Internal States referred to the goals, emotions, thoughts and personality characteristics of the story characters. Examples of Internal States were: "Michael really wanted to attend the concert"; "Diane felt offended"; "Steve missed his best friend very much"; "She knew he needed the money for the concert"; "Steve thinks Roberta does not want to be his friend anymore." These internal states were then used in conjunction with the actions and outcomes undertaken by a character to lend support to or denial of a position.

Future conditions included three distinct subcategories. *Predictions* were positive or negative outcomes that *might* result from the current conflict situation should one side prevail. Examples were: "Diane and Michael won't ask each other for favors anymore"; "They might stop their friendship temporarily." *Prescriptions* were behaviors that subjects felt should be carried out by the characters in the conflict scenario. Examples were: "Sharon should understand the importance of Robert's making new friends." *Resolutions* were ways in which the two characters in the conflict could resolve their conflict. Examples were: "Richard could ask Sharon to meet some of his new friends and everyone could hang out together"; "They could remain friends and if Marsha needs money, she could borrow it from her parents."

Each reason was classified into one of the four primary content categories. Three coders achieved a 95% rate of agreement in classifying all reasons. The data presented in Table 1 indicate the mean proportion of reasons that subjects generated for each of the four content categories when generating supporting and problem-oriented reasons.

Table 1. *Mean proportions of each of four types of reasons generated in support of or against (problem-oriented) a position*

	Supporting Reasons	Problem-Oriented Reasons
Claims/Repudiations	0.08	0.12
Current and Past Beliefs		
Constraining Conditions Action-Outcomes	0.56	0.28
Internal States	0.20	0.19
Future Predictions Prescriptions Resolutions	0.16	0.41

A three-way ANOVA was carried out on the proportion data with Experimental Condition (compromise vs. control) as a between-subjects factor. Content Category (claims/repudiations, current conditions, internal states, future conditions) and Knowledge Type (supporting vs. problem-oriented reasons) were within-subjects factors. Experimental Condition was not significant as a main effect and did not interact with any other factor. Likewise, the main effect of Knowledge Type was not significant. However, the main effect of Content Category, $F(3,417) = 58.58$, $p < 0.0001$ and the interaction between Content Category and Knowledge Type, $F(3,417) = 33.38$, $p < 0.0001$, were significant.[1]

The main effect of Content Category was due primarily to the less frequent generation of claims/repudiations and internal states relative to the generation of reasons that focused on either current or future conditions. Claims/repudiations and internal state evaluations were generated at approximately equal rates as reasons for and against a position. However, subjects generated proportionately more past and current conditions when offering support for a position (56%) than when criticizing the position (28%), $F(1,417) = 51.83$, $p < 0.0001$. Conversely, subjects generated proportionately more future conditions when generating problem-oriented reasons (41%) than when supporting a position (16%), $F(1,417) = 45.91$, $p < 0.0001$. Thus, our working assumption, that reasons most often highlight the negative and positive consequences of a position, were born out by these data analyses. In our discussion of the content of conflict talk between arguers, we will show that focusing on the future is strongly associated with one type of conflict outcome while focusing on past operating conditions is associated with a different outcome.

3.2. *The relationship between commitment, desired strategy and initial knowledge*

The mean level of commitment to the favored position was 3.67 ($S.D. = 1.05$), for both arguers in a dyad. The level did not vary as a function of experimental condition or gender. On a five point scale, this score indicated a moderately high level of commitment. The results of an ANOVA showed no relationship between commitment and the content of reasons generated for either position. Likewise, the correlation between commitment and the total number of reasons generated was -0.02, indicating a clear independence between the two factors. Thus, initial knowledge and commitment were not associated with each other.

When asked how they wanted to resolve differences of opinion just prior to negotiation, 87% ($n = 155$) of the students wanted to compromise, 12% ($n = 21$) wanted to win and no one wanted to lose. One percent ($n = 2$) chose "other" negotiation strategies. Differences in the number of students opting for each strategy were significant, χ^2 (3, $N = 178$) = 371.89, $p < 0.0001$. A clear bias in favor of compromising was evident. However, no relationship was found between the desired strategy for resolving the conflict and the quantity of initial knowledge ($r = 0.01$), nor was the desired strategy related to the strength of commitment to the favored position ($r = -0.12$). Thus, subjects could have few reasons for favoring a position, yet be highly committed to the position and still want to compromise.

3.3. *Predicting the outcomes of negotiation*

Arguers could choose to end the negotiation in one of three ways: a win–loss, a compromise, or a stand-off. The method for identifying the outcome of each negotiation was always based upon explicit statements made by both arguers as to how the negotiation ended.

A *win–loss* occurred when the following two criteria were satisfied: (1) one arguer maintained support for his or her original position *and* explicitly stated that his or her original position had been upheld; (2) the other arguer in the dyad capitulated and stated that he or she had, indeed, lost and switched positions. The following is an example of a negotiation ending in a win–lose outcome:

B: Well, I still think Dwayne is right.
A: He was.
B: Don't you think both of them should just understand each other?
A: No. I think she shoulda paid up.
B: O.K., she shoulda paid up on time.
A: Yeah, Marsha shoulda paid up on time. I lost.

B: You lost. Marsha shoulda paid up on time.

A: Yeah.

A *compromise* resulted when both arguers explicitly stated that they changed their original positions and effected a compromise. According to our theory, a compromise is defined as a resolution in which some element of each position is changed so that common ground can be created between two arguers. Most compromises are achieved by two arguers agreeing to support one side of the argument but with new conditions that constrain the way the favored position will be supported in the future. The following is an example of a compromise negotiation:

A: Well, we can change it. We can compromise.

B: Compromise. That's it. Yeah, O.K.

A: So, they can talk a little, see how things go. They both have to understand their positions. They can't see each other all the time like they used to. Steve has to realize this and Roberta can't be a jerk about it. So, they can still talk and fix up some dates.

B: Right and maybe Roberta can get her new friends together with Steve.

A: So then she could see more of Steve.

A *stand-off* resulted when the two arguers each maintained their original positions and refused to change. In stand-off negotiations, arguers continually justified their own position and criticized their opponent's position until the time allotted for the negotiation elapsed. A small number of dyads reached a stand-off by "agreeing to disagree", or by adopting the bogus resolution of supporting both of the incompatible positions simultaneously.

Despite the possibility that arguers could disagree about what outcome they arrived at, subjects in only two dyads (2%) did so. Arguers in four dyads (4%) resolved their differences in an ambiguous fashion so that the outcomes of their negotiations could not be categorized. The data from these six dyads were removed from further analysis. Thus, only 166 students were included in the outcome analyses. Three judges achieved 96% agreement in classifying the outcomes attained by the dyads.

3.3.1. *The effect of instructions to compromise on negotiated outcomes*

Figure 2 depicts the proportion of subjects who ended their negotiations in a win–loss, compromise, or stand-off. The results of a chi-square analysis, collapsed across all dyads (i.e., all male, all female, or male-female) within a condition, indicated that instructions differentially affected the frequency of negotiating the three different outcomes, $\chi^2 (2, n = 166) = 7.06, p < 0.05$.

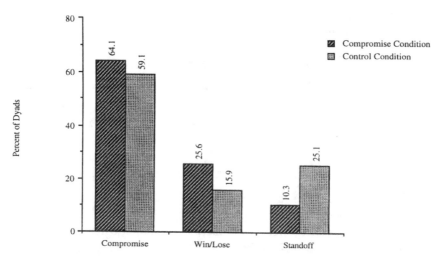

Figure 2.   *Proportions of dyads in the compromise and control conditions achieving a compromise, win–loss, or a stand-off*

Post-hoc tests revealed that instructions did not affect the proportion of compromises across the two experimental conditions. Approximately 59% of the dyads compromised whether instructed to or not. Instructions, however, did affect the proportion of dyads who chose to end negotiations in a stand-off or win–loss, χ^2 (1, $n = 64$) $= 6.89$, $p < 0.01$. Couples asked to compromise ended in a stand-off less frequently (10%) than those in the control condition (25%). Conversely, instructions to compromise *increased* the proportion of couples who ended with win–loss resolution (26%) in comparison to the proportion in the control condition (16%). Thus, one result of compromise instructions was in the reduction of the number of unproductive stand-off dialogues. If a compromise could not be reached, a win–loss ending was then chosen. Negotiating win–loss outcomes, like compromises, requires that common ground and agreement be established, despite the fact that one arguer capitulates to another. Stand-off solutions do not create common ground and clearly, no agreement exists between the two arguers.

3.3.2. *The effect of gender on negotiated outcomes*
A chi-square analysis focusing on differences among the types of dyads (i.e., all male, all female, or male-female) indicated that in the Control condition, couples in the three different dyads chose to compromise at different rates, χ^2 (2,

$n = 26) = 14.19$, $p < 0.001$. Differences among the dyads were not found in the Compromise Condition.

Table 2. *Proportion of dyads in each gender type that ended negotiations in a win–loss or compromise in the control condition*

	Mean	Male–Male	Female–Female	Male–Female
		Dyad Type		
Compromise Ending	0.59	0.67	0.75	0.37
Win–Loss Ending	0.16	0.09	0.06	0.31

Table 2 illustrates the rate of compromise and win–loss outcomes in the control condition across the three types of dyads. Subjects in the all male (67%) and all female dyads (75%) were more likely to compromise than were subjects in the male–female dyads (37%). Conversely, subjects in the all male (9%) and all female dyads (6%) were less likely to chose a win-lose ending than subjects in the male–female dyads (31%), χ^2 (2, $n = 7) = 12.21$, $p < 0.005$. The rate at which subjects in the male–female dyads chose a win-lose outcome was *triple* that for subjects in the two other dyads.

Males and females negotiating together differed on one significant dimension. When choosing to end the negotiation in a win–loss, females won the argument 88.9% of the time and men won 11.1% of the time. A Fisher exact probability test indicated this difference to be significant, $p < 0.005$. The data from the male–female dyads were unambiguous and clearly incompatible with the notion that females compromise more with males and do not win negotiations (Gilligan 1982; Tannen 1990). The results from the studies of Gottman and his colleagues (Gottman 1993; Gottman and Krokoff 1989), Christensen and Heavy (1990, 1993) and Weiss (1990), who reported women to be more tenacious, are more in keeping with our data.

3.3.3. *The relationship between initial knowledge and negotiated outcome*
To determine whether arguers' initial knowledge affected the outcomes of negotiation, a four-way ANOVA was carried out on the total number of reasons generated, with Negotiated Outcome (compromise vs. win vs. loss vs. stand-off) and Condition (compromise vs. control) as between-subjects factors. Position (favored vs. opposed) and Knowledge Type (supporting vs. problem-oriented) were within-subjects factors.

A significant main effect was found for Negotiated Outcome, $F(3,158) = 6.89$, $p < 0.0001$. Scheffe's post-hoc tests revealed that subjects who negotiated compromises generated more total reasons (M = 10.21, *S.D.* = 4.80) than subjects who lost (*M* = 6.23, *S.D.* = 4.57) or ended in a stand-off (*M* = 6.62, *S.D.* = 2.82), $p < 0.05$. The mean number of reasons generated by compromisers did not differ from the mean generated by winners (*M* = 8.53, *S.D.* = 4.43). Winners did not differ significantly from losers or those ending in stand-offs and occupied a middle ground in terms of their initial knowledge.

To determine whether compromisers also had more *types* of argument knowledge as well as more total reasons, a chi-square analysis was carried out on the number of knowledge categories (e.g., supporting favored position, supporting opposed position, problems with favored position, problems with opposed position) each subject generated. Subjects were classified into one of two groups, based upon the number of argument categories they generated. Subjects who generated 1 or 2 categories (*n* = 77) were included in the Low group and subjects generating 3 or 4 categories (*n* = 89) were included in the High group.

Proportionately more compromisers than any other type of arguer were classified in the High group. Sixty-six percent of the compromisers generated at least three categories of knowledge, compared to 47% who ended in stand-offs, 29% who ended in a win and 18% who ended in a loss. These differences were highly significant, χ^2 (3, *n* = 166) = 19.41, $p < 0.001$.

Analyses were then carried out to determine how the knowledge pairing of arguers affected the outcomes. Approximately half of the subjects generated up to 8 reasons, while the other half had 9 or more reasons. To determine the matching of knowledge across pairs of arguers, each arguer who generated up to 8 reasons was placed in a "Low" generation category (*n* = 84) and each one who generated 9 or more reasons was placed in a "High" generation category (*n* = 82). The knowledge pairing of each dyad could then be characterized in one of three ways: High-High (*n* = 25), High-Low (*n* = 30) and Low-Low (*n* = 28).

The results of a chi-square analysis showed that the type of outcomes negotiated varied significantly as a function of arguers' pairings on initial knowledge, χ^2 (4, *n* = 83) = 11.78, $p < 0.02$. The data are presented in Table 3.

Table 3. *Proportion of dyads effecting different outcomes as a function of the dyadic composition of initial knowledge (number of reasons)*

	Compromise	Win–Lose	Stand-off
High–High	0.84	0.12	0.04
High–Low	0.63	0.17	0.20
Low–Low	0.39	0.32	0.29

Those couples who received a High–High classification on the *total number of reasons generated* compromised more frequently (84%) than those who received a Low–Low classification (39%), χ^2 (1, $n = 32) = 4.31$, $p < 0.05$. The knowledge pairings were also significantly related to the proportion of dyads ending in a stand-off. Dyads that were classified as Low–Low ended in a stand-off 29% of the time, whereas dyads who received a High–High classification ended in a stand-off 4% of the time, χ^2 (1, $n = 5) = 4.45$, $p < 0.05$. The knowledge pairings did not differ in the proportions of win–losses attained.

The same pattern of findings was observed when the *number of argument categories* was used as the criterion variable. Seventy-seven subjects generated a "Low" number of categories (i.e., 1 or 2 initial knowledge categories) and 89 subjects generated a "High" number of categories (i.e., 3 or 4 categories). This new knowledge matching could then be described in one of three ways: High–High ($n = 30$), High–Low ($n = 30$), Low–Low ($n = 24$).

Table 4. *Proportion of dyads effecting different outcomes as a function of the dyadic composition of initial knowledge (number of categories)*

	Compromise	Win–Lose	Stand-off
High–High	0.87	0.03	0.10
High–Low	0.52	0.21	0.27
Low–Low	0.42	0.42	0.16

The results of a chi-square analysis, presented in Table 4, showed that outcomes varied as a function of the knowledge match within dyads, χ^2 (4, $n = 83) = 17.21$, $p < 0.001$. Subjects who were both high on number of argument categories generated were more likely to effect a compromise (87%) than subjects who were unequal (52%) or both low on the number of argument categories generated (42%), χ^2 (1, $n = 36) = 4.63$; $p < 0.05$. Conversely, subjects who were both low on the number of argument categories generated were more likely to end with a win–loss (42%) than subjects who were unequal (21%) or both high on number of argument categories (3%), χ^2 (1, $n = 11) = 9.57$, $p < 0.01$. The frequency of ending in a stand-off did not vary significantly as a function of the knowledge match between arguers.

3.3.4. *The relationships between initial knowledge, desired strategy, commitment and negotiated outcome*

Loglinear regression analyses were carried out to determine the relationships among initial knowledge, desired strategy, commitment and outcome. Given that initial knowledge was a strong correlate of the type of outcome negotiated, we sought to determine whether desired strategy and commitment interacted in any significant way to increase the power with which the outcome could be predicted. The results of the loglinear regression analyses showed that the desired strategy and commitment, coupled with knowledge, *did not* add any significant variance to the equation when predicting the outcomes of negotiation. Thus, despite the importance of commitment and desire, these two factors were not as important as prior beliefs and knowledge subjects held about both positions in predicting negotiated outcomes.

The only time the desired strategy was found to be significant was in predicting the frequency of wins and loss, $\chi^2(3, n = 169) = 9.19$. $p < 02$. Post hoc tests showed that the desire to win versus the desire to compromise affected the frequency of winning. Thirty percent of those subjects who wanted to win actually won, compared to 8% of those who wanted to compromise. Furthermore, only 5% who wanted to win incurred a loss compared to 11% who wanted to compromise.

3.4. *Biases in position selection as a function of outcome*

An analysis was carried out to determine whether the position arguers upheld at the end of the negotiation would differ for compromisers versus winners and losers. As we previously argued, a prototypical compromise negotiation entails supporting one side of an issue, but with new constraints placed upon *how* the position is to be supported. Compromisers should be significantly biased in terms of what position they choose to conditionalize. They most often support the position that ensures a continuation of a social relationship between the parties involved in the conflict and minimizes the harm suffered by either party.

Table 5 shows the proportion of dyads who supported each side of the issue as a function of the negotiated outcome. The data were collapsed across condition and scenario because no significant differences were found on either dimension. Ninety-six percent of all compromising dyads supported the side of the argument that allowed the friendship to be continued, χ^2 $(1,53) = 45.30$, $p < 0.0001$. Furthermore, during the negotiation, almost all dyads who compromised stated *explicitly* that their support of one side would allow the two story characters to remain friends. Dyads who ended with a win–loss, however, supported each side of the argument with equal frequency. Approximately half of the dyads voted to maintain and renegotiate the conditions for continued friendship, while the other half supported the abandonment of the friendship or the abandonment of the necessity to loan money.

Table 5.   *Positions upheld in compromise and win-lose outcomes*

Negotiations Ending in Compromise Outcomes	Proportion of dyads
Break off friendship/Do not lend money	0.04
Reevaluate how friendship/lending money should be conducted	0.96
Negotiations Ending in Win-Lose Outcomes	
Break off friendship/Do not lend money	0.53
Reevaluate how friendship/lending money should be conducted	0.47

3.5. *Explanations for ending the negotiation in a compromise or a win–loss*

The reasons that arguers offered in explaining why they arrived at a compromise or a win–loss were identified from the statements generated by the arguers at the end of the negotiation dialogues. Clauses that were identified as explanatory typically provided an answer to the question: Why was a particular outcome negotiated? Two coders achieved a 94% agreement in identifying these explanatory clauses. Each dyad generated a mean of 3.27 ($S.D. = 1.44$) explanations. The mean did not differ across outcomes or the two story themes.

   The explanation data were then coded into three distinct categories: a focus on past conditions, a focus on positive future action-outcomes and a focus on negative future action-outcomes. Two coders achieved 96% agreement in classifying the explanation data into the three content categories. The proportion of explanations falling into each of the three categories is presented in Table 6.

Table 6.   *Content of the explanations offered for compromise and win-lose outcomes*

	Compromise	Win–Lose
Focus on past events and the laying of blame	0.23	0.56
Focus on positive future plans and events	0.63	0.11
Focus on negative future predictions and events	0.16	0.34

   An ANOVA was carried out on the proportion data with Story Theme (borrowing money vs. friendship) and Dyad Outcome (compromise vs. win–lose) as between subjects variables. Focus of Explanation (past, positive future action, or negative future action) was the within subjects variable. Results indicated that the proportion of explanation in each of the three categories differed for the two outcome types, $F(2,128) = 15.92$, $p < 0.0001$. This difference held up for both story themes.

Compromisers focused a clear majority of their explanations on positive future actions identifying the conditions necessary for the maintaining the relationship between the story characters, as well as suggesting long range plans to ensure that their new conditions be met and that future conflict should be avoided. Winners and Losers, on the other hand, focused their explanations on the past, imputing blame and responsibility for harm to one party. When winners and losers did focus on the future, they cited negative future actions and consequences that would occur if the opposition were supported.

3.6. *Conflict talk among compromisers versus winners and losers*

To determine whether different time orientation focuses differentiated the conflict talk of compromisers versus winners and losers, all clauses in the negotiations were coded in terms of their focus on the past, present or the future. Two coders yielded a 98% reliability estimate in coding the time orientation of clauses. Table 7 presents the mean proportion of clauses generated for each of the three time orientation categories.

Table 7. *Mean proportion of clauses focusing on the past, present and future generated by dyads effecting compromise and win-lose outcomes*

	Compromise	Win–Lose
Past	0.27	0.46
Present	0.46	0.47
Future	0.28	0.07

The data indicated that the time focus of the negotiations was significantly associated with the outcome of the negotiation, $F(2,132) = 28.56$, $p < 0.0001$. All arguers focused about 46% of their clauses on the present. These present-oriented clauses typically focused on the task at hand and included remarks such as "What position do you support?", "Why do you think that?", "Let's get this thing resolved." Significant differences were found, however, for the proportion of clauses that focused on the past versus the future. Dyads effecting a compromise generated proportionately more future-oriented clauses (28%), compared to dyads resulting in win–lose outcomes (7%). On the other hand, dyads effecting a win–loss generated proportionately more clauses focusing on the past (46%) than compromisers (27%). Thus, these results converge on those found for the explanation data above: Compromisers focus on the future, while winners and losers focus predominantly on the past.

4. Discussion

The results of this study have clear implications for theories of argumentative decision making and reasoning, particularly in validating the hypotheses that Stein and Miller (1993a, b) derived from their model. Arguers' initial knowledge states, their desires and their conversational styles were all significant predictors of the outcomes of negotiation.

4.1. *Initial knowledge*

4.1.1. *Amount and type of argument knowledge*
The amount of knowledge subjects had about the favored and opposed positions were not equivalent. Subjects offered more knowledge about their favored position than the stance they opposed. The relative amounts of supporting and opposing reasons for the favored position were the inverse of those for the opposed position. Subjects offered more supporting reasons for their favored position than for their opponent's position and they revealed more problem oriented reasons for their opponent's position than for their own position. These data are similar to findings reported in the hypotheses testing literature (McKenzie 1994; Klayman and Ha 1987, 1989), where people focus primarily on evidence in favor of rather than against their working hypothesis.

The asymmetrical nature of argument knowledge may be a critical factor in explaining the perceived "bias" in evidence generation during hypothesis testing. Our data suggest that arguers do not have access to knowledge that would disprove their hypothesis. Subjects who had minimal knowledge about an issue focused primarily (75% of the time) on reasons supporting their favored position. They generated problem oriented knowledge about their opposition 21% of the time and offered knowledge in support of the opposition or against their own position less than 4% of the time. Even when subjects were more knowledgeable and could generate two or three categories of argument knowledge, they still had difficulty (56% of the time) generating any problems with their own position.

Subjects may not be "biased" implicitly for or against a position, as Ross and Lepper (1979) have suggested. Rather, they may show a bias in favor of a position *because* they have acquired more knowledge about the benefits of that position and have yet to acquire any evidence that would qualify or contradict that position. This suggestion runs counter to the "bias" hypothesis and provides an alternative conception about the causal relationship between biases in decision making and knowledge. We suggest that the content and structure of acquired knowledge provide the regulatory force for desire and bias, as much as desire and bias constrain knowledge access. Rather than desiring to dominate access to available knowledge, the process is bi-directional and may be even more weighted in the direction of knowledge controlling desire and bias.

4.1.2. *The content of supporting and opposing reasons*

The reasons generated for and against a position provided insight into the thinking that occurs when subjects focus on their favored versus their opponent's stance. When providing reasons in support of a claim, subjects drew upon *current beliefs* and conditions in conjunction with *past events*. For example, in supporting the story protagonist who wanted to maintain a friendship with an old friend despite the protagonist's current activities of making new friends, subjects in our study would say, "Well, I support Sharon's desire to maintain her friendship with Steve because she has been Steve's friend for a very long time and they have had a special relationship. Furthermore, Sharon has not done anything wrong. She is currently at a new school and she needs to make new friends in order to survive in the new school."

When criticizing a position, over 40% of all reasons were future oriented and included prescriptives as well as possible solutions for resolving the conflict. Explicit references to the past rarely occurred in mentioning problems. Talk about the future is important, especially in terms of the social origins of argument knowledge. Although most formal theories of argumentation acknowledge the social origins of evidence, the role that social knowledge plays in generating evidence is rarely explicated. With the exception of Hart and Honore (1959), two legal theorists who use concepts of social responsibility and justice to examine the validity of evidence, the role of personal goals, preferences, beliefs and moral standards is ignored. Any systematic examination of the content of reasoning during argumentation or hypothesis testing, however, must acknowledge that intentional language (i.e., reference to personal goals and actions) is continually used. Most important, however, is that arguers almost always look to the future in constructing a resolution. Rather than merely focusing on the past or present circumstances, even before they begin negotiation, arguers attempt to deal with the past and present in the light of future possibilities.

4.2. *The effects of instructions on the outcomes of negotiation*

In two of the three types of dyads, instructions to compromise did not increase the number of compromise solutions, relative to a control group, but compromise instructions proved significant in lowering the rate of stand-off outcomes and in increasing the number of compromises between men and women. Without compromise instructions, men and women compromised 37% of the time compared to 64% of the time with compromise instructions. Men and women negotiating in the control condition differed from the two other types of dyads in the number of compromises and win–loss outcomes that resulted. Unconstrained male–female negotiations ended in a win–loss significantly more than the negotiations of same sexed couples.

Many explanations can be generated for differences in male–female negotiations, when compared to same gender negotiations. One finding was clear, however, from our data. When men and women chose to end their negotiation in a win–loss, women almost always won, bringing into question results from previous studies and observations that women compromise more than men and that men usually win when arguing with women (Gilligan 1982; Tannen 1990). Our women were not compromisers any more than the men. As Christensen and Heavy (1990), as well as Gottman and Krokoff (1989), observed in married couple interaction, wives are often more demanding, more tenacious and more focused in their on-line negotiations with their husbands, often causing husbands to feel "flooded" or to feel intense physiological arousal in reaction to conflictual interchange (Gottman 1994).

When the emotional intensity of the interaction increased in the present study, many men capitulated to their partners. A more detailed analysis of these male–female negotiations (Bly and Stein 1993) indicated that women were as emotionally involved in the dialogues as men, interrupting men more frequently when they were winning, than when they compromised or ended in stand-offs. In fact, the relative number of interruptions each partner generated proved to be a sensitive indicator of who was winning with the winner always interrupting more than the loser (Bly and Stein 1993).

4.3. *Relationships among initial knowledge, desired strategy, commitment and outcome*

The fact that we found a strong relationship between the amount of prior knowledge and the outcomes of negotiation strongly suggests that cognitive, as well as emotional, factors play a significant role in determining the process and outcomes of negotiation. Having access to supporting reasons for an opposing point of view in combination with problematic knowledge about one's own position puts a person in an ideal position to compromise, if the desire is present. When subjects did not have access to these two categories of knowledge, they were more at risk for ending their negotiation in a loss or a stand-off, despite the fact that the clear majority of arguers *wanted* to compromise when negotiating. In our negotiation settings, wanting to compromise was not enough to ensure that a compromise occurred.

Our data indicated that inferences made *during* the negotiation and prior knowledge about each position overpowers initial desire. Although subjects wanted to compromise, their ability and skill as well as that of their opponent's, may affect their interactional stances and the types of outcomes they can tolerate. The fact that men and women had difficulty compromising under more "natural" conditions, where no instructions were provided, may indicate that these couples have other agendas that are not experienced by couples of the same sex. In our visual and verbal analysis of the male–female negotiations, considerably more 'off-task' conversation occurred, involving flirting, attempts on the part of men to deploy the woman's attention and attempts to impress one another with information not related to the negotiation. These added factors, however, do not explain the fact that almost all wins were attained by women.

A better explanation may be that many of the wins given to women were temporary, especially from the men's viewpoint. In debriefing our subjects after the negotiations ended, many men indicated that they would have said just about anything to get out of the negotiation with their female partner. They felt trapped in the situation and reported that continued opposition wasn't worth the effort. The predictions these men made about future interactions corroborated their spontaneous accounts of the negotiation process. Over half of the men who lost did not believe they had lost, even though they fully acknowledged that they *said* they had lost on video tape.

It may be that the argument is not really over after a negotiation when a winner and loser are declared. Although win–loss solutions appear to be stable at the time of the resolution, the loser may not think of the outcome as fixed. Indeed, the working strategy of the loser may be to end a situation where losses are accruing, get out and plan a subsequent move where winning will be more probable. We offer this suggestion because all too often, the dynamic and changing nature of negotiations are forgotten. Arguments occur because important personal goals of two or more people come into clash with each other. When one of the disputant's goals is blocked by another, the blockage is rarely accepted as a permanent blockage. Indeed, the loser often became more motivated in subsequent interactions to gain control or to win, especially if the loser has received poor treatment at the hands of the victor. "Covert" loser behaviors have been well documented in the business and organizational literature (Stern and El-Ansary, In press), as well as in the family interaction literature. Thus, the dynamic, longitudinal quality of a relationship, via negotiation, is of primary concern. In fact, this more dynamic, long range quality is what Tannen (1990) and Gilligan (1982) may be sensing. We need data, however, to corroborate their intuitions. As we found in the present study, women are quite able to maintain the floor and to negotiate on their own behalf. Whether these gender differences hold over time, within the same relationship and over multiple contexts, must be investigated in future research.

4.4. *The relationship between the conversational focus and the outcome*

As previous studies on conflictual interchange (Gottman 1993, 1994), negativity and violence (Beck 1988) indicate, the content and process of negotiation really do matter. Different outcomes have different precursors during conversational interaction. In our study, win–loss negotiations differed substantially from compromises. Two differences were particularly apparent.

First, the side of the issue that the two arguers chose to uphold at the end of the negotiation differed markedly as a function of whether they compromised or opted for a win–loss solution. Couples choosing to compromise almost always supported the side that permitted the social relationship between two disputants to continue and grow. Winners (and losers), however, chose to support each side with equal probability, with winners sometimes advocating the maintenance of the relationship and sometimes the dissolution of the relationship.

Second, the focus of attention during the negotiation was significantly different. Compromisers were primarily oriented toward creating a new plan of action that would incorporate some of the concerns of each participant. Thus, they were engaged in choosing the claim of the arguer who chose to support the continuation of a social relationship between two disputants and setting mutually agreed upon constraints on this goal. In the building of a new plan of action, some of the concerns of each party were being addressed.

Winners and losers, on the other hand, focused more on blame and responsibility in past actions. In effect, winners and losers were engaged in the type of decision making that often occurs in legal settings or courts of law, where juries attempt to assess blame, impute responsibility and mete out punishment (Hart and Honore 1958; Pennington and Hastie 1993). Although we do not characterize the feelings and emotions of couples in the present paper, it was clear from the video tapes and the dialogues that those subjects who argued for positions that cut off a relationship often displayed anger in both verbal and non-verbal interaction. The main reason for their anger, which was also their primary reason given for seeking a win, was that one of the disputants had intentionally violated a moral standard or contract previously negotiated by the two disputants. According to Stein, Trabasso and Liwag (1992, 1994), unexpected violations of moral or social standards are the most frequent reasons given for anger and an angry person's attempt to seek revenge or to guarantee that these violations never occur again.

5. General conclusions

We have shown that the study of on-line arguing and negotiating is indeed a rich source for the study of conversational analysis. Further, our data illustrate that natural occurring language behavior can be studied quite easily within an "experimental" setting, without disrupting the natural flow of negotiation or conversation. Indeed, those investigators who are involved in discerning the most constructive course of action during negotiation procedures almost always attempt to manipulate and constrain the strategies that two disputants use. Although constructive interaction is always a possibility in natural "uncontrolled" negotiation, our data suggest that the probability decreases markedly in some situations.

The necessity for intervention was particularly true with respect to men and woman negotiating. Without compromise instructions, men and women negotiated compromises only 37% of the time. With compromise instructions, they negotiated compromises 59% of the time. Furthermore, compromise instructions decreased the frequency of stand-off resolutions and increased the frequency of win–loss solutions. Thus, intervention is necessary when the moral and social outcomes of conversation are of equal importance as the study of conversation itself.

The results of our study also have implications for theories of conversational analysis such as the framework and postulates developed by Grice (1989a, b). Negotiation often involves deception and hurtful communication and in this regard, the parties privy to argumentative interactions make very different assumptions about each other than when they are in agreement with each other. Consequently, in situations of deceit and harm, what two participants infer that the other person knows and what they want the other person to know varies markedly from situations in which accord and agreement are present.

The study of conversation also has major implications for theories of everyday memory and eyewitness testimony (see Stein, Wade and Liwag 1996 for a current essay on this topic). Although we did not present the memory data that we collected after our on-line negotiations ended, all of our subjects were asked to recall their entire conversational interchange in as much detail as possible. When both source memory (who said what) and memory for content (what was said) were analyzed, the data analyses revealed that overall, losers had the best source memory, with winners not far behind. Compromisers had the *least* accurate source memory, in comparison to winners and losers. For content memory, compromisers and losers had the best memory while winners included significantly less detail about the actual content of the conversation.

These data illustrate that the outcome of a conflict, as well as the conversational interaction leading up to the outcome, are strong determinants of memory accuracy. Compromisers have very different goals from those of winners and winners have different goals from losers. Our hypothesis is that the goals of the arguer during negotiation hold the key to describing the resulting memory representation of conversation, primarily because the goal predicts and directs the focus of attention, as well as the constructive meaning analysis carried out during the conversational input.

Winners have the goal of persuading throughout their conversation. They ask fewer questions about their antagonist's position and offer twice as many repudiations and rebuttals to their opponent than do arguers who compromise. When asked to remember the conversation, winners focus primarily on two types of information: support they offered for their own position and counter-arguments against their opponents position. Thus, the content of their conversational interaction corresponded quite nicely to the organization of their prior knowledge.

Winners did not include much information about their opponent's position and they rarely, if ever, included any information about the weaknesses of their own position. Thus, according to Ross and Lepper (1980), winners indeed preserved their initial belief structure and in the process they also failed to learn anything relevant about their opponent's position.

Losers, on the other hand, were able to give a more accurate account of what both they and their opponent said. The goals of the losers, however, were different from those of winners. Although losers may have initially desired to convince their opponent about the legitimacy of their position, losers were the ones with the least knowledge about the issue. Even though winners' knowledge was highly constrained, they had more knowledge than losers and their knowledge was more causally coherent than losers' knowledge.

The differences in knowledge structures were revealed in the number of questions losers asked about the winner's position. Losers also showed explicit evidence of switching their goals from support of their own stance to support of their opponent's stance. This switch in goals served losers well because they were able to acquire accurate information about the winner's position as well as retain information about the strengths of their own position.

The fact that most compromisers had the goal of compromising very early on in their conversations may explain why their content memory was the highest. Much of their conversation was directed toward the mutual construction of a new plan of action that took into consideration interests of both parties. The goal of creating common ground among themselves may require very accurate and precise interpretation of what the other person has said, primarily because the next suggestion in the conversation is dependent upon the previous one. Furthermore, the construction of a new plan may involve causally representing the new constraining conditions in a highly coherent manner, making the interchange more memorable. The focus on a "joint" plan, however, may predispose compromisers to give priority to what was said rather than to who said it. The important goal in a compromise is to arrive at a workable solution that is independent of who suggested the solution.

If we are able to replicate these results, then it becomes imperative to describe the specific goals of people in conflict as well as the content and structure of the conversation associated with different goals. The goals determine the focus of attention and possible biases that operate during the encoding process. Clearly, the conflict paradigm is one way of providing a more accurate account of constructive memory processes for personally meaningful interaction.

Acknowledgements

This research was funded in part by grants from the Smart Foundation and the University of Chicago Biomedical Grant to Nancy L. Stein, the National Institute of Child Health and Human Development (Grant No. HD 25742) to Tom Trabasso and Nancy L. Stein and the Spencer Foundation to Tom Trabasso. We are grateful to the students at Rich Central High School and to Dr. Anthony Moriarty, Associate Principal, for their help, participation and insight into the process of compromise. We are indebted to Maria D. Liwag, for her generosity in craftsmanship and intellectual collaboration, without which this article would not have been completed. Our appreciation is also extended to Mike Ross and Tom Trabasso for their advice and comments on an earlier version of this paper and to John Holmes for suggestions and scholarship on conflict resolution and sex differences. We would also like to thank Anne Wright, Joshua Stein, Rebecca Hutton and Sharon Lieberman for their help in data collection, transcription and administration of the study.

Notes

1. The ANOVA was conducted on the $y' = 2$ arcsin $(y^{1/2})$ transformation of the proportion data. This transformation was conducted in all the succeeding ANOVA's involving proportion data.

References

Beck, A.T. 1988. *Love Is Not Enough.* New York: Harper and Row.

Bleckman, E.A. and M.J. McEnroe. 1985. "Effective Family Problem Solving." *Child Development* 56.429–437.

Bly, B. and N.L. Stein 1993. "Differences in Interruptions when Arguers Compromise versus Win or Lose." Paper presented at the Winter Text Conference, Jackson Hole, Wyo.

Chi, M.T.H., J.D. Slotta and N. de Leeuw. 1993. "From Things to Processes: A theory of conceptual change for learning science concepts." *The Journal for the European Association for Learning and Instruction.*

Christensen, A. and C.L. Heavey. 1990. "Gender and Social Structure in the Demand/ Withdraw Pattern of Marital Conflict." *Journal of Personality and Social Psychology* 59.73–81.

Christensen, A. and G. Margolin. 1988. "Conflict and Alliance in Distressed and Non-distressed Families." In *Relationships within families*, R.A. Hinde and Stevenson-Hinde (eds), 263–282. New York: Oxford University Press.

Christensen, A. and C.L. Heavey. 1993. "Gender Differences in Marital Conflict: The demand/withdraw interaction pattern. In *Gender Issues in Contemporary Society*, S. Oskamp and M. Costanzo (eds). Newbury Park, Calif.: Sage.

Cummings, E.M. and P. Davies. 1994. *Children and Marital Conflict: The impact of family dispute and resolution.* New York: Guilford.

Dunn, J. 1989. *The Beginnings of Social Understanding.* Cambridge, Mass.: Harvard University Press.

Dunn, J. 1992. *Young Children's Close Relationships: Beyond attachment.* London: Sage.

Eisenberg, A.R. and C. Garvey. 1981. "Children's Use of Verbal Strategies in Resolving Conflicts." *Discourse Processes* 4.149–170.

Ericsson, K.A. and J. Smith. 1991. *Toward a General Theory of Expertise: Prospects and limits.* New York: Cambridge University Press.

Fisher, R. and S. Brown. 1988. *Getting Together: Building a relationship that gets to yes.* Boston: Houghton Mifflin.

Forgatch, M. 1989. "Effects of 'Negative' Emotion on Family Problem Solving." *Journal of Marriage and Family* 51.115–124.

Gilligan, C. 1982. *In a Different Voice: Psychological theory and women's development.* Cambridge, Mass.: Harvard University Press.

Goodwin, M.H. 1990. *He-Said-She-Said: Talk as social organization among black children.* Bloomington, Ind: Indiana University Press.

Gottman, J.M. 1993. "The Roles of Conflict Engagement, Escalation and Avoidance in Marital Interaction: A longitudinal view of five types of couples." *Journal of Consulting and Clinical Psychology* 61.6–15.

Gottman, J. 1994. *Why Marriages Succeed or Fail.* New York: Simon and Schuster.

Gottman, J. M and L.J. Krokoff. 1989. "Marital Interaction and Satisfaction: A longitudinal view." *Journal of Consulting and Clinical Psychology* 57.47–52.

Gottman, J.M. and R.W. Levenson. 1991. *Marital Processes Predictive of Later Dissolution: Behavior, physiology and health.*

Grice, P. 1989a. "Logic and Conversation." In *Studies in the Way of Words*, P. Grice, 22–40. Cambridge, Mass.: Harvard University Press.

Grice, P. 1989b. "Further notes on logic and conversation." In *Studies in the Way of Words*, P. Grice, 41–57. Cambridge, Mass.: Harvard University Press.

Grotevant, H.D. and C.R. Cooper. 1985. "Individuation in Family Relationships: A perspective in individual differences in the development of role taking skill in adolescence." *Human Development* 29.82–100.

Hart, H.L.A. and A.M. Honore. 1959. *Causation and the Law.* Oxford: Oxford University Press.

Hofer, M. and B. Pikowsky. 1993. "Validation of a Category System for Arguments in Conflict Discourse." *Argumentation* 7.135–148.

Klayman, J. and Y.-W. Ha. 1987. "Confirmation, Disconfirmation and Information in Hypothesis Testing." *Psychological Review* 94.211–228.

Klayman, J. and Y.-W. Ha. 1989. "Hypothesis Testing in Rule Discovery: Strategy, structure and content." *Journal of Experimental Psychology: Learning, Memory and Cognition* 15.596–604.

Koehler, J. 1989. "Judgments of Evidence Quality among Scientists as a Function of Prior Beliefs and Commitments." Unpublished Ph.D. dissertation, University of Chicago.

McKenzie, C.R.M. 1994. "Taking into Account the Strength of an Alternative Hypothesis." Unpublished Ph.D. dissertation, University of Chicago.

Murray, F.B. 1972. "Acquisition of Conservation through Social Interaction." *Developmental Psychology* 6.1–6.

Pennington, N. and R. Hastie. 1993. "The Story Model for Juror Decision Making." In *Inside the juror*, R. Hastie (ed.), 192–221. New York: Cambridge University Press.

Piaget, J. 1932. *The Moral Judgment of the Child.* New York: Free Press.

Resnick, L.B. 1991. "Shared Cognition: Thinking as social practice." In *Perspectives on socially shared cognition*, L.B. Resnick, J.M. Levine and S.D. Teasley (eds), 1–20. Washington, D.C.: American Psychological Association.

Reyna, V., W. Woodruff and C. Brainerd. 1992. "Attitude Change in Adults and Adolescents: Moderation versus polarization, statistics versus case histories." Unpublished manuscript, University of Arizona.

Ross, H.S. and C.L. Conant. 1993. "The Social Structure of Early Conflict: Interaction, relationships and alliances." In *Conflict in Childhood and Adolescence*, C.U. Shantz and W.W. Hartup (eds), 153–185. New York: Cambridge University Press.

Ross, L. and M.R. Lepper. 1980. "The Perseverance of Beliefs: Empirical and normative considerations." In *New Directions for Methodology of Behavioral Science: Fallible judgment in behavioral research*, R.A. Shweder and D. Fiske (eds). San Francisco: Jossey-Bass.

Ross, M. and D. Holmberg. 1990. "Recounting the Past: Gender differences in the recall of events in the history of a close relationship." In *Self-inference Processes: The*

Ontario symposium. Vol. 6, M. Olson and M.P. Zanna (eds), 135–152. Hillsdale, N.J.: Lawrence Erlbaum.

Ross, L. and C. Stillinger. 1991. "Barriers to Conflict Resolution." *Negotiation Journal*, October, 1991.389–404.

Sherif, M. and C.W. Sherif. 1953. *Groups in Harmony and in Tension*. New York: Harper and Row.

Sherif, M. and C.W. Sherif. 1979. "Research on Inter-group Relations." In *The Social Psychology of Intergroup Relations*, W.G. Austin and S. Worchel (eds). Monterey, Calif.: Brooks-Cole.

Smetana, J.G. 1989. "Adolescents' and Parents' Reasoning about Actual Family Conflict." *Child Development* 60.1052–1067.

Smetana, J.G., J. Yau and S. Hanson. 1991. "Conflict Resolution in Families with Adolescents." *Journal of Research on Adolescence* 1.189–206.

Stein, N.L. and M. Liwag. 1996. "A Goal Appraisal Process Approach to Understanding and Remembering Emotional Events." In *New Approaches to the Development of Memory*, P. Van den Broek, P. Bauer and T. Bourg (eds). Hillsdale, N.J.: Lawrence Erlbaum.

Stein, N.L. and C.A. Miller. 1990. "I Win – You Lose: The development of argumentative thinking." In *Informal Reasoning and Instruction*, J. Voss, D. Perkins and J. Segal (eds), 265–290. Hillsdale, N.J.: Lawrence Erlbaum.

Stein, N.L. and C.A. Miller. 1993a. "A Theory of Argumentative Understanding: Relationships among position preference, judgments of goodness, memory and reasoning." *Argumentation* 7.183–204.

Stein, N.L. and C.A. Miller. 1993b. "The Development of Memory and Reasoning Skill in Argumentative Contexts: Evaluating, explaining and generating evidence." In *Advances in Instructional Psychology*. Vol. 4, R. Glaser (ed.), 285–335. Hillsdale, N.J.: Lawrence Erlbaum.

Stein, N.L., R.S. Bernas, D.J. Calicchia and A. Wright. 1995. "Understanding and Resolving Arguments: The dynamics of negotiation." In *Models of Understanding*, B. Britton and A.G. Graesser (eds). Hillsdale, N.J.: Lawrence Erlbaum.

Stein, N.L., T. Trabasso and M.D. Liwag 1993. "The Representation and Organization of Emotional Experience: Unfolding the emotion episode." In *Handbook of Emotions*, M.L. Lewis and J. Haviland (eds.) 279–300. New York: Guilford.

Stein, N.L., T. Trabasso and M.D. Liwag 1994. "The Rashomon Phenomenon: Personal frames and future-oriented appraisals in memory for emotional events." In *The Development of Future-oriented Processes*, M. Haith, J. Benson, R. Roberts and B. Pennington (eds), 409–436. Chicago: The University of Chicago Press.

Stein, N.L., E. Wade and M.D. Liwag. In press. "A Theoretical Approach to Understanding and Remembering Harmful Events." In *Memory for Everyday and Emotional Events*, N.L. Stein, P.A. Ornstein, B. Tversky and C.J. Brainerd (eds). Hillsdale, N.J.: Lawrence Erlbaum.

Stern, L.W. and A.I. El-Ansary. In press. "Marketing Channels: Strategy, design and management." In *The Logistics Handbook*, J. Robeson and W. Copacino (eds). New York: Free Press.

Tannen, D.J. 1990. *You Just Don't Understand: Women and men in conversation.* New York: William Morrow.

Tesla, C. and J. Dunn. 1992. "Getting along or Getting Your Own Way: The development of young children's use of argument in conflicts with mother and sibling." *Social Development* 1.107–121.

Trabasso, T., P. van den Broek, and S. Suh 1989. "Logical Necessity and Transitivity of Causal Relations in Stories." *Discourse Processes* 12.1–25.

Ury, W.L. 1991. *Getting Past No: Negotiating with difficult people.* New York: Bantam Books.

Vallone, R.P., L. Ross and M.R. Lepper. 1985. "The Hostile Media Phenomenon: Biased perception and perceptions of media bias in coverage of the Beirut massacre." *Journal of Personality and Social Psychology* 49.577–585.

Valsiner, J. and R. Cairns. 1992. "Theoretical Perspectives on Conflict and Development." In *Conflict in Child and Adolescent Development.* C.U. Shantz and W.W. Hartup (eds), New York: Cambridge University Press.

Vuchinich, S. 1987. "Starting and Stopping Spontaneous Family Conflicts." *Journal of Marriage and Family* 49.591–601.

Vuchinich, S. 1990. "The Sequential Organization of Closing in Verbal Conflict." In *Conflict Talk*, A. Grimshaw (ed.), 118–138. New York: Cambridge University Press.

Vuchinich, S. and J. Angelleli. 1995. "Family Interaction during Problem Solving." In *Perspectives on Family Communication*, M.A. Fitzpatrick and A. Vaneglisti (eds). Newberry Park, Calif.: Sage.

Vuchinich, S., J. Angelelli and A. Gatherum. 1995. *Context and Development in Family Problem Solving.* Unpublished manuscript, Oregon State University, Corvalis, Oregon.

Weiss, R. 1990. *Staying the Course: The emotional and social lives of men who do well at work.* New York: Free Press.

West, C. and D.H. Zimmerman. 1977. "Women's Place in Everyday Talk: Reflections on parent-child interaction." *Social Problems* 24.521–529.

Appendix: Borrowing money scenario

Diane and Michael became friends when they entered junior high school and started playing in the band. They have been friends for about five years now. When they don't have a band rehearsal on a Friday afternoon, they usually go to the mall. There, they visit their friend who works at 'The Gap' or play video games. When the stores close, they often go to a movie in the mall.

A couple of months ago, Diane wanted to buy a shirt at Merry-Go-Round, but she didn't have enough money to pay for it. Michael offered to lend her the extra money, so

Diane could buy the shirt. Diane borrowed the money from Michael and paid him back the next Monday at school.

A few weeks ago, Michael was getting his car tuned-up but he didn't have enough money to pay the whole bill. Since Diane was with him, she offered to loan Michael the extra $40 he needed. Michael thanked Diane and told her that he would try to pay her back early in the next week. But when the next week came, Michael did not have the money. Michael told Diane that he would try to borrow money from his parents so he could pay Diane back the following week. Diane told Michael that she would really appreciate it if Michael paid her back soon since she wanted to buy tickets to a concert that she thought would sell out. But Michael did not pay Diane back in this second week either.

Finally, Michael did pay Diane back in the third week. Michael told Diane that his parents had given him the money several days beforehand so that he could pay her back. But Michael kept forgetting to bring the money to school. However, Diane was still able to get tickets to the concert that she wanted to attend. Diane was upset that it took Michael so long to pay her back. Diane stated that she would not lend Michael money again. Diane felt that Michael was irresponsible in taking so long to repay her. Michael disagreed with Diane. He thought that Diane should loan him money in the future. Michael believed that he made an honest attempt to repay Diane.

Friendship scenario

Richard and Sharon have lived a block away from each other as long as they can remember, and they have always gone to the same public schools. They often eat dinner over at each other's houses, do homework together and talk about the people that they are interested in. They also really enjoy practicing new dance steps together. They usually practice in Richard's basement, because there is a lot of room and Richard's mom does not mind the music.

This fall they both started ninth grade, but for the first time, they are going to different schools. Richard is going to a Catholic school and Sharon is going to the local public school. Ever since school started, Richard and Sharon have been spending a lot less time together. While Sharon is still getting together with her old friends, Richard is making a lot of new friends. Sharon often asks Richard to join her and Richard's old friends, but Richard usually declines. Richard has explained to Sharon that since he is going to be at this Catholic school for the next four years, he needs to spend time getting to know new people.

Wednesday after school, Sharon walked over to Richard's house. Sharon asked Richard if he wanted to practice some new dance steps soon, because there was a dance scheduled for the next Saturday night at Sharon's high school. Sharon also invited Richard to come to the dance with her. Richard thanked Sharon for the invitation, but told Sharon that someone from his new school had already invited him to a party on Saturday.

Sharon was upset that Richard was spending so much time with his new friends. Sharon told Richard that they would not be able to maintain their friendship. Sharon felt that Richard did not think it was important enough to get together with her. Richard disagreed with Sharon. Richard believed that he and Sharon will always be friends. Richard felt that Sharon did not try to understand his need to make friends in a new school.

Communicating Evaluation in Narrative Understanding

Tom Trabasso and Aslı Özyürek
The University of Chicago

> No utterance can be put together without value judgment. Every utterance is above all an *evaluative orientation*. ... the disjuncture between referential meaning and evaluation is totally inadmissible. Referential meaning is molded by *evaluation* and it is *evaluation* after all which determines that a particular referential meaning may enter the purview of speakers"
>
> (Voloshinov/Bakhtin 1973:105)

Narratives, be they personal, third person, or fictional, are the main means by which we interpret, represent, and communicate life experience and its personal significance. This paper examines how a person evaluates the narrative life experience of another. The context in which the evaluations are communicated is one in which the person talks about what the narrative means as it is read sentence by sentence. Since the narratives are about the narrator's personal well-being and inter-personal interaction, *evaluation* processes are central both to the narrator and to the comprehender of the narrative communication. We report what comprehenders of narratives evaluate, how they evaluate them, and the kinds of linguistic devices they use in expressing evaluations when they talk about their understanding of the narrative life experience of another person to a third party listener.

Labov and Waletsky (1967) and Labov (1972) were the first to examine and report on the "evaluative" function of personal narratives. They asked the narrator to tell what happened during an experience where the narrator had been in serious danger. They regarded evaluation as "the means used by the narrator to indicate the point of the narrative, its raison d'être, why it was told, and what the narrator was getting at" (Labov 1972:366). In Labov and Waletsky's (1967) view, narration is a temporally ordered sequence of clauses. Evaluation was a disruption of the temporal order of events by the narrator in order to reflect upon and express the significance of the narrative. By departing from the temporal sequence, the narrator communicates something more important than the reference or mere recapitulation of the events. To make a point, the narrator uses evaluative devices that mark some narrative units off as more important than others. The point was to show which events were dangerous or unusual, strange, uncommon, or valenced and non-neutral and was often accompanied by expression of emotion.

In Labov and Waletsky's (1967) study, the narrators were under an instruction to report on events that were life threatening. It is not surprising, then, that their narrators reported and reflected upon events that were dangerous and emotionally charged. The key assumption of their analysis is that people, through narration, *evaluate* events in terms of their personal significance and express how the events affect the narrator's well-being. It is through narration, then, that one can understand how the narrator construes events in terms of the possible harms or benefits that ensue from them.

Goodwin and Goodwin (1987) examined how people make evaluations in spontaneous conversation among multiple participants. Evaluations for them are "assessments" and serve important interactional functions in building collaboratively a conversation. An assessment is a particular type of speech act through which the speaker evaluates objects or events in a conversation. As such, the speaker takes a position toward the phenomena being assessed as well the participants in the conversation. By assessing something, say as "beautiful", the speaker publicly commits himself to a particular evaluation of what he has witnessed and is now communicated to others. In turn, recipients are affected by the speaker's assessments and can judge whether the speaker can properly evaluate the events. The public display of the experience of one participant also provides resources for the interactive organization of co-experience with participants. As such, affect and emotions are public displays that constitute assessments and are pervasive and central to the organization of the interaction.

In our study where a reader is asked to talk about sentences, the author of the written text or the written text itself is analogous to the role of the speaker. Here the reader talks about the experience of a third (fictional) party. The author, in effect, describes and makes to the reader assessments or evaluations about the experiences of the characters and their emotional displays. The reader of the text is thus in the role of a recipient. The reader, in turn, reports to the experimenter how the reader understands and evaluates the life experiences of the characters in the story. The reader's talk is a kind of "reported speech" phenomena (Bakhtin 1981) in that the reader is retelling and evaluating the other's experience as the narrative unfolds. The reader, in reporting her interpretations, explanations, and evaluations, can, in effect, co-construct the narrative by assuming the perspective of the characters.

In this paper, we address the question of why assessments or evaluations occur, where they occur, how they occur, and what is evaluated during understanding and talking about the experiences of another in a narrative. For us, evaluation is a means of reflecting upon events that affect us personally. Evaluation is very general and is not restricted to narration. Appraisal or evaluation processes may constitute the basis for personal and inter-personal understanding and interaction. Appraisal or evaluation is believed to underlie all emotional experience (Lazarus 1991; Stein and Levine 1989). We often appraise events in terms of our own or other's well-being. Evaluative understanding enables us to generate coping strategies that deal with changes that events bring about in our lives (Folkman and Lazarus 1990). Evaluation of what others do and say affect the goals and plans that govern how a person interacts with another.

We studied how, when, and under what circumstances a person would make and communicate *evaluative* inferences when he or she tried to understand the experiences of other people. We asked people to read about the fictional experience of another and to tell us about how they understood that person's experience, one event at a time. In effect, we asked people to read, interpret, and reflect upon a story character's experience. We allowed the readers opportunity to engage in evaluative processes while they read and tried to comprehend the story. Their talk about how they understood particular events allowed the study of how different kinds of events *constrain* the ways of evaluation as well as which linguistic expressions were used to communicate these evaluations. The situation we studied was one where the comprehender is communicating about a fictional person's life experiences to a third party so that it allowed the comprehender to take different perspectives, voices, or positions of evaluation. The comprehender could take on the voice of the character in the narrative or evaluate events from his or her own perspective or from that of a third person (Bakhtin 1981, 1984).

In understanding events, readers engage heavily in trying to explain why something is happening (Graesser, Singer, and Trabasso 1994; Singer, Graesser, and Trabasso 1994; Schank 1986; Trabasso and Magliano 1994). Evaluations can serve an explanatory function as well as making a point. They can be used as reasons to justify why a course of action is appropriate as a means or why a particular end is desirable, attainable, or beneficial. If so, then evaluation serves a rationality function, consistent with the belief that rational beings operate in their best interests by deliberately choosing appropriate means and ends (Rescher 1988).

An episode of a narrative is highly structured and its clauses are meaningfully related by causal and logical as well as temporal relations. In our view, the narrative clauses refer to interpreted events and include not only those that are externally referenced with respect to states of the world but also those that are richly subjective, mental, and internal. Evaluations, as internal states, form a part of the interpretation expressed in any clause within an episode and do not stand apart from the narration. What and how the narrator feels, thinks, believes, desires, or values are mental states that are part of the experience being narrated and can be referential as well as evaluative. These internal states, responses, or reactions are meaningfully related, constrained by, and dependent upon other events in the narration. As such, evaluation can occur throughout the episode.

To begin our study of how evaluations are communicated during comprehension of a narrative, an example of an episode from a narrative is presented. We then describe and define its episodic content and structure. Following this orientation, we present a verbal protocol of someone who is reading, and communicating her understanding of each sentence in the narrative as she reads it. An experiment is then described in which we collected 64 verbal protocols during comprehension of narratives, subjected them to an analysis of the ways of evaluation, and examined how they were linguistically expressed. We conclude by discussing our findings with reference to issues of rationality, adaptation and emotion, and narrative meanings.

1.1. *Example narrative episode and structure*

Consider the following episode from a three-episode narrative, called the Betty story (taken from Suh and Trabasso 1993):

1. There was a girl named Betty.
2. Betty found that her mother's birthday was coming soon.
3. She really wanted to give her mother a present.
4. She went to the department store.
5. She found that everything was too expensive.
6. She could not buy anything for her mother.
7. Betty felt sorry.

In the first sentence (1), we are introduced via a Setting statement to the main character and we are told that she is a girl. Settings typically introduce characters and set the space and time circumstances in which a story occurs (what Labov 1972 termed "orientation"). Settings or the circumstances that they provide enable the episodic events to occur (Stein and Glenn 1979).

Sentence (2) opens the episode that begins the story. This sentence contains what is termed an Initiating Event (Stein and Glenn 1979). Initiating Events happen to or are experienced by the main protagonist. They are the main events of personal significance in that they typically have profound effects on the protagonist's goal states and well-being (Stein, Trabasso and Liwag 1993, 1994). We therefore expect that initiating events would be evaluated frequently in terms of their consequences.

In the present case, Betty's discovery of that her mother's birthday is coming soon has important personal and social implications and consequences for her in her relationship to her mother. In sentence (3), the personal significance of the discovery by the story character causes or results in a Goal. The Goal is expressed as a desire to attain some state, namely of her mother having a present. This desire to attain a particular goal state then motivates Betty to carry out various actions as Attempts in sentences (4), (5), and (6) to attain the goal. The Attempts in sentence (5) and (6) are enabled by the attempts in sentence (4). However, the Outcome, expressed in sentence (5), results in a failure to attain a desired goal object in sentence (6). This failed goal Outcome psychologically causes Betty to feel sorry in sentence (7). The last sentence is an Emotion, one of several kinds of internal events that can occur in response to an Outcome or an Initiating Event.

The sentences of the Setting and the first Episode of the Betty story can be represented as a causal network, following Trabasso, van den Broek and Suh (1989). Figure 1 presents a general, causal network representation of an episode, of which the sequence in the Betty story is specific case. The arrows in the causal network representation in Figure 1 indicate that the Setting allows or enables all events that follow it. The Initiating Events are typically references to external events. They can cause or enable other external events. Of importance here is that Initiating Events are interpreted and expressed through Internal Responses by the person. Internal responses include mental states, reactions, and processes. The content of internal responses is expressed as thoughts, beliefs, values, cognitions, perceptions, emotions, goals, and plans. Internal responses can psychologically cause or enable other internal responses. Once, however, a goal is formulated along with its plan, the person can intentionally carry it out the actions associated with the plan. Goals are desired or undesired states, activities, or objects. When a goal is about a desired state, activity, or object, the person would be motivated to attain or maintain it; when the goal is undesired, then the person is motivated to avoid or escape from it. Goals motivate plan formulation and the Attempts that follow from it. The Attempts carried out can enable other Attempts in the plan to also be accomplished. Attempts can also result in Outcomes that signify goal success or failure. Goal success or failure, as expressed in Outcomes, refer to whether or not the person has attained or maintained a desired state, activity, or object or has avoided or escaped from an undesired state, activity, or object. Outcomes of goal success or failure can also become initiating events in that they can, in turn, psychologically cause a variety of Internal Responses that can lead to new episodes.

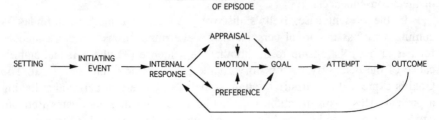

Figure 1.   *Causal network representation of an episode from a story*

Internal responses are the main means by which the narrator or reader can express *evaluations* of events. Internal responses can be positively or negatively valenced in the expression of personally meaningful and significant evaluations. Does the narrator or reader view the event as good or bad, liked or disliked, as wanted or unwanted, or negative or positive emotionally? These expressions in the narrative or in understanding the narrative inform us about the valence of the evaluation of the events as well as the way in which the evaluation is communicated.

1.2. *Verbal protocols*

A principal way of finding out how people understand other people's lives is to give them an opportunity to talk about their understanding of particular events, states, and actions. In order to study how different people interpret the same events, we asked them to tell us about how they understood a series of sentences in narrative episodes that depicted the experiences of a fictional person or animal. In the psychological study of problem solving and understanding, what someone reports on how he or she thinks about a problem is known a *verbal protocol* and the protocols obtained are taken as basic data (Ericsson and Simon 1984). Verbal protocols may be obtained by asking questions after the person hears, reads, or sees an event (e.g., Stein and Levine 1987, 1990; Magliano and Graesser 1991). A second way is to ask the reader to "think-aloud" during comprehension of the text (Ericsson 1988; Trabasso and Suh 1993). In either case, the protocols may be regarded as a special form of communication in which one person communicates to another his or her understanding of a third person's narrative communication. Thinking-aloud was the method used in the present study since it was judged to be less constraining than question-answering.

2. "Thinking aloud": A study of communicating one's understanding during reading

In our study, people were asked to tell us about their understanding (i.e., to "think aloud") while they read and tried to understand each narrative text, one sentence at a time. This procedure reveals information that the person mentally accessed in evaluations of events as they are experienced and interpreted. The think-aloud data came from a dissertation study carried out by Suh (1988; see Suh and Trabasso 1993, or Trabasso and Suh 1993 for details).

Eight college students each read eight three-episode stories where a protagonist was engaged in personal problem-solving and experienced events that affected personal well-being, that the protagonist tried to do something about, and to which the protagonist expressed positive or negative emotions when goal success or failure occurred. For example, a young woman named Jane, who is overweight, tries in the first episode to lose weight by jogging. In one version, she fails. In the fail version, in episode two, she takes up racquetball and, in episode three, she succeeds in losing weight. She is "frustrated over her failure" at the end of episode one but "happy" with the success in episode three.

The stories were identified by the character's name. Half of the characters were female; half were male. There were eight stories with two versions each and each version had either a success or a goal failure in the first episode. In the Betty Story versions, the character wants to give her mother a birthday present and either succeeds or fails by buying a gift or not at a department store. She then knits a sweater which she either gives to her mother or puts away. In the Bill Story versions, the character is initially blind and tries to regain his eyesight medically. He either succeeds or fails. He then goes and takes water from a magical lake that either makes him younger or restores his eyesight. In the Ivan Story versions, an archer tries to kill a giant who has been terrorizing a village and succeeds or fails in his first attempt with a bow and arrow. Ivan then learns to use a sword and returns to the village as a hero or finally succeeds in killing the giant. In the Fred Story versions, a student who is poor in mathematics, takes a math course and either passes or fails an exam. He then forms a study group and becomes a good student or he finally passes the math exam. In the Jane Story versions, Jane is overweight and tries dieting. She either succeeds or fails. She then takes up racquetball and enjoys it or finally loses weight. In the Jimmy Story versions, a boy asks his mother for a bicycle and either gets it or is refused. He then obtains a delivery job at a grocery store, earns money, and buys a basketball or finally buys his bicycle. In the Mickey Story versions, a hungry mouse tries to get into a barn and either succeeds in finding food or fails to get in. He then gets into a house and has a lot of fun or finally finds food.

Finally, in the William Story versions, a second son wishes to become king. He attempts to impress his father and succeeds or fails. He becomes king and kills his brother or he kills his brother and then becomes king.

The stories ranged from 13 to 18 sentences in length (mean = 15 sentences). Each of the eight college students who participated as readers in the study was instructed to read the stories, one sentence at a time, and to tell the experimenter about his or her understanding of the events referred to in the sentence in the context of the story. The reader's communication was tape recorded and transcribed.

The readers generated an average of 2.70 clauses per sentence as they communicated their understanding. Of these, 75 per cent were inferences. Of the inferences, 68 percent were explanations. Thus, explanations of the content of the sentences predominated (Trabasso and Magliano 1994).

2.1. *Example Protocol*

Consider the following verbal protocol obtained from one of the college students (Reader E, Betty Story, TEXT Sentences 1–7):

Setting (1).   ONCE THERE WAS A GIRL NAMED BETTY.

Reader: "There's a young female person whose name is Betty."

Initiating Event (2).   ONE DAY, BETTY FOUND THAT HER MOTHER'S BIRTH-
DAY WAS COMING SOON.

Reader: "Betty, like all, like most children who <u>love</u> their parents, Betty found out that her mother's birthday was coming soon. Most children eventually discover that their parents birthday is around the corner or somebody tells them."

Goal (3).   SHE REALLY WANTED TO GIVE HER MOTHER A PRESENT.

Reader: "This shows that Betty <u>loved</u> her mother and she <u>wanted to thank her</u> for all the things she had done by giving her something for her birthday."

Attempt (4).   SHE WENT TO THE DEPARTMENT STORE.

Reader: "Betty decided that, you know, something *really fancy* would suit, <u>show her feelings</u> toward her mother instead of some *homemade* card that may or may not look any <u>good</u>."

Outcome (5). SHE FOUND THAT EVERYTHING WAS TOO EXPENSIVE.

> Reader: "This is Betty discovering that on her childhood budget, she *really* has not the money necessary to buy the kind of gift that she wants to give to her mother."

Outcome (6). SHE COULD NOT BUY ANYTHING FOR HER MOTHER.

> Reader: "This was because everything was *so* expensive."

Internal Response (7). BETTY FELT SORRY.

> Reader: "Uhm, this is because she wanted to give her mother something *special*, as you can buy in a department store, but she didn't have the money and she felt that maybe she'd be short-changing her mother, without giving, if she didn't give her something from the department store."

In this protocol, we have underlined those words that index an evaluation on the part of the Reader E. In addition, we have italicized words that served as intensifiers. The first evaluation is made to the initiating event from the perspective of the character but is stated as a generalization (i.e., "like all") and involves an emotional state (love). The goal of the story character is explained by her emotional disposition, a preference of loving her mother. In addition, the goal is explained by another, superordinate goal of wanting to thank her mother. This goal is explained by what the mother has done for Betty in the past. The attempt in fourth sentence is also evaluated and explained as actions taken to express feelings and to find something "really fancy" and not something "homemade" that would not look *good*, an appraisal of the kind of gift. The outcome in the fifth sentence is interpreted as a goal failure and is explained by the Reader as a lack of money. This explanation is repeated for the explicit goal failure in the sixth sentence. The narrative then expresses the character's emotional reaction to the failure in her goal. Note how the Reader now explains why the character feels this way in terms of her goal and the circumstances that lead to its failure and in terms of not being able to provide an appropriate goal of value for her mother.

The protocol, of course, was elicited by asking the reader to talk to the experimenter about her understanding of each sentence in a story. Despite this constraint of elicitation, the reader co-participates in the construction of the narrative with author and the experimenter. Furthermore, she and other readers employed spontaneous conversational markers (e.g., "Uhm", well, so etc.) along with assessments and intensifiers etc. in taking turns with the author. Furthermore, there is an advantage to eliciting conversation about understanding in that all the readers talk about the same content thereby permitting us to study how they evaluate particular kinds of events such as initiating events, emotions, outcomes, etc.

2.2. *Linguistic Devices*

In this protocol, then, we see that evaluations occurred throughout the episode and provided coherence of interpretation. The evaluations were expressed primarily from the perspective of the character as either explanations of goals, attempts, or emotions or as causal consequences of events and outcomes. The evaluations were communicated as emotions and goals.

Readers made a wider range of evaluations than are illustrated here. They also used a range of linguistic devices for each of these evaluations. Table 1 (next page) summarizes the kinds of evaluations that we have observed over the 64 protocols that we examined for 8 readers.

In Table 1, we have indicated whose perspective is associated with each kind of evaluation. When readers evaluated events from their perspective, we found that they often used *appraisals*. Appraisals are summary evaluations that were expressed linguistically as "good" or "bad". Appraisals are positive or negative in value. Appraisals reflect an evaluation of how appropriate something is according to a social norm or how beneficial or harmful something is according to a moral standard. Good or bad appraisals occurred rarely from the perspective of characters, although Reader E did make such an evaluation in understanding the Betty Story. Readers generally use their own or a third party perspective in making appraisals of external, initiating events, actions, or outcomes as good or bad. In contrast, internal responses were evaluated almost entirely from the character's perspective. On rare occasions, readers took an emotional stance towards an outcome or emotional state of the character by expressing compassion or empathy.

Readers assumed the character's perspective and expressed evaluations linguistically in four other ways. They expressed positive or negative valenced *preferences*. Preferences express a disposition or stance towards an object and carry with them a tendency to approach or avoid the object (Lazarus 1991). They are communicated as likes and dislikes.

Another form of evaluation that is expressed both non-verbally and through language is that of *emotion*. Emotions were expressed via a variety of discrete emotional states and reactions (e.g., 'happy' or 'sad') that were readily inferred as to their positive or negative valence.

A third form of evaluation occurs in an expressed desire to change the

Table 1. *Evaluative linguistic devices*

Perspective of Evaluation	Ways of Evaluation	Valence	Linguistic Device
Reader/ Third Party/ Character	Appraisal	Positive	"Good"
		Negative	"Bad"
Character	Preference	Positive	"Like"
		Negative	"Dislike"
Character/ Reader	Emotion	Positive	"Happy"
		Negative	"Sad"
Character	Goal	Desired	"Want"
		Undesired	"Don't Want"
Character	Goal Attainment/ Maintenance/ Avoidance/ Escape	Positive	"Success"
		Negative	"Failure"

current states of the character through *goals*. Goals were frequently marked by 'want' and negatively valenced by auxiliaries involving negation such as 'don't'. They also indexed by 'need,' 'have to', 'decided', 'desired', etc. Goals are important in that they organize the actions taken to achieve them and they result in *outcomes* of success or failure. Success or failure of goals is, of course, valenced from the perspective of the character's well-being.

3. Evaluations of episodic constituents

Evaluation is inferential in nature (Graesser *et al.* 1994). The linguistic expressions and devices used to report inferred evaluations of events are constrained by the circumstances of the story, the content of the current sentence, and by the reader's relevant world knowledge (Trabasso and Magliano 1994). The event in the current sentence, when interpreted from the character's perspective in the causal network, has causal antecedents or consequences. Evaluations, then, may be viewed as attempts by the reader to infer how and why the character responded to a particular event.

We now detail how the content and role that each episodic constituent plays in the episode constrains how it is evaluated and how it is explained or how causal consequences are inferred from it. For each type of sentence in the episode, we describe the possible options that readers follow for valenced linguistic expressions from either the Reader's, the Third Party's, or the Character's perspective. For each episodic event, we then provide examples from protocols that illustrate the event's constraints on evaluative expression.

3.1. *Initiating events*

Initiating events, along with outcomes, are probably the most important events in a narrative (Stein and Glenn 1979; Trabasso and Sperry 1985). Together, initiating events and outcomes tell us what happened. Initiating events and outcomes are the main changes that occur in minimal plots of state, transformation, state change.

Initiating events begin the complicating action of a plot or episode (Labov 1972; Mandler and Johnson 1977; Stein and Glenn 1979), result in a causal chain of events over several episodes (Trabasso, Secco and van den Broek 1984), and are highly connected causally to other events (Trabasso and Sperry 1985). In the causal network of Figure 1, initiating events cause psychologically a variety of internal responses. The changes brought by initiating events can thus be "good" or "bad" for the person. They can be beneficial and satisfy goals or they can be harmful and threaten or fail goals. The internal responses reflect appraisals and evaluations of the initiating events in terms of their impact on the person's well-being. The initiating events can violate expectations, beliefs, or values (Stein, Trabasso and Liwag 1993, 1994) and can result in high emotional arousal. However, the resultant states of these processes are valenced appraisals or evaluations that are expressed or summarized behaviorally and linguistically.

We found five evaluations of initiating events. All of these evaluations were judged to be causal consequences. The ways of evaluation of initiating events are listed below in Table 2.

Table 2. *Evaluations of initiating events*

Episodic Clause	Causal Relation	Ways of Evaluation	Valence	Linguistic Devices	Perspective
Initiating Event	Consequence	Appraisal	Positive	"Good"	Reader/ Third Party/ Character
			Negative	"Bad"	
	Consequence	Preference	Positive	"Like"	Character
			Negative	"Dislike"	
	Consequence	Emotion	Positive	Emotion States, e.g., "Pleased"	Character
			Negative	Emotion States, e.g., "Disappoint-ed"	
	Consequence	Emotion	Positive	Emotion States (no examples)	Reader
			Negative	Empathy or Compassion, e.g., "Feel Sorry"	
	Consequence	Goals	Desire	"Want"	Character/ Reader/ Third Party
			Don't Desire	"Don't Want"	

3.2. Reader appraisals of initiating events

Initiating events, it will be recalled, are often outcomes that signal a realized or a potential success or failure in a goal. They have major causal consequences to the Character. The Reader, as an observer, appraises and judges them as "good" or "bad". For example, Reader R, in understanding a story about Jimmy, the boy who wanted a bike, has read that Jimmy had asked his mother to buy him one, but she refused. Reader R then interpreted the initiating event (1) of the second episode as follows:

(1) Text:

Next day, Jimmy's mother told him that	
he should have his own savings	(Initiating Event/Attempt)

Reader:

"Mothers tell their children that	(Initiating Event)
That is **not a bad idea**	(Internal Response, (+) Reader appraisal)
It's a **good way** to build responsibility	(Internal Response/Goal, (+)Reader appraisal)
But this may be so that he can help pay for the bike"	(Goal)

In this example, the initiating event of the narrative leads to a positive appraisal and this appraisal, in turn, leads to goals. Evaluations by the Reader, then, can be seen as inferences that fill in missing events in a mental model or causal network representation of a story. This sequence, initiating event → appraisal → goal, is repeated by Reader R for the initiating event in a narrative about Ivan the Warrior where the appraisal is negative rather than positive as in (1):

(2) Text:

They said that the giant came to village at night and hurt people	(Initiating Event)

Reader:

"**That's not good**	(Internal Response, (−)Reader/Third Party appraisal)
That is <u>not</u> something you <u>want</u> to happen	(Goal)
giant coming to the village at night	(Initiating Event)
and I guess Ivan would <u>not be happy</u> with that"	(Internal Response,(−) Character emotion)

3.3. *Character preferences for/against initiating events*

Reader E interpreted the initiating event of the second episode of the narrative in the Jane story with a positive preference from the perspective of Jane. Recall that Jane was overweight, had tried to lose weight by dieting, and had failed. In (3), Reader E's causal sequence conforms to that of the causal network model of Figure 1: initiating event → positive preference → goal. Example (3) is from Reader E's protocol.

(3) Text:

One day, Jane saw a racquetball game   (Initiating Event)

Reader:

"Well, she saw this game   (Initiating Event)
Maybe she **likes it**   (Internal Response, (+) Character
                                         preference)
and she's <u>going to get</u> involved in it"   (Goal)

Reader M, in (4), evaluated the initiating event of the first episode of the Ivan Story as: initiating event → negative preference → goal → attempt. This evaluative sequence also conforms to the expectations of the causal network. Ivan was described in the first sentence of the story as a Warrior. The initiating events were in the second and third sentences.

(4) Text:

They said that the giant came to the village at night (Initiating Event)
and hurt people.   (Initiating Event)

Reader:

"They **didn't like** being hurt by the giant   (Internal Response,
                                                    (−) Character preference)
No doubt that these people turned to Ivan   (Attempt)
and said why don't you go and kill the giant"   (Goal)

Reader M's evaluation in (4) contrasts with Reader R's evaluation of the same initiating event in (2) in that Reader R took his own or a third party perspective in appraising the event, whereas Reader M expressed the Character's perspective in terms of a preference. These two examples illustrate how the same event can be construed in different ways by different people, depending upon whose perspective and which goals are being affected (cf. Stein *et al.* 1993, 1994, and Stein and Trabasso 1993, for how the same external events can lead to different valenced reactions).

3.4. *Emotions as reactions to initiating events*

Another way in which an evaluation of an event can be expressed is through an emotion. Linguistically, emotions are lexical entries and refer to valenced internal states or reactions, or expressions of an internal reaction. In the causal sequence for (5) conforms to that of the model in Figure 1: initiating events → emotion → goal. Examples of positive and negative emotions from the perspective of the Character for the Betty Story by Reader P in (5) and for the Ivan Story by Reader R in (6) are:

(5) Text:

One day Betty found out that her mother's birthday was
    coming soon   (Initiating Event)

Reader:

"Betty will try to get a present for her mother (Goal)
or other wise **make her happy** for her birthday" (Internal Response, (+)
                                       Character Emotion)

    (6)   Text:

They said that Ivan came to village at night   (Initiating Event)
and hurt people

Reader:

"That's not good   (Internal Response,(−) Reader
                                         appraisal)

That is not something you want to happen   (Internal Response/ Goal,
                                       (−) Reader appraisal)

giant coming to the village at night   (Initiating Event)
and I guess Ivan would **not be happy with that**" (Internal Response,
                                       (−) character emotion)

  Reader emotions, while rare in the protocols, represent the Reader's response to the events of the narrative. They could be reactions to the events as if they are happening to the Reader, albeit vicariously and at a safe distance, or they could be empathic or compassionate expressions of identification with character's plight. One example of compassion is expressed by Reader M to Jane's initiating event of becoming overweight in (7).

(7) Text:

Jane was very heavy.	(Initiating Event)

Reader:

"I immediately **feel sorry** for Jane	(Internal Response, (−)Reader emotion)
probably she got teased a lot about being overweight	(Initiating Event)
especially difficult when you are teenager"	(Internal Response,(−) Reader/Third Party appraisal)

In this example, Reader M expresses her compassion but justifies with an explanation involving a possible consequence of Jane's state and how teenagers, in general, appraise this kind of untoward situation. The appraisal of difficulty might represent yet another perspective, namely the voice of a disinterested, third party or a shared norm.

3.5. *Goals as evaluations of initiating events*

Since Goals were often conjoined with other evaluations in (1), (3), (4), (5), and (6), we do not discuss them separately. We note that Goals may be expressed in terms of "want" or "don't want" but there are a variety of ways of stating or implying them. Some of the main ways are to use infinitives (to buy), prepositions (for), attempts (try to), etc. in conjunction with the desired goal state, activity, or object.

3.6. *Evaluations of goals*

Goals are evaluated in terms of the antecedent events that precede and cause them. Goals, then, are to be understood in terms of the initiating events, preferences, and emotions that occur or are inferred prior to them. They can also be understood as purposes or desires about future changes in states of attainment, maintenance, escape, or avoidance. Goals are "appropriate" when they can achieve these desired states that are caused by evaluations of initiating events. Table 3 summarizes our evaluation of goals.

3.7. *Character preference for/against goals*

Reader E, in reading that Jane, the overweight girl, decided to learn racquetball, explained this goal in (8) by reason of a positive preference and a future, desired outcome. These explanatory, causal antecedents are consistent with the expectations of the causal network model in Figure 1.

Table 3.   *Evaluation of goals*

Episodic Clause	Causal Relation	Ways of Evaluation	Valence	Linguistic Devices	Perspective
Goal	Antecedent/ Explanation	Preference	Positive	"Like"	Character
			Negative	"Dislike"	
	Antecedent/ Explanation	Appraisal	Positive	"Noble"	Reader/ Third Party
			Negative	"Not admirable"	
	Antecedent/ Explanation	Emotion	Positive	Emotion States, e.g., "Love"	Character
			Negative	Emotion States, e.g., "Upset"	
	Consequence	Goal Attain/ Maintain/ Escape/ Avoid	Positive	"Success"	Character
			Negative	"Failure"	

(8) Text:

Jane decided to learn racquetball   (Goal)

Reader:

"Well Jane obviously **liked** racquetball   (Internal Response,
                                                                     (+)character preference)

Maybe she decided this could be a form of exercise   (Goal)
she could use to lose a few pounds"   (+ Outcome)

In contrast, Reader C justified Jane's original desire to lose weight in (9) by antecedent reasons of the initiating event of being overweight and a negative preference regarding this state, a causal sequence consistent with Figure 1.

(9) Text:

Jane wanted to lose weight	(Goal)

Reader:

"Well obviously if you are *50 pounds* overweight	(Internal Response)
and you **do not like** your body	(Internal Response, (−)character preference)
you want to lose weight"	(Goal)

3.8. *Reader appraisal of goals*

Readers react to Goals by appraising their appropriateness or value to the character. Reader R, in (10) evaluates the value of character Fred's goal to pass a course in response to a history of having not done well in mathematics. The evaluation is stated as a positive appraisal, using "noble" rather than "good".

(10) Text:

This time Fred was determined to pass the course	(Goal)

Reader:

"That's a **noble** thing	(Internal Response, (+)Reader appraisal)
to pass a math course"	(Goal)

Subject R, however, expressed in (11) a negative appraisal of the goals and plans of a king named John who wanted to dispose of his older brother who was a rival to the throne. Negative preferences for one goal may be stated along with a preferred alternative goal/plan.

(11) Text:

John decided to poison William	(Goal)

Reader:

"Well that is **not a particularly admirable behavior** for a king	(Internal Response, (−)Reader appraisal)
but apparently he decided to poison William	(Goal)
and apparently kill him	(Goal)
I guess I suppose being king there are other ways to get rid of William	(Goal)
but he decided to poison"	(Goal)

3.9. *Character emotion*

Readers can evaluate goals in terms of emotions as well as the initiating events and preferences that are antecedent to them. In (12) Reader C understood Jimmy's goal by justifying it causally in terms of its initiating event → positive appraisal → positive emotion → goal(s), a sequence consistent with the causal network model. She takes the Character's perspective by first referring to his perception of the event, and then the Character's emotional reaction to it. The emotion is explained by the Character's appraisal of a future, desired use of the goal object. The interpretation ends by quoting the Character's goals as thoughts:

(12) Text:

Jimmy wanted to buy a bike   (Goal)

Reader:

"So Jimmy saw this beautiful bike (Initiating Event)
it was purple that his friend had (Initiating Event)
and he is all **keen**   (Internal Response, (+) character emotion)
because he thinks bike racing
is a *really good sport*   (Internal Response,(+) character appraisal)
and said "Ah I have got
to get myself a bike   (Goal)
I want to join your team"   (Goal)

Reader J, in (13) provides an example of explaining a goal with a negative emotion closely related in meaning to a negative preference that is caused by the initiating event of being overweight.

(13) Text:

Jane wanted to lose weight   (Goal)

Reader:

"Jane was **not happy**   (Internal Response, (–) character emotion)
being fat   (Initiating Event)
she *wanted* to become thinner"   (Goal)

3.10. *Character outcome*

Goals may be evaluated in terms of their potential success or failure and these possible outcomes are used to explain or justify them. Subject R, in (14), provides an example where a goal is explained by a preference for the desired activity or by its possible, future benefits:

(14) Text:

Jane decided to learn racquetball   (Goal)

Reader:

"Again may be she decided to learn it   (Goal)
to help her become thinner   (+ Outcome)
or may be she just *liked* the game"   (Internal Response, (+) Character preference)

3.11. *Evaluation of attempts*

When attempts are observed as external actions, they are evaluated from the Reader's perspective as appropriate means to achieve a desired end. The focus of the evaluation of attempts can be on the means and whether or not they are the best way to attain the goal or they can be expressed in terms of successful or failed consequences to the goal. Table 4 (next page) summarizes the possible evaluations of attempts.

3.12. *Appropriate means to achieve goals*

Positive appraisals represent the Reader's evaluation of observed actions. Reader R, in (15), evaluates Ivan's second attempt to kill the giant with a positive appraisal but justifies the appraisal in terms of the Character's ability (from the Setting), a goal, and the means available to the goal plan:

(15) Text:

When the giant came, Ivan shot an arrow at him   (Attempt)

Reader:

"Uh, being an archer   (Setting)
It is a *good way*   (Internal Response, (+) Reader appraisal)
to kill the giant   (Goal)
I suppose with a bow and an arrow"   (Attempt)

Possible negative outcomes are future consequences of attempts and may, in themselves, be evaluated. Reader M, in (16), evaluates attempts by Bill, a blind person, to cure his blindness by medication as not a good plan because it cannot attain his goal. The causal reasoning follows the sequence: goal →

Table 4. *Evaluation of attempts*

Episodic Clause	Causal Relation	Ways of Evaluation	Valence	Linguistic Devices	Perspective
Attempt	Antecedent/ Concurrent	Appraisal	Positive	Appropriate Means, e.g., "Good" or "Correct Way"	Reader/ Third Party
			Negative	Inappropriate Means, e.g., "Not a good way"	
	Consequence	Goal Attain/ Maintain/ Avoid/ Escape	Positive	Goal "Success"	Reader/ Third Party
			Negative	Goal "Failure"	

attempt → possible negative outcome → negative preference, a sequence consistent with the expectations of Figure 1.

(16) Text:

Bill tried every medicine available   (Attempt)

Reader:

"I think that's probably **not a good strategy**   (Internal Response
                                                                             (−) reader appraisal)

because you don't get cured blindness by medicine   (− Outcome)
but he probably wanted to try everything possible"   (Goal)

3.13. *Appropriate outcomes (ends)*

Attempts are evaluated in terms of the beneficial, successful or harmful, failed outcomes that they could produce. In the next example, (17), Reader D evaluates Betty's attempts to knit a sweater in terms of its positive outcomes and her appraisal:

(17) Text:

| Betty followed the instructions in the article | (Attempt) |

Reader:

"So she is making this sweater *correctly* (Attempt)
she knitted it **the way it was supposed to be knitted** (+ Outcome)
so it should turn out a **good** sweater" (+ Outcome, reader
appraisal)

3.14. Evaluation of outcomes

Outcomes are evaluated in terms of their possible causal consequences to goals and emotions. Outcomes are judged in terms of whether or not the Reader believes that the Character succeeded in attaining or maintaining a desired state, or escaping or avoiding an undesired state. Table 5 (next page) summarizes the kinds of evaluations that readers made of outcomes.

Table 5. *Evaluation of outcomes*

Episodic Clause	Causal Relation	Ways of Evaluation	Valence	Linguistic Devices	Perspective
Outcome	Consequent	Goal Attain/ Maintain/ Escape/ Avoid	Positive	"Success"	Character/ Reader/ Third Party
			Negative	"Failure"	
	Consequent	Emotion	Positive	Emotion States, e.g., "Pleased"	Character
			Negative	Emotion States, e.g., "Frustrated"	

3.15. *Goal success or failure*

Goal success evaluations are a consequence to outcomes in stories. They are often followed by a positive emotion. Reader R, in (18) makes such a goal success evaluation when a mouse named Mickey finally finds food. The causal sequence, consistent with the model, is: outcome → goal success → positive emotion.

(18) Text:

Mickey found lots of food   (+ Outcome)

Reader:

"I guess the story ends <u>happily</u>   (Internal Response, (+)
                                          character positive emotion)
after **successfully getting a good meal**"   (+ Outcome)

Outcomes that result in goal failure may be evaluated by the reader as unsuccessful and failed goals that result in negative emotions. Reader R, in (19), interprets Betty's failure to find a present for her mother as a causal sequence: outcomes → goal failure → negative emotion, in line with Figure 1.

(19) Text:

Betty couldn't find anything for her mother   (– Outcome)

Reader:

"Well apparently I guess everything was too expensive   (Outcome)
she did not have enough money   (Outcome)
she **can't buy** a present for her mother   (–Outcome)
and I suppose she is kind of <u>disappointed</u>"   (Internal Response,
                                                         (–)character emotion)

3.16. *Emotions*

Examples (18) and (19) showed that emotions can serve as evaluations of goal success or failure. Emotions are ascribed to the character by the reader on the basis of an evaluation of outcomes in terms of success or failure of goals. When goal success is appraised, then a positive emotion is assumed to be the causal result; when goal failure is inferred, then the a negative emotion is inferred as a causal consequence. Reader M, in (20), evaluates Bill's restoration of his eyesight by water from a lake as a "miracle" and predicts that Bill will be *very* happy. Thus, the causal sequence is outcome → positive appraisal → emotion.

(20) Text:

Bill's eyesight was restored	(+Outcome)

Reader:

"I guess it was a <u>miracle</u> after all	(Internal Response, (+) Reader appraisal)
he was no doubt *very* **happy**"	(Internal Response, (+) Character emotion)

Likewise, negative emotions follow from inferred goal failures. Reader M, in (21), evaluates an outcome as a goal failure that causes a negative emotion. She provides the listener with enough information to infer the goal failure, namely with a goal and an attempt, that in conjunction with the narrative outcome, and the negative emotion, are sufficient to infer a goal failure. The causal network sequence for this example is: goal → attempt → negative outcome → emotion.

(21) Text

Mickey found that the door to the barn was closed	(– Outcome)

Reader:

"He probably was **disappointed**	(Internal Response, (–) character emotion)
since he was trying to get into the barn	(Goal/Attempt)
and get some food"	(Goal)

3.17. *Evaluations of emotion*

Emotions, when explicitly stated in the narrative, represent the expressed results of appraisals of events by characters. In the cognitive theories of emotion (Arnold 1960; Lazarus 1991), emotions are a result of an appraisal of precipitating events in terms of one's well being. In some appraisal theories of emotion, the success or failure to attain or to maintain desirable states, and to escape or avoid undesirable states constitute appraisals of one's well being (Roseman 1984; Stein and Levine 1987, 1989, 1990). If an event is appraised as putting the person into a state of not having something that one desires or having something that one does not desire, negative emotions are experienced. If one is put into a state of having something that one wants or not having something that one did not want, positive emotions are experienced. In these appraisal theories, the *causal antecedents* of an emotional reaction would be a goal that has an outcome in which it either succeeds or fails. Goals and outcomes as causal antecedents of emotions provides the basis for relational meanings between the events appraised and emotion (Lazarus 1991).

According to this analysis, readers would use goals and outcomes of goal success or failure to jointly explain a character's narrative emotion. Trabasso and Magliano (1994) analyzed the current corpus of protocols and found substantial support for this claim. Emotions are explained or justified in terms of the goals and outcomes, the character's preferences or the reader's appraisals, and other character emotions that precede them. Table 6 summarizes the evaluation of emotions.

Table 6. *Evaluation of emotions*

Episodic Clause	Causal Relation	Ways of Evaluation	Valence	Linguistic Devices	Perspective
Emotion	Antecedent Explanation	Preference	Positive	"Good"	Reader/ Third Party
			Negative	"Bad"	
	Antecedent Explanation	Goal Attain/ Maintain/ Avoid/ Escape	Positive	"Success"	Character/ Reader/ Third Party
			Negative	"Failure"	
	Antecedent Explanation	Emotion	Positive	Emotion States, e.g., "Proud"	Character
			Negative	Emotion States, e.g., "Desperate"	

3.18. *Positive emotions*

Positive emotions are a consequence of goal success. In (22), Reader E predicts a positive emotion and makes a positive appraisal of the whole causal sequence: goal → successful outcome → emotion → Reader appraisal. The goals are stressed with intensifiers.

(22) Text:

Bill was happy	(Emotion)

Reader:

"Well this is <u>good</u>	(Internal Response, (+)Reader appraisal)
because he *desperately*	
wanted his eyesight back	(desired Goal, Character)
We know he was *so determined*	
at getting his eyesight back	(desired Goal)
and he was <u>successful</u>	(+Outcome, (+)Reader appraisal)
and that would make him *happy*"	(Internal Response, (+) Character emotion)

Reader's naive theories of emotion frequently embody the more sophisticated ones referenced above (e.g., Stein and Levine 1989) in that they make generalizations from their perspective and use a Third Party voice to explain or justify the emotions. Example (23), taken from Reader R's protocol on Bill the Blind Man has the following causal sequence: initiating event → goal → successful outcome → emotion.

(23) Text:

Bill was happy (Emotion)

Reader:

"That's understandable	(Internal Response)
if you're blind for a long time	(Setting/Initiating Event)
you want to see again	(Goal, Reader)
and <u>it comes through</u>	(+Outcome)
<u>Getting what you want</u>	(+Outcome Reader)
that's a reason to be <u>happy</u>"	(Internal Response, (+)character emotion)

In explaining emotions, Readers may omit goals but imply them by referring to the outcome and predicting the emotion (cf. Trabasso and Magliano 1994, for several examples). Reader E does this in (24) in justifying Betty's positive emotion.

(24) Text:

Betty was very happy	(Emotion)

Reader:

"She was probably very <u>happy</u>	(Event)
because she **finished this *beautiful* sweater**"	(+Outcome)

3.19. *Negative emotions*

Negative emotions in a narrative are evaluated and justified in the same way as positive emotions. However, Trabasso and Magliano (1994) found that when expectations of success fail, the readers often provide the attempted goal and contrast it explicitly with its failure. The contrast is often marked with "but" or "and". Example (25) by Reader M on the Jane Overweight story provides this kind of goal → failed outcome → emotion causal explanatory sequence.

(25) Text:

Jane was frustrated   (Emotion)

Reader:

"I bet she tried to lose weight   (desired Goal)
and she <u>didn't lose weight</u>   (–Outcome)
She is probably still being teased"   (–Outcome)

Failed outcomes need not be explicit. They, too, can be inferred from a series of reasons that involve a goal, its attempt, and a negative emotion, i.e., goal → attempt → implied goal failure → negative emotion. Reader C does this in (26) where she interpreted Bill's emotional reaction to the failure of the drugs to restore his eyesight.

(26) Text:

Bill was desperate   (Emotion)

Reader:

"Obviously this guy was *pretty* <u>desperate</u>   (Internal Response,
                                               (–)character emotion)
He *really* <u>wanted to see</u>   (desired goal)
and he's trying all these medications"   (Attempt)

Another means of expressing an evaluation of goal failure is to make a general evaluation of failure. This is done by Reader R in (27) for the Jane Story. Here, using Third Party generalizations, Reader R explains the emotion in a causal sequence that reinstates the episode: initiating event → goal → attempt → failed outcome → emotion → appraisal.

(27) Text:

Jane was frustrated	(Emotion)

Reader:

"It's <u>hard</u>	(Internal Response, (−)Reader appraisal)
when you are a few pounds overweight	(Initiating Event)
and you try *really hard* <u>to lose them</u> because your	(Goal/Attempt)
<u>goal is to get more friendship</u> out of people	(Goal)
and you fail"	(−Outcome)

3.20. *Preference and emotion explanations*

Emotions in a narrative are interpreted and explained less frequently by preferences or other emotions. Example (28) is a case where Reader C explained an emotion with a Character appraisal and a Character preference: appraisal → preference → emotion.

(28) Text:

Her mother was happy	(Emotion)

Reader:

"Obviously because her mother thought that the amount of money Betty <u>spent was a lot</u>	(Internal Response,(−)Reader appraisal)
and she really **liked** the purse"	(Internal Response, (+)Character preference)

Example (29) is a case where Reader M used a successful goal attainment and preference as well as a future successful outcome and an emotion to explain an emotion. The causal sequence is: successful outcome → positive outcome → positive emotion → positive emotion).

(29) Text:

Betty was very happy	(Internal Response/Event)
Reader: "She was probably <u>happy</u>	(Internal Response, (+) character emotion)
because she finished this <u>beautiful</u> sweater	(+Outcome)
and anticipated lots of compliments	(+Outcome)
she was **proud** of it"	(Internal Response, (+)Character emotion)

4. Discussion

The analysis of what people talk about in reporting their understanding of a narrative to a listener reveals that evaluation or appraisals occurred throughout the narrative episode and pervaded the talk of the readers. The ways of evaluation and their valences depended upon what was appraised. The evaluations differed across the categories of the episode with initiating events having the greatest variation in evaluative devices or expressions. Initiating events caused a variety of internal responses that were evaluative in nature and support appraisal theories of emotion (Arnold 1960; Lazarus 1991; Roseman 1984; Stein and Levine 1987, 1989, 1990).

The present study of narratives supports our claim that evaluation plays a important role in comprehension of the lives of others as expressed in narratives. Readers engage in extensive appraisal of experiences of others throughout the episode. Narrators, likewise, use evaluation and appraisal processes as a basis for selecting and reporting of the events in their past, how they felt about these events, how they coped with them, and what they learned from them. Appraisal and coping constitute what people talk about when they interpret and deal with events that affect their well being.

The present analysis is consistent with and complements those of Labov and Waletsky (1967) and Goodwin and Goodwin (1987). Our speakers (readers) publicly displayed their assessments of events, and used various linguistic devices to communicate their evaluations. In addition, we showed how these evaluations are used to communicate one's understanding of the experience of another in terms of how the speaker construes the events as affecting the well-being of the other. The kinds of evaluations we identified and which events to which they are applied occur in everyday, spontaneous conversation. We found, as did Labov and Waletsky (1967) and Goodwin and Goodwin (1987) that emotion terms are used to characterize evaluations of experience. Moreover, we also found that preferences, general appraisals, goals, and outcomes were means by which speakers express their evaluations or assessments. These, too, are likely to occur throughout spontaneous conversation and may well serve the organization functions that structure collaborative conversation especially in the co-construction of conversational narratives (see, for example, Chafe, This Volume, and Ervin-Trip, This volume). In our view, the shared understandings of events is an important aspect of the conversational interaction and also serves to achieve an organization among multiple participants.

Stein, Folkman, Trabasso, and Christopher (In press) analyzed thirty narratives made shortly after bereavement by a caregiver of a partner who died from AIDS. The analysis of the events reported in the narratives was done terms of the caregiver's positive and negative beliefs, outcomes, and emotions. The relative frequency of positive appraisals predicted standardized measures of the caregiver's mental health at the time of bereavement and twelve months later. The greater the proportion of positive appraisals, the more likely the caregiver would evidence goals and plans for the future, high positive morale, and high positive mood states. Similarly, the greater the proportion of positive appraisals, the less likely the caregiver would feel depressed or have trouble in coping with his new life without his partner.

Stein, Trabasso and Liwag (1993, 1994) examined the appraisals that young children, two to seven years in age, make in narratives about events that cause emotions. Stein and Liwag (In press) report an extensive analysis on the ways of appraisal that these children use in evaluating the events in terms of goals and outcomes that caused their positive and negative emotions. In both cases, the children express evaluative understanding of what occurred to them in terms of emotions, beliefs, expectations, values, goals, and outcomes.

Appraising or evaluating events is believed to be adaptive. Appraising events in terms of possible harms and benefits to ourselves enables us to generate coping strategies that deal with these changes (Folkman and Lazarus 1990). In theories of causation, we evaluate events in terms of their causes so that we can learn to prevent either produce or prevent them (Collingwood 1938/1961). That is, by tracing causes or conditions and by assigning responsibility to agents (Hart and Honore 1956/1961, 1959), we can determine what it is that is affecting our well being and formulate plans to do something about it. This kind of causal reasoning appears to be quite general and applies to understanding not only our own experience but to the understanding of the experiences of others, be they real or fictive in nature (Hilton, Mathes and Trabasso 1992; Stein, Trabasso and Liwag 1993, 1994).

Appraisals are not limited to events that impact on our well being. Within a theory of rationality of means and ends (Rescher 1988), appraisals and evaluations can be made of goals and plans (ends and means) that are generated in response to events. These evaluations can be done in terms of the appropriateness of the goals and plans and whether their attainment would result in benefits. Further, actions carried out as attempts are also evaluated and monitored as to whether they are consistent with the goal plan, and whether they are an efficient and effective means to the desired ends. Actions can be evaluated as to whether they are within the resources and skill of the person and whether things are going well or badly. Outcomes of actions are also evaluated in terms of success or failure in achieving one's goals, and whether they result in harm or benefit. Our view of others as rational beings is expressed in our understanding of how and why they act and feel and whether these actions are carried out in our best interests.

In seeking to understand another person in rational terms, we engage in seeking explanatory coherence. In the present study, the causal sequences of thoughts provided a causally coherent interpretation of why and how the person reacted to and dealt with the events that impacted on him. The positive or negative valence of the evaluations of events, namely, appraisals, preferences, emotions, goals, and outcomes also provide a semantic coherence. The readers maintained the valence of these categories over several sentences of the narrative. We may, in observing or vicariously experiencing the life of another, achieve coherence by posing why- and how-questions privately to ourselves. However, this understanding is more likely to be shared as part of a conversational interaction in which we communicate explanations and reasons for human action. The explanations and reasons may or may not refer to a factual state of affairs. They may be types of justification communicated to others which reflect implicit or explicit references to evaluation (Polkinghorne 1983).

Acknowledgment

The research reported in this paper was supported by a grant from the Spencer Foundation to the first author. The second author was supported by a fellowship from the Harris Foundation.

References

Arnold, M.B. 1960. *Emotion and Personality*. Vols. I and II. New York: Columbia University Press.
Bakhtin, M.M. 1981. *The Dialogic Imagination*. C. Emerson and M. Holquist (ed. and trans.). Texas: Texas University Press.
Bakhtin, M.M. 1984. *Problems of Dostoyevsky's Poetics*. C. Emerson (ed. and trans.). Minneapolis: University of Minnesota Press.
Chafe, Wallace. This volume. "Polyphonic Topic development."
Collingwood, R.G. 1938/1961. "On the So-called Idea of Causation." In *Proceedings of the Aristotelian Society*, 85–108. Reprinted in H. Morris (ed.) 1961. *Freedom and Responsibility: Readings in philosophy and law*, 303–313. Stanford: Stanford University Press.
Ericsson, K.A. 1988. "Concurrent Verbal Reports on Text Comprehension: A review." *Text* 8.295–235.

Ericsson, K.A. and H.A. Simon. 1984. *Protocol Analysis: Verbal reports as data*. Cambridge, Mass.: MIT Press.

Ervin-Tripp, S. and Aylin Küntay (This volume). "The Occasioning and Structure of Conversational Stories."

Folkman, S. and R.S. Lazarus. 1990. "Coping and Emotion." In *Psychological and Biological Approaches to Emotion*, N.L. Stein, B. Leventhal and T. Trabasso (eds), 309–317. Hillsdale, N.J.: Lawrence Erlbaum.

Goodwin, C. and M.H. Goodwin. 1987. "Concurrent Operations on Talk: Notes on the interactive organization of assessments." *IPRA Papers in Pragmatics* 1.1–54.

Graesser, A.C., M. Singer and T. Trabasso 1994. "A Constructionist Theory of Inference Generation during Narrative Text Comprehension." *Psychological Review* 101.371–395.

Hart, H.L.A. and A.M. Honore. 1956. "Causation in the Law." *Law Quarterly Review* 72.58–90. Reprinted in H. Morris (ed.), 1961. *Freedom and Responsibility: Readings in philosophy and law*, 325–342. Stanford: Stanford University Press.

Hart, H.L.A. and A.M. Honore. 1959. *Causation in the Law*. Oxford: Oxford University Press.

Hilton, D.J., R.H. Mathes and T. Trabasso. 1992. "The Study of Causal Explanation in Natural Language: Analyzing reports of the Challenger disaster in the New York Times." In *Explaining One's Self to Others*, M.L. McLaughlin, M.J. Cody and S.J. Read (eds), 41–60. Hillsdale, N.J.: Lawrence Erlbaum.

Labov, W. 1972. *Language in the Inner City: Studies in the Black English vernacular*. Philadelphia, Pa.: University of Pennsylvania Press.

Labov, W. and J. Waletsky. 1967. "Narrative Analysis." In *Essays on the Verbal and Visual Arts*, J. Helm (ed.), 12–44. Seattle, Wash.: University of Washington Press.

Lazarus, R.S. 1991. *Emotion and Adaptation*. New York: Oxford University Press.

Magliano, J.P. and A.C. Graesser. 1991. "A Three-pronged Method for Studying Inference Generation in Literary Text." *Poetics* 20.193–232.

Mandler, J. and N. Johnson. 1977. "Remembrance of Things Parsed: Story structure and recall." *Cognitive Psychology* 9.111–151.

Polkinghorne, D. 1983. *Methodology for the Human Sciences*. Albany, N.Y.: State University of New York Press.

Rescher, N. 1988. *Rationality*. Oxford: Clarendon Press.

Roseman, I. 1984. "Cognitive Determinants of Emotions: A structural theory." In *Review of Personality and Social Psychology*. Vol. 5: *Emotions, Relationships, and Health*, P. Shaver (ed.), 11–36. Beverly Hills: Sage.

Schank, R.C. 1986. *Explanation Patterns: Understanding mechanically and creatively*. Hillsdale, N.J.: Lawrence Erlbaum.

Singer, M., A.C. Graesser and T. Trabasso. 1994. "Minimal or Global Inferences in Comprehension?" *Journal of Memory and Language* 33.1–21.

Stein, N.L., S. Folkman, T. Trabasso and A. Christopher-Richards (In press). "The Role of Appraisal and Goal Processes in Predicting Psychological Well Being."

Stein, N.L. and C.G. Glenn. 1979. "An Analysis of Story Comprehension in Elementary School Children." In *New Directions in Discourse Processing*, R.O. Freedle (ed.), Vol. 2 in the series *Advances in discourse processes*. Norwood, N.J.: Ablex.

Stein, N.L. and L.J. Levine. 1987. "Thinking about Feelings: The development and organization of emotional knowledge." In *Aptitude, Learning, and Instruction: Cognition, conation, and affect*. Vol. 3, R.E. Snow and M. Farr (eds), 165–198. Hillsdale, N.J.: Lawrence Erlbaum.

Stein, N.L. and L.J. Levine. 1989. "The Causal Organization of Emotion Knowledge: A developmental study." *Cognition and Emotion* 3(4).343–378.

Stein, N.L. and Levine, L.J. 1990. "Making Sense of Emotion: The representation and use of goal structured knowledge." In *Psychological and Biological Approaches to Emotion*, N.L. Stein, B. Leventhal and T. Trabasso (eds), 45–73. Hillsdale, N.J.: Lwarence Erlbaum.

Stein, N.L. and M.D. Liwag. In press. "A Goal Appraisal Process Approaches to Understanding and Remembering Emotional Events." In *Developmental Spans in Event Comprehension and Representation: Bridging fictional and actual events*, P. van den Broek, P. Bauer and T. Bourg (eds). Hillsdale, N.J.: Lawrence Erlbaum.

Stein, N.L., T. Trabasso and M. Liwag. 1993. "The Representation and Organization of Emotional Experience: Unfolding the emotional episode." In *Handbook of Emotions*, M.L. Lewis and J. Haviland (eds), 279–300. New York: Guilford.

Stein, N.L., T. Trabasso and M.D. Liwag. 1994. "The Rashomon Phenomenon: Personal frames and future-oriented appraisals in memory for emotional events." In *The Development of Future Oriented Processes*, M.M. Haith, J.B. Benson, R.J. Roberts Jr. and B.F. Pennington (eds), 409–435. Chicago: The University of Chicago Press.

Suh, S. 1988. "Converging Evidence for Causal Inferences during Comprehension." Unpublished Ph.D. dissertation, University of Chicago.

Suh, S. and T. Trabasso. 1993. "Inferences during On-line Processing: Converging evidence from discourse analysis, talk-aloud protocols, and recognition priming." *Journal of Memory and Language* 32.279–301.

Trabasso, T. and P.A. Magliano. 1994. "Understanding Emotional Understanding." In *Proceedings of International Society for Study of Emotion*, N. Frijda (ed.), 78–82. Storrs, Conn.: ISRE Publications.

Trabasso, T., T. Secco, and P. van den Broek. 1984. "Causal Cohesion and Story Coherence." In *Learning and Comprehension of Text*, H. Mandl, N.L. Stein and T. Trabasso (eds), 83–111. Hillsdale, N.J.: Lawrence Erlbaum.

Trabasso, T. and L.L. Sperry. 1985. "Causal Relatedness and Importance of Story Events." *Journal of Memory and Language* 24.595–611.

Trabasso, T. and S. Suh. 1993. "Understanding Text: Achieving explanatory coherence through on-line inferences and mental operations in working memory." *Discourse Processes* 16.3–34.

Trabasso, T., P. van den Broek and S. Suh. 1989. "Logical Necessity and Transitivity of Causal Relations in Stories." *Discourse Processes* 12.1–25.

Voloshinov, V.N. 1973. *Marxism and the Philosophy of Language*, L. Matejka and I.R. Titunik (trans.). Cambridge, Mass.: Harvard University Press.

In the series TYPOLOGICAL STUDIES IN LANGUAGE (TSL) the following titles have been published thus far:

1. HOPPER, Paul J. (ed.): *Tense-Aspect: Between semantics & pragmatics.* 1982.
2. HAIMAN, John & Pamela MUNRO (eds): *Switch Reference and Universal Grammar. Proceedings of a symposium on switch reference and universal grammar, Winnipeg, May 1981.* 1983.
3. GIVÓN, T.: *Topic Continuity in Discourse. A quantitative cross-language study.* 1983.
4. CHISHOLM, William, Louis T. MILIC & John A.C. GREPPIN (eds): *Interrogativity: A colloquium on the grammar, typology and pragmatics of questions in seven diverse languages, Cleveland, Ohio, October 5th 1981-May 3rd 1982.* 1984.
5. RUTHERFORD, William E. (ed.): *Language Universals and Second Language Acquisition.* 1984 (2nd ed. 1987).
6. HAIMAN, John (Ed.): *Iconicity in Syntax. Proceedings of a symposium on iconicity in syntax, Stanford, June 24-26, 1983.* 1985.
7. CRAIG, Colette (ed.): *Noun Classes and Categorization. Proceedings of a symposium on categorization and noun classification, Eugene, Oregon, October 1983.* 1986.
8. SLOBIN, Dan I. & Karl ZIMMER (eds): *Studies in Turkish Linguistics.* 1986.
9. BYBEE, Joan L.: *Morphology. A Study of the Relation between Meaning and Form.* 1985.
10. RANSOM, Evelyn: *Complementation: its Meaning and Forms.* 1986.
11. TOMLIN, Russel S.: *Coherence and Grounding in Discourse. Outcome of a Symposium, Eugene, Oregon, June 1984.* 1987.
12. NEDJALKOV, Vladimir (ed.): *Typology of Resultative Constructions. Translated from the original Russian edition (1983). English translation edited by Bernard Comrie.* 1988.
14. HINDS, John, Shoichi IWASAKI & Senko K. MAYNARD (eds): *Perspectives on Topicalization. The case of Japanese WA.* 1987.
15. AUSTIN, Peter (ed.): *Complex Sentence Constructions in Australian Languages.* 1988.
16. SHIBATANI, Masayoshi (ed.): *Passive and Voice.* 1988.
17. HAMMOND, Michael, Edith A. MORAVCSIK and Jessica WIRTH (eds): *Studies in Syntactic Typology.* 1988.
18. HAIMAN, John & Sandra A. THOMPSON (eds): *Clause Combining in Grammar and Discourse.* 1988.
19. TRAUGOTT, Elizabeth C. and Bernd HEINE (eds): *Approaches to Grammaticalization, 2 volumes (set)* 1991
20. CROFT, William, Suzanne KEMMER and Keith DENNING (eds): *Studies in Typology and Diachrony. Papers presented to Joseph H. Greenberg on his 75th birthday.* 1990.
21. DOWNING, Pamela, Susan D. LIMA and Michael NOONAN (eds): *The Linguistics of Literacy.* 1992.
22. PAYNE, Doris (ed.): *Pragmatics of Word Order Flexibility.* 1992.
23. KEMMER, Suzanne: *The Middle Voice.* 1993.
24. PERKINS, Revere D.: *Deixis, Grammar, and Culture.* 1992.
25. SVOROU, Soteria: *The Grammar of Space.* 1994.
26. LORD, Carol: *Historical Change in Serial Verb Constructions.* 1993.
27. FOX, Barbara and Paul J. Hopper (eds): *Voice: Form and Function.* 1994.

28. GIVÓN, T. (ed.) : *Voice and Inversion*. 1994.
29. KAHREL, Peter and René van den BERG (eds): *Typological Studies in Negation*. 1994.
30. DOWNING, Pamela and Michael NOONAN: *Word Order in Discourse*. 1995.
31. GERNSBACHER, M. A. and T. GIVÓN (eds): *Coherence in Spontaneous Text*. 1995.
32. BYBEE, Joan and Suzanne FLEISCHMAN (eds): *Modality in Grammar and Discourse*. 1995.
33. FOX, Barbara (ed.): *Studies in Anaphora*. 1996.
34. GIVÓN, T. (ed.): *Conversation. Cognitive, communicative and social perspectives*. 1997.
35. GIVÓN, T. (ed.): *Grammatical Relations. A functionalist perspective*. n.y.p.